THE BEDFO
HISTORICAL
SOCIE
199€

G000164879

THE CONGREGATIONAL CHURCH.
LUTON. BEDS.

J. CORNEY SC.   O'PENED. MAY. 29ᵗ. 1866.

Frontispiece: Luton: The Congregational Church in Stuart Street, designed by John Tarring and built in 1866. It was demolished c.1971.

(*Engraving: Thomas Corney, c.1866*)

THE PUBLICATIONS OF THE BEDFORDSHIRE
HISTORICAL RECORD SOCIETY
VOLUME 75

Bedfordshire
Chapels and Meeting Houses
Official Registration 1672-1901

Edited by
Edwin Welch

PUBLISHED BY THE SOCIETY 1996

©
THE BEDFORDSHIRE
HISTORICAL RECORD SOCIETY
AND THE EDITOR, 1996

ISBN 0 85155 058 4
First published in 1996 by the Society

The volume has been published with the help of a grant from Bedford Museum.

Cover design by Justin March, Park Farm Studios Ltd.,
Riseley Road, Bletsoe, Bedford MK44 1QU

Printed and bound by
Newnorth Print Ltd

CONTENTS

LIST OF ILLUSTRATIONS

Sources of Illustrations and acknowledgements

All the pictures are reproduced from originals or copies held in the County Record Office apart from the illustrations of Potton Congregational church which were provided by Potton History Society.

Owners who have kindly allowed reproduction of their material include the County Record Office (Frontispiece, 1, 11, 14, 16, 26, 27, 28, 41, 46, and 47), Mrs. Ballantyne (44), Bedfordshire County Council Photographic Services (19, 29, 30, 43), Bedford Borough Council (5, 8), The Charter Partnership (architects) (cover, 6, 7, 38), Alan Cirket (49), Harold Clements (25), Mrs. I. N. Cooper (13), Mr. S. H. Davey (3, 4), Mr. R. W Douglas (9), Mr. R. B. Hobourn (21), Mr. R. A. Hodgkin (23), Mrs. M. Houlgate (24), Keith Lazenby (12, 22, 42, 45), Mrs. Manton (18), Mr. V. Norris (34), Potton History Society and Daphne Wilkins (31, 32), Ridgmont Baptist Church (33), Maurice Rust (36, 37), the Shuttleworth collection (39), Mr. C. D. Smith (15, 20), Society of Friends (2), Mrs. M. Stevens (40), Miss D. Stringfellow (17), Andrew Underwood (48), John Wainwright (10), and Richard Wildman (35).

Acknowledgements

Patricia Bell for her hospitality and assistance; Chris Pickford and the staff of the Bedfordshire Record Office for their help (and patience); Bedford Borough Council; the Registrar General and the staff of Churches & Chapels and the Library, Office of Population, Censuses and Surveys, who did much to ease my task; Dr K. Thompson, Hertfordshire County Archivist, Dr P.C. Saunders, Cambridgeshire Deputy County Archivist; Dr David Wykes of Leicester University; Mr J. Creasey & Mrs J. Barnes of Dr Williams's Library; Mr R.H.A. Cheffins of the British Library; Public Record Office; Birmingham Reference Library. H.M. Stationery Office for permission to reproduce official records; Dr Williams's trustees for permission to reproduce the Bedfordshire sections of the Evans and Thompson lists; Nigel Lutt and Chris Pickford for help with the selection of the illustrations and, lastly, the General Editor, Gordon Vowles, for seeing the volume into print from its origins half a world away.

Vancouver, February 1996   Edwin Welch

ABBREVIATIONS

ABN	Archdeaconry of Bedford records in BRO
B.H.R.S.	Bedfordshire Historical Records Society
BRO	Bedfordshire Record Office
CRO	Cambridgeshire Record Office at Huntingdon
HRO	Hertfordshire Record Office
MOR	Bedford Moravian Church records in BRO
occ.	occupation
OPCS	Office of Population, Censuses & Surveys
OR	*Original Records of Early Nonconformity*, vol. 2
PB	Biggleswade Peculiar Jurisdiction records in BRO
poss.	possession
PRO	Public Record Office, London
QSM	Quarter Sessions minute books in BRO
QSR	Quarter Sessions rolls in BRO
Reg.	Registered
RI	Leighton Buzzard Peculiar Jurisdiction records in BRO
RG	Registrar General's records in PRO
RG(M)	Registrar General's licence for marriages
RG(W)	Registrar General's licence for worship
S.A.	Salvation Army (Salvationist)
X	Parish record in BRO

N.B. The complete title of *Dunstable Methodist Circuit,* quoted in the Calendar is *The Dunstable Methodist Circuit: One Hundred and Fifty Years of Witness* (Dunstable, 1993)

INTRODUCTION

The system of registration of dissenters' meeting houses (including Roman Catholic buildings), later described as the registration of places of religious worship, appears to be confined to England and Wales. It is a typical English institution, in having evolved slowly over two centuries, and being a voluntary system. It began in 1672 when Charles II, wishing to help his Roman Catholic subjects, issued a Declaration of Toleration for Protestants dissenting from the Church of England. This was a short-lived experiment which never achieved his goal of toleration for Roman Catholics, but it left behind an invaluable record in the form of lists of meeting houses and preachers who had registered with the Secretary of State. A second Declaration of Toleration issued by James II in 1687 was strenuously opposed by Anglicans and dissenters and has left few or no records at all. In 1689, when William III rewarded with a Toleration Act the dissenters who had supported him, the same precedent of voluntary registration was followed. However the responsibilty of receiving applications was placed on the courts of quarter sessions and the bishops. Registration was popular because it provided protection against persecution and riot. Magistrates, however unsympathetic, were obliged to protect them – a duty which could be enforced by mandamus from superior courts. Until the mid-eighteenth century most registrations were made by quarter sessions probably because of objections to Anglicanism, but then registrations with bishops and archdeacons became more popular. This was because the licence was issued by the registrar at any time (rather than four times a year with the clerk of the peace), and the registrar made fewer objections to the certificate than the magistrates.

As persecution slowly declined in England and Wales the system of registration might have disappeared but for various pieces of legislation introduced in the nineteenth century. The first permitted registered buildings to claim exemption from poor rates. Another released them from the control of the Charity Commission, and a third allowed the Registrar General to license the building for the performance of marriages. The system remained voluntary because even when the Act said otherwise no provision was made for enforcing it. However it became difficult for an active congregation to avoid registration.[1] Therefore when in mid-century bishops complained of being obliged to register Mormon and similar buildings the duty was transferred to the Registrar General. There it has remained with very few changes in either legislation or administration. Non-Christian religious bodies are now included, and from time to time difficulties arise with the appearance of new religions.[2]

The result of the legislation has been the creation of a body of information about the development of dissent and religious activity in England and Wales. It has not been used as extensively as the religious census of 1851 because of the difficulties of interpreting the information and because the information itself is widely scattered. Before 1852 most of the licences are to be found in the episcopal and archdeaconry archives of the Anglican Church, but others are with county and borough quarter sessions records. However the incomplete returns[3] of licences issued before 1852 made to the Registrar General are now in the Public Record Office, together with the record of licences issued in 1672. After 1837 when the Registrar General began to issue licences to allow marriages to be performed in dissenting chapels, and after 1852, when he took over the duty of licensing places of religious worship the records are to be found in his office – now the Office of Population, Censuses and Surveys. The purpose of this volume is to bring together in one place summaries of all the Bedfordshire licences issued before 1902. It should however be noted that missing records and incomplete registration by quarter sessions mean that very few licences before 1740 are recorded. The calendar has been supplemented by four lists of dissenting chapels made in 1715, 1772, 1842 and 1908, and a list of trust deeds registered in Chancery from 1736 to 1865. Since the 1851 religious census has already been published by the Record Society[4] this will make all the official records of chapels and meeting houses easily accessible.

The Legislation

The first two attempts to permit limited toleration were made not by Act of Parliament, but by royal proclamation. Neither was ultimately successful, but the first, issued by Charles II in 1672, set a precedent which has been followed up to the present day. The Declaration of Indulgence issued on 15th March 1671/2 states that because the persecution of dissenters over the past twelve years had failed to bring them to conform to the Established Church all penal measures were to be suspended against both Protestants and Roman Catholics.[5] In addition 'a sufficient number of places' were to be allowed to Protestant Dissenters as long as both the meeting house and the preacher were approved by the Crown. For the greater part of 1672, until Charles II was obliged to withdraw his promise of toleration, a registry was established in the Secretary of State's office which received petitions and issued licences for England and Wales. Almost a century ago these were printed by Lyon Turner in his *Original Records of Nonconformity.*

On 4 April 1687 James II issued a similar Declaration of Indulgence suspending all the penal laws and permitting all dissenters to meet 'in private houses and places purposely hired or built for that use' so long as they were 'peaceably, openly and publicly held.'[6] On this occasion the licensing of meeting houses was to be by one or more justices of the peace. but it is improbable that much use was made of the Declaration during the remaining twenty-one months that James II remained in power. When he ordered the Declaration to be read in all parish churches the Seven Bishops protested and were put on trial. The failure of the jury to convict them was the first step towards the Glorious Revolution.

Because prominent Protestant nonconformists had sympathised with and often actively supported the Bishops rather than James II, they received their reward from William III and the Convention Parliament. The Toleration Act which it passed was intended to provide 'some ease to scrupulous consciences in the exercise of religion.'[7] Any Protestant dissenter who took the oaths of allegiance and supremacy already passed by Parliament[8] was to be relieved of all the penalties in certain listed Acts, and were to be allowed to serve parish offices by deputy if they wished. Nonconformist preachers were obliged to take the oaths in order to be licensed at Quarter Sessions.[9] Special provisions were included for Baptists and for Quakers. Section 5 of the Act withdrew exemption for services held 'with the doors locked, barred or bolted.' The last section, which appears as something of an afterthought, requires meetings to be

> certified to the bishop of the diocese, or to the archdeacon of that archdeaconry, or to the justices of the peace at the general or quarter sessions of the peace for the County, city, or place in which such meeting shall be held.

The ecclesiastical registrar or the clerk of the peace was to provide the congregation with a certificate of registration for a fee of sixpence.[10]

In 1711 an Act 'for preserving the Protestant Religion' extended the right of Quakers to make a declaration instead of taking an oath.[11] It further provided that if the meeting place had been registered then the preachers need not have been licensed in that county or city. This was an important concession for ministers who itinerated, as the Methodists were to do later in the century. In 1779 a further concession was made by substituting a simple declaration of Protestantism for the 39 Articles of the Church of England which had previously been the standard used in the oaths.[12] The Roman Catholic Relief Act of 1791 allowed that denomination similar privileges to those granted to Protestant Dissenters more than a century earlier.[13] Buildings which they used for worship could be registered at quarter sessions (but not with the ecclesiastical authorities) for the same sixpenny fee. Their ministers had to take an oath of allegiance and meeting houses were 'not to be locked, barred or bolted' during services. The principal difference from the earlier Acts is that meeting houses were not to have a steeple or bells – an injunction not repealed until 1926, but generally ignored.

An agitation in Parliament against itinerating Methodist preachers caused the legislation to be revised in 1812.[14] The licence fee was increased to two shillings and sixpence and the fines for non-observance of the Act increased by considerable amounts. Preachers were to be exempt from parish offices or service in the militia only if they did not engage in trade or business. On the other hand it provided that no dissenter was to be summoned to go more than five miles from his home to answer for any offence under the Act, and in court he might insist on taking the oaths. Disturbers of nonconformist meetings could be bound over by the magistrates to keep the peace. For the first time the meeting was defined as an assembly of more than twenty persons. Although this Act in particular implied that registration was compulsory, there was no attempt made to enforce it, and few licences to dissenting ministers can be found. Licences were only obtained when meetings were attacked by rioters or ministers were persecuted by the magistrates.

A year later toleration was extended to Unitarians.[15] Although 'impugning the doctrine of the Holy Trinity' had always been a very serious offence, Unitarianism under various names had flourished during the eighteenth century. Many of the original Presbyterian and General Baptist congregations had adopted these opinions, and towards the end of the century Theophilus Lindsey, an Anglican clergyman, had founded a Unitarian congregation in London without being prosecuted.[16]

A further concession, and one which increased the popularity of licensing meeting houses, was made by Parliament in 1833. There had been considerable controversy about the payment of parish and church rates for nonconformist places of worship. In some parishes they had been exempt, but in others the rates had been levied. In 1818 Lendal Congregational chapel in York had appealed against rates collected both on the building and on collections made there. The case was lost and the congregation had to pay £150 in costs. Similar examples could be found in other parts of the country.[17] Now 'all churches, chapels, and other places of religious worship' were exempt from rates if they were solely used for worship or 'the charitable Education of the Poor.'[18]

The passing of Hardwicke's Marriage Act in 1753, which was intended to prevent irregular marriages in the Fleet Prison and elswhere, had incidentally prevented all nonconformists except Quakers and Jews (who were exempted by the Act) from being married anywhere except in an Anglican parish church and by a minister in holy orders.[19] In 1837 this was corrected to some extent by a Marriage Act which regulated marriages in Anglican and nonconformist churches.[20] For the first time a system of civil registration of births, marriages and deaths was established, making use of the recently-instituted system of Poor Law Unions. By this Act a Superintendent Registrar of Marriages (usually the Clerk to the Poor Law Guardians) was permitted to issue licences for the performance of marriages (seven days after notice was given to him) and certificates of notice (twenty-one days after notice). The marriage could take place in the registrar's office before a registrar of marriages or in a licensed place of worship in the presence of a registrar, and at least two witnesses. The application for a licence to perform marriages in a nonconformist place of worship had to be signed by twenty householders who attended the meeting, and to state that the building had been registered with the bishop, archdeacon or clerk of the peace for at least one year previously.[21] The completed application in duplicate was then sent to the General Register Office at Somerset House to be entered 'in a Book to be kept for that Purpose' by the Registrar General. Public notice of the application was printed in the *London Gazette* and in a local newspaper.[22] One copy of the application was then returned to the Superintendent Registrar who issued a licence on parchment for a fee of £3.[23] If a congregation moved to a new site, then a new licence for marriages could be issued without a year's delay for the same fee.[24] For the first time provision was made for the cancellation of licences when the building ceased to be used by the congregation which had licensed it. Previously there had been no provision for cancellation, either compulsorily or voluntarily, in the legislation. Voluntary cancellations in ecclesiastical or quarter sessions records are very rare, and often a different denomination would take over both building and licence. Another provision of the Act (to be discussed later in this introduction) required the Registrar General to print an annual list of buildings registered for the performance of marriages.

Although the Marriage Act was amended later in the same year, the only provision affecting meeting houses was permission for the Registrar General to make changes in the boundaries of registration districts,[25] and it was not until 1852 that any further legislation was passed. In that year the power to license meeting houses for worship was transferred from the ecclesiastical and quarter sessions authorities to the Registrar General, and the present system of registration of places of religious worship came into existence. Bishops and archdeacons had complained at being obliged to register chapels used by Unitarians, Plymouth Brethren, Irvingites (Catholic Apostolic), Swedenborgians and Mormons (Church of Latter Day Saints). The Act is short and gives the appearance of a hurriedly assembled piece of legislation.[26] A similar procedure to that already in existence was used, and the fee for registration was still only two shillings and sixpence. Bishops, archdeacons and clerks of the peace were to make returns within three months to the Registrar General of all licences which they had issued. The intention was probably to discover how many of the licences were still in use, but this proved impossible, and the lists were incomplete because no attempt was made to collect the same information from the registrars of peculiar jurisdictions. The Registrar General was required to print a list of the licences which he issued and supply copies to the Superintendent Registrars for the use of the public, but the pre-1852 licences were not printed.

Three years later an amending Act 'concerning the certifying and registering of Places of Religious Worship' was necessary.[27] Roman Catholics, Jews and others were now included specifically in its scope, and the forms already being used by the Registrar General were included as schedules to the Act. Only one person was required to sign the application, but the Superintendent Registrar was required to persuade him to provide the name of the denomination,

> but if those Persons decline to describe themselves by any distinct Appellation erase the Words "calling themselves," and insert "who object to be designated by any distinctive Religious Appellation."

The procedure for cancelling a licence was also enacted for the first time. Trustees, owners or occupiers could notify the Superintendent Registrar of the closure of a chapel. If no such person could be found then the Registrar General could cancel the licence by advertising his intention in the *London Gazette* and a local newspaper. Almost all of these procedures were already in place, but without parliamentary sanction. The amending Act has remained the basis of the procedures up to the present time, and is remarkably similar to that instituted in 1689. Fees are increased from time to time, the requirement that a building should be registered for worship for twelve months before being registered for marriages was abolished in 1959, and other minor changes were made in 1953, but the system would be familiar to an eighteenth century registrar or clerk of the peace.

Marriages

After 1837 Quakers and Jews continued to have the privileged status which they obtained under Hardwicke's Marriage Act. Quaker marriages need not be solemnised in a licensed building, neither is there any restriction on the time of the ceremony. It is only necessary for the parties to obtain permission from a registering officer of the Society of Friends, and for the ceremony to be carried out in conformity with the Society's rules.[28] As a result Quaker meeting houses are not normally licensed for marriages, and there was less incentive to register for worship.

Jewish marriages on the other hand are restricted to persons 'professing the Jewish religion' and must take place in the synagogue and according to Jewish law. However it does not appear that the Jewish community in Bedford (1803-1827) ever registered its synagogue for worship.

After the new procedures were introduced in 1837 it was still necessary for a registrar of marriages to be present at marriages performed in chapels. In rural areas this could produce problems of timing when the registrar had to travel long distances, and particularly when the hours for marriages were so restricted.[29] As an alternative after 1898 the trustees of a chapel were allowed to nominate an 'authorised person' who would take the place of the registrar at the ceremony.[30] Congregations which have taken advantage of this provision have 'A.P.' in the lists published by the Registrar General, but this information has not been noted in this calendar. In 1995 a final change permitted marriages in buildings which were neither places of religious worship nor registars' offices. Even boats, if securely moored, are acceptable.

Bedfordshire Sources – Ecclesiastical

Until 1837, when it was transferred to the diocese of Ely, Bedfordshire was an archdeaconry in the diocese of Lincoln. It was customary for the bishops of Lincoln to appoint a commissary to exercise their jurisdiction in each archdeaconry, and usually the archdeacons appointed the same civil lawyer as their official. Since the registrar of both courts was usually the same person, there was normally one court system for the archdeaconry. After the archdeaconry was transferred to Ely the same officials continued in office. This simplifies the records because however a request for a licence was addressed – to bishop, archdeacon, commissary, official or surrogate – it inevitably came to the deputy registrar or his assistant for attention. These records which only begin in 1740 are now in the Bedforshire Record Office. In the earliest years it appears to have been usual for one or more members of the congregation to appear before the deputy registrar, or a locum tenens, and for the certificate to have been written by his clerk.[31] Later a certificate written and signed by members of the congregation would be prepared beforehand and brought or even sent by mail to the registrar's office. The final development in the early nineteenth century was to use a printed form which had two parts. The first part was the certificate and the second was filled out by the registrar to turn it into the licence. It was presumably always given to the registrar in duplicate. The Wesleyan Methodists, from their printing office in City Road, London, initiated this, but the forms were soon copied by local printers for the use of other denominations.

There were two exceptions to the archdeaconry records – the peculiar jurisdictions of the parish of Biggleswade, and the parish of Leighton Buzzard with Billington, Egginton, Heath and Reach, and Stanbridge. Both peculiars claimed to have archidiaconal jurisdiction which was only suspended during the bishop's triennial visitations. The judge of the peculiar was therefore entitled to issue dissenters' meeting house licences.[32] Biggleswade had the same officers as the archdeaconry of Huntingdon, whereas Leighton Buzzard had its own registrar residing in the town.[33] However, as the calendar shows, only three Biggleswade licences were issued by that peculiar jurisdiction and three by the archdeaconry court. Leighton Buzzard peculiar makes a better showing, but still faced competition from the archdeaconry court. By the eighteenth century eccesiastical courts were in decline and the half-crown fee was hardly worth a lengthy dispute.

The ecclesiastical authorities, unlike the clerks of the peace, normally kept a register of the licences issued. This was particularly important after 1812 when annual returns had to be made to the clerk of the peace. Bedford Archdeaconry has two registers. The first (BRO, ABN 1/1), begun towards the end of the eighteenth century, consists of eight pages ($15\frac{1}{2}$" $\times$ $9\frac{1}{2}$") with entries from 1740 to 1816. It gives the name of owner or occupier of the property, the parish or hamlet, the date of registration and very little else. It was assembled from the original certificates because when the clerk had reached 1792 a further batch of certificates from 1770 to 1780 were found and inserted out of chronological order. The other register (BRO, ABN 1/2 fills seventeen pages of a book (8" $\times$ $6\frac{1}{2}$") from 1818 to 1852.[34] Despite its smaller size it manages to include the name of the first 'petitioner' as well as the information given in the earlier register. As an entry was made when the certificate was received it is in much better order.[35] There is a third list of licences from 1818 to 1832 (BRO, ABN 3/3) which is a draft of the return made to the Registrar General in 1852. In addition there are the original certificates (ABN 2) from 1740 to 1852, now arranged by parish. A considerable number of those earlier than 1818 were already missing in 1852. Three more certificates can be found in BRO, ABC 24. There are a number of discrepancies between these sources and the return of 1852.

The returns made to the Registrar General in 1852 are now in the Public Record Office (RG 31/2 for Bedford Archdeaconry). Thomas Mann, the Registrar General's Chief Clerk, encountered some difficulty in obtaining a complete return from the archdeaconry registrar. A circular letter enclosing a copy of the Act and blank forms was sent to Messrs Bailey and Leech of Bedford on 29 June 1852. On 30 July a further circular was sent asking if extra copies of the form were required.[36] The offer was declined. At the beginning of August Charles Bailey's son Samuel wrote from Southill to say that he was unable to find any record of licences amongst his late father's papers and suggesting that the return should begin in 1818 with the second register because earlier records were incomplete. On 20 August Mann sent out new forms for episcopal and archidiaconal returns respectively, and six days later Bailey and Leech sent ten sheets of the archidiaconal form for the period from June 1813 to May 1852. On the first sheet it was added that 'No Register or record [was] found previous to this date.' Mann's enquiry about earlier licences on 31 August met with the same response, but on 28 September he received a further seven sheets (using the episcopal form) giving details of licences from 1740 to May 1813, which was probably compiled from the original certificates as a number of entries in the first register, for which there are no certificates, are omitted from the list. In all a return of 463 licences was made.[37]

The peculiar jurisdictions in Bedfordshire did not compile registers of licences. For Biggleswade one original certificate is in the Bedfordshire Record Office, and two in the Cambridgeshire Record Office at Huntingdon. All the original certificates for Leighton Buzzard are in the Bedfordshire Record Office. In addition to this, four licences for Kensworth, which was transferred from Hertfordshire to Bedfordshire in 1897, have been found amongst the records of the Archdeaconry of Huntingdon in the Hertfordshire Record Office, and two for Swineshead, which was transferred from Huntingdonshire to Bedfordshire in 1888, have been found in the Huntingdonshire Record office.

Bedfordshire Sources – Quarter Sessions

Applications for licences were made to the clerks of the peace for the county and the borough, but less often than to the deputy registrar. This was because quarter sessions was only held four times a year and there would be a delay in obtaining a licence. In addition the magistrates were much more likely to object to an application than the deputy registrar, and the minutes of the Protestant Dissenting Deputies in London are full of complaints about refusal to license and application to higher courts for redress.[38] However no cases of refusing a licence have been noted in Bedfordshire. The Clerks of the Peace produced no register of applications, and they were not listed until 1852 when the Registrar General required one. The County Quarter Sessions minute books only begin in 1711, and the rolls in 1714, and even after that date they are incomplete. The problems of listing the licences are made worse by the failure of the clerk of the peace to enroll the certificate, and register it in the minute book. As the record of one licence is all that the Bedford Borough Clerk of the Peace recorded it is difficult to draw any conclusions about the procedures used there.

Until the mid-eighteenth century one or more members of the congregation attended the Quarter Sessions and the certificate was written in the Clerk of the Peace's office. In the nineteenth century a printed form similar to that used in the Anglican courts was also developed. The normal practice in the County was to place the original application on the quarter sessions roll, and to make an entry in the minute book, but examples can be found when either no enrolment or minute was made. The Bedford borough quarter sessions had few applications and only one has survived in its records, though the existence of others is known from the 1852 list and the Moravian church records. Neither Clerk of the Peace routinely kept the returns of licences made by the Archdeaconry after 1812.

The clerks of the peace for the County and the Borough made returns of all the licences in 1852 (PRO, RG 31/6 & 8), but the only correspondence preserved is a letter of 9 March 1853 forwarding a copy of the Parliamentary Paper providing statistics drawn from the returns to the County Clerk of the Peace.[39]

Bedfordshire Sources – Registrar General[40]

The system established by the Registrar General in 1837 for marriages was to provide a printed form to be signed by twenty householders who were members of the congregation. Although a copy of the worship licence issued by ecclesiastical or quarter sessions officials was presumably produced to the superintendent registrar this information was not recorded by him. This form was sent to the Registrar General and entered under a consecutive number in a large ledger. A licence, originally on parchment, was provided for the congregation after it had been registered at Somerset House.

The procedure adopted for worship in 1852 which has persisted in its original form until the present day incorporates elements of the 1689 and the 1837 methods. Printed forms, similar to those used by the Methodists, are provided for each application, completed in duplicate and checked by the Superintendent Registrar. Two copies are sent to Somerset House[41] where all the information (except the names of the applicants) is entered in a large ledger – one for marriages and one for worship. Two separate numerical sequences are in use, and each application is assigned the next number in the appropriate series.[42] One copy of the application is returned to the Superintendent Registrar who prepares the licence; the other copy is bound up in numerical order (500 to a volume) by the Registrar General's office. The only index is to the ledgers and arranged by registration districts, but where district boundaries have since changed this information is usually added to the index. Cancellations, substitutions and name changes are added to the ledgers. Cancellations are either voluntary or made upon revision by the superintendent registrars. Since the former are more likely to provide an accurate date for the disappearance of the congregation, those said to have been cancelled on revision have been noted. To extract all the information for Bedfordshire before 1902 it was necessary to search four marriage registers and eleven worship registers.

The printed lists of registered places of worship have a complicated history. They were not published until 1908, previous lists being only supplied to superintendent registrars for the public to consult.[43] The most complete set is in the OPCS Library in St Catherine's House, London. Although both the Marriage Act and the Worship Act required the Registrar General to produce lists for marriages and worship the earliest is *Lists of Chapels belonging to the Church of England . . . [and] . . . Places of Public Worship registered for the Solemnization of Marriages* (1843). It is arranged alphabetically by registration districts and then chronologically – the current arrangement of the present *List* – and includes a list of all superintendent registrars. In 1852 details about authorised persons for the marriage of Jews and Quakers are included, but places registered for worship are not listed. That information appears for the first time in the 1903 edition. The *Official List* was then divided into three parts:

Part I List of registration officers arranged by districts

Part II List of Church of England buildings registered for marriages, arranged by districts

Part III List of Places of Religious Worship arranged by districts.

In part III for the first time entries in bold type indicate which buildings are also registered for marriages, and A.P. added to show that an authorised person has been appointed. In addition the *Official List* included instructions to registrars, statistics, and lists of registering officers of Quakers and secretaries of synagogues. Part II soon ceased to be published, and after 1915 parts I & III were published separately. Part I was published annually, but part III less often and was kept up to date by annual amendments.

Bedfordshire Denominations

These brief notes are intended to provide basic information about the different denominations active in Bedfordshire and a list of denominational histories which can be consulted for further information.[44] Titles such as 'unsectarian' or 'mission' are self-explanatory and not included here

Baptists

The Baptists were divided into two groups by their theological opinions – Calvinistic or Particular Baptists, and Arminian or General Baptists. Most Particular Baptist congregations belong to the Baptist Union, but Strict and Particular Baptists do not. The latter are again divided between the Gospel Standard Baptists and the Earthen Vessel Baptists.[45] There were also differences over the practice of open communion – admitting persons not baptised as adults. Most of the Baptist congregations in Bedfordshire were Calvinist, but often joined with Congregationalists in Union churches.

General Baptist congregations were divided between those which belonged to the General Baptist Assembly and the New Connexion of General Baptists. Most of the former had their origins in the seventeenth century, and by the end of the eighteenth had adopted Unitarian views. The New Connexion began in Leicestershire in the early eighteenth century as a result of the Methodist Revival, and is now part of the Baptist Union. The only General Baptist licence in Bedfordshire is for Eaton Socon in 1778 (31/4) and was probably for a General Baptist Assembly congregation as an earlier licence there was for Presbyterians (31/2) who also adopted Unitarian views.[46]

Bereans

This small denomination was founded by John Barclay (1734-98) at Edinburgh in 1773. He adopted a modified form of Calvinism which placed great emphasis on the scriptures. Bedford (8/48) was one of the few congregations in England.[47]

Brethren

More usually known as the Plymouth Brethren, the denomination was founded by an Irish Anglican clergyman, John Nelson Darby, who moved to Plymouth. It has no paid ministry and places great emphasis on communion – 'breaking bread'. Over the years it has divided frequently, but the congregations fall into two main groups – Exclusive Brethren who limit their contacts with 'the World', and Open Brethren who are prepared to associate with others to a limited extent. There have been several congregations in Bedfordshire in addition to that licensed at Biggleswade (10/18).[48]

Catholic Apostolic Church (Irvingites)

The Catholic Apostolic Church (a title rejected by many of its members) began with the preaching of Edward Irving (1792-1834), a Scottish Presbyterian minister, in London. In preparation for the Millennium it developed an elaborate hierarchy in which ministers were called angels, and the leaders of the Church were twelve apostles. As no provision was made for replacing the apostles the Church was unable to renew its ministry when they died and has almost ceased to exist. The Bedford congregation (8/73 & 74) closed before 1954.[49]

Congregational or Independent Churches

The Independents were Calvinists, but unlike the Presbyterians believed in the independence of each congregation, though they joined together in voluntary organisations. In Bedfordshire they often formed a Union Church with the Baptists, and although this could cause problems it has persisted to the present day. The Congregational churches have joined with the Presbyterian Church of England and the Churches of Christ to become the United Reformed Church, but some have chosen to remain outside the union.[50]

Society of Friends (Quakers)

The Religious Society of Friends was founded by George Fox (1624-1691). They had no paid ministry and were noted for their speech, dress and refusal to swear oaths. The Society was not particularly successful in Bedfordshire though a number of meetings still exist.[51]

Methodists

The early Methodists were divided in their opinions between Arminianism and Calvinism. Except in Wales where they form a separate denomination, the Calvinistic Methodists either joined the Congregational Union or belong to the Countess of Huntingdon's Connexion. The congregation at Wootton (115/9) may be their only representative in Bedfordshire.

The Arminian Methodists owed their allegiance to John Wesley (1703-91), but after his death divided into different denominations. Only the (original) Wesleyan

Methodists and the Primitive Methodists are represented in Bedfordshire. The latter began in Staffordshire in 1811 when the Wesleyan hierarchy objected to the 'Camps' – revival meetings held at Mow Cop. The different groups of Methodists slowly united, and the Methodist Church was formed in 1932. A few groups of congregations refused to do so, and the Free Methodist Church at Wilshamstead (113/8) is part of one such group.[52]

Moravian Church (United Brethren)

The Moravian church originated in Czechoslovakia as a result of the introduction of John Wycliffe's works into that country. After being driven underground by persecution it experienced a great revival in the early eighteenth century in parts of Germany. As a result of their missionary activities throughout the world some Moravians came to London where they influenced the early Methodists. The Bedford settlement, founded in 1754, was responsible for founding several congregations in Bedfordshire and Northampton.[53]

Mormons (Church of Jesus Christ of Latter Day Saints)

This denomination was founded by Joseph Smith of Manchester, New York (1805-44) after receiving the Book of Mormon in a revelation. After several moves caused by persecution the Mormons settled at Salt Lake City in Utah, and all its members were encouraged to settle there. This is the reason why all the early Mormon churches in Bedfordshire closed, though they have been replaced by others in more recent years.[54]

Presbyterians

The Presbyterians are Calvinists and differ from the Independents by believing in a centralised administration through synods and assemblies. However after 1662 much of this hierarchical structure which had never been complete in England and Wales during the Commonwealth disappeared because of persecution, and it is sometimes difficult in the eighteenth century to differentiate between Presbyterians and Congregationalists. Many of the Presbyterian congregations adopted Unitarian views, but a revival in the nineteenth century encouraged by the Scottish and Irish Churches led to the formation of the Presbyterian Church of England (now part of the United Reformed Church).[55] There were very few Presbyterians in Bedfordshire.

Proprietary Church of England

This was Bedfordshire's own denomination if a small and short-lived effort can be so described. For its founder, the Rev. Timothy Matthews, 1795-1845 (8/31 & 78/3) and his pilgrimage through various denominations, see P.L. Bell, *Belief in Bedfordshire* (Bedford, 1986), p. 152-6 and J. Varley, 'A Bedfordshire Clergyman' in *B.H.R.S*, vol. 57, pp. 113-140.

Salvation Army (Salvationists)

The Salvation Army was founded by William Booth (1829-1912), a Methodist preacher, in 1861, and adopted its present name in 1878. Its hierarchy is based on the military, and it demands unquestioning obedience from its members.[56]

Union Chapels
These were mixed congregations of Baptists and Independents (see above)

Bedfordshire Calendar of Chapels and Meeting Houses
In this calendar I have tried to include all the known licences issued up to the end of 1901. Included here also are the three parishes which have not always been part of Bedfordshire:

> Kensworth, transferred from Hertfordshire in 1897
> Swineshead, transferred from Huntingdonshire in 1888
> Tilbrook, transferred to Huntingdonshire in 1888

Entries in the Registrar General's records which claimed to relate to the County (e.g. at Eynsbury and St Neots) have been ignored as mistakes of the applicants or the clerks. The parishes have been arranged alphabetically and assigned a number, and each entry has a sub-number for easy reference. In general the parishes are those of the ancient ecclesiastical parish, but exceptions have been made for Bedford and Luton – the former because not all applications give the name of the parish, and the latter in order to include the hamlets now incorporated in the town under one heading.

Where the denomination is given in the application or the licence this appears on the first line of the entry. When it is only deduced from other evidence the probable denomination is given at the end of the entry. Considerable care is required in such cases. The person making the application may be acting as an agent and not a member of the congregation, or there may have been a secession from the original congregation. Before 1852 licences often passed from one denomination to another with the building, and it is not impossible for the same to have happened since 1852.

The second line gives the issuing authority and the date. The former may be the archdeaconry, peculiar jurisdiction or quarter sessions, or (after 1837) states whether it was for worship or marriages. Where two dates are given the first is the date of the application and the second the date of the licence. The third line provides the description of the building. For early entries round brackets indicate alternative descriptions or spellings which differ materially in the various sources. For the Registrar General's records square brackets are used for later alterations of importance made to the entry in the register.

The fourth line gives the names of persons registering the building if known.[57] The last line gives the references to the records used to compile the entry. For the Registrar General's records subsequent changes are noted. 'Cancelled' means that a member of the congregation signed a cancellation: 'Cancelled on Revision' that it was cancelled after advertising. The latter often implies that several years elapsed between the demise of the congregation and cancellation. A reference number followed by 'Substituted' and a date means that another licence was obtained. 'Substituted for' gives the number of a licence which was replaced.

Because of the difficulties of providing accurate descriptions of denominations before 1852 no attempt has been made to add this information to the first line, but where there is good evidence of the probable denomination – original licence with the congregation, or use of Methodist printed form – this has been noted at the end of the entry.[58] Certain peculiarities in Bedfordshire have been noted while compiling the calendar. One is the disappearance of licences for rooms after 1852 which has not been found elsewhere in England. It may be that the rural nature of much of the County is responsible. Another is the appearance of marks rather than signatures before 1852, a practice which ends abruptly when the Registrar General took over. It was probably the custom to allow the owner of the building, if he was a member of the congregation, to sign the certificate first even if he was illiterate, but the Registrar General's form required one signature only.

A note of the 1672 licences, extracted from G. Lyon Turner's *Original Records of Nonconformity under Persecution and Indulgence* (London, 1911, 2 vols), vol. 2 has been added for completeness. Readers are urged to consult those invaluable books. In addition four appendices give cross-sections of existing congregations in 1715, 1772, 1842 and 1908. A fifth appendix lists the nonconformist trust deeds registered in Chancery from 1736-1870.

NOTES

1. I was once told that although the Shipping Registration Act only prescribes voluntary registration, it would be impossible to sail from any British port without registration. Although meeting houses could exist without registration they usually complied with the Act
2. It should be noted that the term Dissent means 'dissenting from the Established Church of England' and includes Roman Catholics (who are more usually called recusants). 'Protestant Dissenter' excludes Roman Catholics, but still includes Methodists and more recent Christian denominations. Confusion is caused by some dissenters objecting to the title (or to that of nonconformist) while others insist on using it
3. The returns are incomplete because the Registrar General apparently never requested returns from the ecclesiastical peculiar jurisdictions, and also because registrars and clerks of the peace could not always find all the surviving records
4. *B.H.R.S.*, vol. 54 (1975)
5. The Declaration of Indulgence is printed in A. Browning (ed.), *English Historical Documents, 1660-1714* (London, 1953), no. 140. Roman Catholics were only permitted to worship in private houses and not in chapels
6. *Ibid.*, no. 146
7. Act, 1 Will. & Mary, c.18. Some confusion has arisen because, although this Act was passed by Parliament in May 1689, it is dated 1688 in most legal works. This is because Acts without a date of implementation were traditionally assigned to the first day of the Parliamentary Session in which they were passed. As this Session began in March 1688[9], all its acts are dated 1688
8. Act, 1 Will. & Mary, c.8. The oaths prescribed in this Act effectively debarred Roman Catholics and Unitarians from taking advantage of the Toleration Act
9. Few ministers took out licences at Quarter Sessions. Samuel Marson qualified as 'a dissenting teacher' at Bedfordshire Quarter Sessions on 16 July 1740 (BRO, QSM 7, p. 65). Two other entries can be found in QSR 1812, 166
10. In this calendar I have used the traditional names of certificate (request for registration) and licence (certificate of registration) regardless of the different terms used in the various Acts

11.   Act, 10 Anne, c.6. This exemption was extended to Moravians in 1748 (Act, 22 Geo. II, c.30)
12.   Act, 19 Geo. III, c. 44
13.   Act, 31 Geo. III, c. 32
14.   Act, 52 Geo. III, c. 155. This Act obliged bishops and archdeacons to make annual returns of new licences to clerks of the peace. A copy of the Bedfordshire Archdeaconry return for 1851/2 appears in BRO, QSM 37, p. 87
15.   Act, 53 Geo. III, c. 160
16.   For Unitarians, whose influence in Bedfordshire was very small, see B.G. Bolam and others, *The English Presbyterians* (London, 1968)
17.   E. Royle (ed.), *A History of the Nonconformist Churches of York* (York, 1993), pp. 43 & 44. B.L. Manning, *The Protestant Dissenting Deputies* (Cambridge, 1952), pp. 166-8
18.   Act, 3 & 4 Will. IV, c. 30. The last clause was no doubt inserted to permit Sunday Schools to meet in chapels
19.   Act, 26 Geo. II, c. 33. Before 1753 dissenters, and especially Baptists, were married in their own meeting houses before witnesses. This constituted a valid, but irregular, marriage
20.   Act, 6 & 7 Will. IV, c. 85
21.   An important source of information was lost in 1837 when the Registrar General failed to collect details of the licences issued for worship when licencing the chapel for marriages
22.   For example, 8/27 & 28 in this calendar appear in the *London Gazette* for 30 May 1837 (p. 1373)
23.   Superintendent registrars usually destroyed their copies when registration ended, so the only complete set is with OPCS
24.   There was some doubt as to whether a completely new building on the original site had to be re-licenced (E. Jakes, *The Ely Methodists,* Ely, 1988, pp. 40 & 41)
25.   Act, 1 Victoria, c. 22. Poor Law Unions, which provided the boundaries for registration districts, had been established without reference to counties. A few parishes in Bedfordshire were included in Hunts. and Northants. Unions
26.   Act, 15 & 16 Victoria, c. 36. Although it is entitles an Act for 'Places of Religious Worship of Protestant Dissenters,' it also applied to Roman Catholics and Jews (see Manning, *op. cit., p. 148)*
27.   Act, 18 & 19 Victoria, c. 81
28.   See *Church Government, Being the Third Part of Christian Discipline in the Religious Society of Friends,* no. 13
29.   The hours for marriages were not extended to 8 a.m. & 6 p.m. until 1949 (Act, 12 & 13 Geo. VI, c. 76). A story by A. Quiller-Couch, 'When the Sap rose' in *The Delectable Duchy* illustrates some of the problems of restricted hours
30.   Act, 61 & 62 Victoria, c. 58
31.   These are the certificates addressed (correctly) to the Commissary and Official of the Archdeaconry
32.   The Registrar General was apparently unaware of this and no returns were obtained from the peculiar jurisdictions in 1852
33.   *Returns: Probate of Wills* (House of Commons Paper, 1845), pp. 30-35
34.   The gap between Aug. 1816 and Feb. 1818 was probably caused by the death of the deputy registrar. This would also account for the delay in registering 28/8
35.   According to BRO, ABN 3/2 this register was begun by Charles Bailey when he was appointed Deputy Registrar in 1818
36.   All this correspondence is to be found in BRO, ABN 3/1 & 2
37.   They had to be re-numbered when the second return was received
38.   See Manning *op.cit.*
39.   BRO, CPC 4. This was a House of Commons Paper issued on 23 Feb. 1853. See *Congregational Historical Society Transactions,* vol. 6 (1913-15), p. 204
40.   The Registrar General's Department is now known as the Office of Population, Censuses & Surveys
41.   Now to Smedley Hydro in Birkdale (Lancs.)
42.   A few duplicate numbers have been noticed in the registers and noted in the calendar

43.   For this reason the British Library set only begins in 1908

44.   For more information about Bedfordshire nonconformity see Patricia Bell, *Belief in Bedfordshire* (Bedford, 1986) and W.M.Wigfield, 'Recusancy and Nonconformity in Bedfordshire' in *B.H.R.S.*, vol. 20. Dr Williams's Library has published *Nonconformist Congregations in Great Britain* (London, 1973) Which lists its holdings by counties. This provides an invaluable list of articles on Beds. chapels written by H.G. Tibbutt and others

45.   They were named after the periodical which they supported. There is a history of the Bedfordshire Gospel Standard chapels in S.F. Paul, *Further History of the Gospel Standard Baptists* (Brighton, 1958)

46.   A.C. Underwood, *A History of the English Baptists* (London, 1947). The Baptist Historical Society has published three volumes of *The English Baptists* – Seventeenth Century by B.R. White (1983), Eighteenth Century by Raymond Brown (1986) & Nineteenth Century by J.H.Y. Briggs (1994)

47.   There is no history of this denomination, but a brief account can be found in the *Oxford Dictionary of the Christian Church*

48.   See for example a *Directory of some Assemblies in the British Isles* (London, 1933) for Beds. congregations. For the Brethren see F. Roy Coad, *A History of the Brethren Movement* (Exeter, 1968) & H.H. Rowdon, *The Origins of the Brethren* (London, 1967)

49.   P.E. Shaw, *The Catholic Apostolic Church* (New York, 1946) & C.G. Flegg, *Gathered under Apostles* (Oxford, 1992). There are several biographies of Irving available

50.   R.W. Dale, *History of English Congregationalism* (London, 1907) & R.T. Jones, *Congregationalism in England*3 (London, 1962)

51.   W.C. Braithwaite, *The Beginnings of Quakerism* & *The Second Period of Quakerism* (reprinted, York, 1981 & 1979)

52.   W.J. Townsend, H.B. Workman & G. Eayrs, *A New History of Methodism* (London, 1909, 2 vols.); H.B. Kendall, *The Origin and History of the Primitive Methodist Church* (London, [1906], 2 vols.); & R. Davies & G. Rupp, *The History of the Methodist Church in Great Britain* (London, 1965-88, 4 vols.)

53.   J.E. Hutton, *A History of the Moravian Church* (London, 1909. J.T. & K.G. Hamilton, *History of the Moravian Church* (Bethlehem, Penn., 1967) should be used with caution

54.   R.L. Evans, *A Century of 'Mormonism' in Great Britain*(Salt Lake City, 1937)

55.   C.G. Bolam and others, *The English Presbyterians* (London, 1968) is chiefly concerned with the congregations which became Unitarian. The only history of the Presbyterian Church of England is A.H. Drysdale, *History of the Presbyterians in England* (London, 1889)

56.   R. Sandall, *The History of the Salvation Army* (London, 1947-55, 3 vols.)

57.   It was not possible to include the names of the twenty householders signing the application for a marriage licence. This information for a specific licence can be obtained from the Churches and Chapels section of OPCS

58.   Note that where the certificate is addressed to the Archdeacon of Bedford, or not addressed to anyone in particular this has not been recorded in the calendar

BEDFORDSHIRE CHAPELS & MEETING HOUSES

Official Registration, 1672-1901

1. AMPTHILL

1/1
Quarter Sessions   5 Oct. 1726
Barn in occ. of Christopher Bennell
Reg. by Joseph Dunham of Haynes, yeoman
BRO, QSR 1726, 84.

1/2
Archdeaconry   30/30 Dec. 1758
Dwelling house of Joseph Crouch at Cow Fair End.
Reg. by William Copperwheat of Ampthill, sen. and William Copperwheat, jun. (his mark) of same, weavers
BRO, ABN 1/1; ABN 2/14. PRO, RG 31/2, 14

1/3
Archdeaconry   3/4 Mar. 1797
Building in Dunstable Street
Reg. by William Coles, Samuel Batchelder
BRO, ABN1/1; ABN 2/78. PRO, RG 31/2, 78

1/4
Archdeaconry   7/7 Dec. 1805
Dwelling house of James Marriott of Ampthill
Reg. by James Marriott, William Clark, Henry Langley, Richard Upton
BRO, ABN 1/1; ABN 2/121. PRO, RG 31/2, 121

1/5   **Methodist**
Archdeaconry   **29 Aug./2 Sept. 1811**
Methodist Chapel at Hog Hill
Reg. by William Baker, James Marriott, William Clark, Samuel Langley
BRO, ABN 1/1; ABN 2/141. PRO, RG 31/2, 140
Certificate addressed to the Bishop of Lincoln

1/6
Archdeaconry   3/3 Dec. 1822
Newly erected Chapel
Reg. by Samuel Hobson of Maulden
BRO, ABN 1/2; ABN 2/197; ABN 3/3, 47. PRO, RG 31/2, 218

1/7   **Primitive Methodist**
Archdeaconry   **23/23 May 1840**
House or building of Samuel Francis in Woburn Street

17

Reg. by Samuel Francis, Thomas Clements, Henry Alderslade
BRO, ABN 1/ 2; ABN 2/348. PRO, RG 31/2, 371
They also registered a chapel in Bedford on the same day

1/8   **Wesleyan**
Marriages   **16 Feb. 1848**
Wesleyan Chapel in Woburn Street
Cancelled 29 July 1885
OPCS, RG(M) 2843

1/9   **Wesleyan**
Worship   **17 Feb. 1854**
Wesleyan Methodist Chapel
Reg. by William Henry Clarkson, 4 Harpur St., Bedford, superintendent minister
Cancelled 29 Aug. 1894
OPCS, RG (W) 2128
He also registered Wesleyan chapels at Haynes, Houghton Conquest, Lidlington, Marston
Morteyne & Maulden on the same day

1/10   **Quaker**
Worship   **1 May 1854**
Friends' Meeting House in Dunstable Street
Reg. by Joseph Marsh Morris of Ampthill, baker (Clerk)
Cancelled 12 Nov. 1933
OPCS, RG(W) 4587

1/11   **Primitive Methodist**
Worship   **6 June 1874**
Primitive Methodist Chapel in Saunders Piece
Reg. by Thomas Reeve, Saunders Piece, Ampthill, Primitive Methodist minister
Cancelled 23 Sept. 1920
OPCS, RG(W) 21822

1/12   **Union Chapel**
Worship   **2 Sept. 1878**
Union Chapel (Baptist & Congregational) in Dunstable Street
Reg. by Richard Goodman jun., of Flitwick, deacon
OPCS, RG (W) 24178

1/13   **Union Chapel**
Marriages   **6 Sept. 1878**
Union Chapel (Baptist & Congregational) in Dunstable Street
OPCS, RG(M) 9560

1/14   **Wesleyan**
Worship   **16 Oct. 1884**
Wesleyan Methodist Chapel in Dunstable Street
Reg. by Robert Raw of Ampthill, Wesleyan minister
OPCS, RG(W) 28162

1/15   **Wesleyan**
Marriages   **29 July 1885**
Wesleyan Methodist Chapel in Dunstable Street
OPCS, RG(M) 11306

Plate 1: Ampthill Methodist chapel: The present chapel in Dunstable Street was built in 1884 to replace the one in Woburn Street which was licensed in 1811.   (*Postcard: c.1905*)

1/16   Salvation Army
Worship   24 Feb. 1893
Salvation Army Barracks in Dunstable Street
Reg. by William Greenwood, 19 Alexandra Rd., Bedford (occupier)
37051 substituted on 24 Feb. 1899
OPCS, RG (W) 33702

1/17   Salvation Army
Worship   24 Feb. 1899
Salvation Army Barracks in Arthur Street
Reg. by Louisa Romeril, Arthur St., Ampthill, Captain, S.A.
Substituted for 33702. Cancelled on 24 Apr. 1909
OPCS, RG(W) 37051

2. ARLESEY

2/1
Quarter Sessions   29 Sept. 1761
House of John Chapman
Reg. by Samuel James, William Thomas, John Child
BRO, QSP43/4
Certificate was addressed to the Archdeacon of Huntingdon and amended to Bedfordshire J.P.s

2/2
Archdeaconry   11 Dec. 1812
A Building
BRO, ABN 1/1

2/3
Archdeaconry   5 Apr. 1819
House of William Seymour
Reg. by Edward Stanford and others
BRO, ABN 1/2; ABN 3/3, 13. PRO RG 31/2, 184

2/4   Wesleyan
Worship   27 Mar. 1854
Wesleyan Chapel
Reg. by William Davies of Hitchin (Herts.), minister
62126 substituted on 5 Nov. 1948
OPCS, RG(W) 3784

2/5   Primitive Methodist
Worship   29 Nov. 1860
Primitive Methodist Chapel
Reg. by James Young, Sun St., Biggleswade, Primitive Methodist minister
Cancelled on revision, 19 Apr. 1895
OPCS, RG(W) 9835
Young registered Primitive Methodist chapels at Biggleswade, Stotfold &
Wrestlingworth on the same day

2/6   Primitive Methodist
Worship   4 July 1876
Primitive Methodist Chapel
Reg. by William Sidebottom of Biggleswade, Primitive Methodist minister
OPCS, RG(W) 22905

2/7   Salvationists
Worship   20 Aug. 1887
Salvation Barracks
Reg. by Frederick Parker of Arlesey, Captain, S.A.
Cancelled on revision 19 Apr. 1895
OPCS, RG(W) 30294

2/8   Salvationists
Worship   5 Jan. 1889
Salvation Army Barracks in High Street
Reg. by Agnes Brown of Arlesey, Officer in charge, S.A.
32054 substituted on 13 Mar. 1890
OPCS, RG(W) 31321

2/9   Salvationists
Worship   13 Mar. 1890
Salvation Army Barracks in Straw Street
Reg. by Annie Tunstall of Arlesey, Captain, S.A. (occupier)
Cancelled on revision 5 July 1954
OPCS, RG(W) 32054

Plate 2: Aspley Guise: The Quaker meeting house at Hogsty End (now in Woburn Sands), established in 1672. No licence is recorded. *(Engraving: c.1820)*

3. ASPLEY GUISE

3/1
Archdeaconry   **2 Nov. 1807**
House of Thomas Candy
BRO, ABN 1/1

3/2
Archdeaconry   **2 Apr. 1808**
House of Eleanor Bosworth
BRO, ABN 1/1

3/3
Archdeaconry   **26 Oct./2 Nov. 1809**
House in occ. of Thomas Candy, bounded on one side by tenement of James Fensam, and on other by dwelling house of Thomas Sear
Reg. by Joseph Sibthorpe sen., Joseph Sibthorpe jun., William Jackson, George Foskett, William Smith, Josiah Chapman, Peter Gilks (all of Aspley).
BRO, ABN 2/136

3/4
Archdeaconry   **7/8 Oct. 1811**
Dwelling house of Joseph Pain
Reg. by William Britten, John Pain, William Bowden
BRO, ABN 1/1; ABN 2/142. PRO, RG 31/2, 141

3/5   **Methodist**
Archdeaconry   **29 July 1815**
Methodist Chapel
BRO, ABN 1/1

3/6
Archdeaconry   **14/19 Apr. 1823**
Dwelling house of William Percival at Hogsty End
Reg. by William Percival
BRO, ABN 1/1; ABN 2/201; ABN 3/3, 50. PRO, RG 31/2, 222

3/7   **Primitive Methodist**
Archdeaconry   **27 Nov. 1849**
Primitive Methodist Chapel bel. to Benjamin Herbert, William Mayne and others (printed form)
Reg. by Henry Yeates, minister in Newport Pagnell
BRO, ABN 1/2; ABN 2/416. PRO, RG 31/2, 444
Certificate addressed to the Bishop of Ely

3/8   **Wesleyan**
Worship   **20 June 1854**
Wesleyan Chapel
Reg. by William Britten of Bow Brickhill (Bucks.), baker (trustee)
Cancelled 31 Dec. 1866
OPCS, RG(W) 5392
Britten registered a Wesleyan chapel at Salford on the same day

3/9   **Primitive Methodist**
Worship   **18 Dec. 1860**
Primitive Methodist Chapel at Woburn Sands
Reg. by Samuel Turner of Aylesbury (Bucks.), minister
Cancelled 29 June 1954 on revision
OPCS, RG(W) 10308

3/10   **Wesleyan**
Worship   **3 Feb. 1863**
Wesleyan Chapel, Chapel St. [Mount Pleasant in 1954]
Reg. by John Shemeld of Aspley, painter (trustee)
Cancelled 5 July 1978
OPCS, RG(W) 15515

3/11   **Wesleyan**
Marriages   **2 Apr. 1863**
Wesleyan Chapel, Chapel St., [Mount Pleasant]
Cancelled 5 July 1978
OPCS, RG(M) 5213

3/12   **Primitive Methodist**
Worship   **17 Aug. 1866**
Primitive Methodist Chapel at Water Hall, Salford Ford
Reg. by John Wilson of Linslade (Bucks.), town missionary
Cancelled 5 Feb. 1897 on revision
OPCS, RG(W) 17406

3/13   Protestant Dissenters
Worship   9 Aug. 1875
A building belonging to Lucy Hart, for Protestant Dissenters
Reg. by Lucy How of Aspley, widow (proprietor)
42930 substituted on 27 Feb. 1908
OPCS, RG(W) 22401

4. GREAT BARFORD

4/1
Archdeaconry   **19/19 Dec. 1766**
Dwelling house of Jeremiah Lee
Reg. by Jeremiah Lee of Great Barford, farmer [husbandman in RG 31/2]; Russell
Chapman (his mark) of Colmworth
BRO, ABN 1/1; ABN 2/12. PRO, RG 31/2, 23
Certificate addressed to the Commissary & Official of Bedford

4/2
Archdeaconry   **10 Mar. 1809**
Chapel built by S. Duncombe on his own land belonging to a cottage
Reg. by S. Duncombe, John Duncombe, John Robertson (his mark)
BRO, ABN 1/1; ABN 2/135. PRO RG 31/2, 131

4/3
Archdeaconry   **17 July 1813**
House of Stephen Dickens
BRO, ABN 1/1

4/4
Archdeaconry   **10/15 Jan. 1825**
Chapel (brick building) (printed form)
Reg. by James Golding of St Neots (Hunts.), William Brocklehurst
BRO, ABN 1/2; ABN 2/219; ABN 3/3, 67. PRO, RG 31/2, 238
Probably Wesleyan as the form was printed by T. Cordeux, 14 City Rd., London.
Certificate addressed to the Bishop of Lincoln

4/5
Archdeaconry   **12/14 Feb. 1833**
Dwelling house of Thomas Pack of Barford
Reg. by Thomas Pack
BRO, ABN 1/2; ABN 2/277. PRO, RG 31/2, 298
Certificate addressed to the Bishop of Lincoln

4/6   Wesleyan
Worship   15 Mar. 1854
Wesleyan Chapel
Reg. by Adam Fletcher of St Neots (Hunts.), Wesleyan minister
Cancelled for 39994 on 5 Nov. 1903
OPCS, RG(W) 3405

5. LITTLE BARFORD

5/1
Archdeaconry   **2 Apr. 1799**
House of John Lewing
BRO, ABN 1/1

6. BARTON

6/1
Archdeaconry   **24/24 Oct. 1803**
Dwelling house of John Ward, farmer
Reg. by John Ward (his mark), Robert Pilter, William Davis, William Boustrad, John
Wingrave, William Prior
BRO, ABN 1/1; ABN 2/111. PRO, RG 31/2, 110
Certificate addressed to the Bishop of Lincoln

6/2
Archdeaconry   **13 Feb. 1819**
House of William Peddit (Pedder)
Reg. by John Pack and others
BRO, ABN 1/2; ABN 3/3, 12. PRO, RG 31/2, 183

6/3
Archdeaconry   **16 June 1821**
Barn in occ. of William Brown (for ocasional preaching)
Reg. by William Brown, Jos. Brown, James Blott, William Blott
BRO, ABN 1/2; ABN 2/178; ABN 3/3, 28. PRO, RG 31/2, 199

6/4
Archdeaconry   **19 Nov. 1823**
House of John Warren
Reg. by John Warren
BRO, ABN 1/2; ABN 3/3, 54.

6/5
Archdeaconry   **9/13 Dec. 1831**
Newly erected Chapel
Reg. by John Warren, James Harris, James Foxen, Thomas Burbidge
BRO, ABN 1/2; ABN 2/263; ABN 3/3, 112. PRO, RG 31/2, 284
Certificate addressed to the Bishop of Lincoln

6/6   **Wesleyan**
Archdeaconry   **19/21 June 1834**
Wesleyan Chapel (printed form)
Reg. by Isaac Wale of Bedford
BRO, ABN 1/2; ABN 2/288. PRO, RG 31/2, 307
Certificate addressed to the Bishop of Lincoln. Wale registered chapels at Dunstable &
Hockliffe on the same day

6/7
Archdeaconry
Wesleyan Chapel (printed form)

Wesleyan
19/19 May 1835

Reg. by Thomas Rogerson of Luton
BRO, ABN 1/2; ABN 2/301. PRO, RG 31/2, 327
Certificate addressed to the bishop of Lincoln. Rogerson registered Wesleyan chapels at
Houghton Regis, Leagrave, Luton, Tebworth, Toddington & Whipsnade on the same day

6/8
Worship
Wesleyan Methodist Chapel in Sharpenhoe Road

Wesleyan
6 Feb. 1854

Reg. by Wright Shovelton, Chapel St., Luton, superintendent minister
OPCS, RG(W) 1753
Shovelton registered Wesleyan chapels at Caddington & Luton on the same day

6/9
Worship
Primitive Methodist Chapel in Bedford Road

Primitive Methodist
3 Nov. 1876

Reg. by John Henry James Beckhurst, High Town, Luton, minister
Cancelled on Revision, 10 Aug. 1954
OPCS, RG(W) 23070

7. BATTLESDEN

7/1
Archdeaconry
House in occ. of James Creamer (printed form)

10/19 Mar. 1851

Reg. by William Stevens of Leighton Heath (Leighton Buzzard), John Bendle (witness)
BRO, ABN 1/2; ABN 2/424. PRO, RG 31/2, 451
Certificate addressed to the Bishop of Ely

8. BEDFORD

8/1
House of Josiah Roughead

Baptist
1 May 1672

O.R., p. 855

8/2
House of John Tingey at Ford End

Congregational
1 May 1672

O.R., p. 854

8/3
House of John Fenn in St. Paul's par.

Baptist
30 Sept. 1672

O.R., p. 854

8/4
Archdeaconry
Barn in occ. of John Randall in St Cuthbert's par.

23 May 1707

Reg. by Ebenezer Chandler, William Nicholls, Henry Whitbread
BRO, ABC 24, f. 115d

Plate 3: Bedford: The Moravian church, school and houses in St. Peter's Street. The chapel was later rebuilt and a new licence was issued in 1867.

(Print: Bradford Rudge, 1851)

8/5
Archdeaconry   **16 Oct. 1740**
Barn of Mrs Anne Okely in St Paul's par.
Reg. by Thomas Craner of Blunham, Mathew Basterfield of Bedford
BRO, MO 42
The licence is in the Bedford Moravian Church records, and printed in *B.H.R.S.*, vol. 68, p.196. When issued the congregation was Particular Baptist

8/6   **Moravian**
Quarter Sessions   **- - 1752**
Moravian Chapel in St Peter's par.
BRO, MO 43
The original licence is missing, and it is not registered in the Quarter Sessions records. Contents reconstructed from 8/7

8/7
Archdeaconry   **3/3 June 1754**
House of Francis Negus in St Cuthbert's par.
Reg. by Joseph Negus of Bedford, woolcomber, Thomas Simpson of Bedford, yeoman
BRO, ABN 1/1; ABN 2/4. PRO, RG 31/2, 4
Certificate addressed to the Commissary & Official of Bedford

Plate 4: Bedford: The Howard chapel in Mill Street, built in 1774 and re-fronted in 1849. It was licensed in 1775. (*Print: John Sunman Austin, 1854*)

8/8   Moravian
Borough & County Quarter Sessions   1/3 Oct. 1759
Vestry added to east side of Chapel
Reg. by George Tranker, William Vowell
BRO, MO 43. PRO, RG 31/6, 4
No entry found in County or Borough Quarter Sessions records

8/9
Archdeaconry   9/9 Feb. 1773
Corn Warehouse at the bottom of Red Lion Yard, High St.
Reg. by Benjamin King, John Costin, Gideon Costin, William Belsham, Richard Leach,
Thomas Askew Leach, William Rayner, Samuel Bigrave
BRO, ABN1/1; ABN 2/33. PRO, RG 31/2, 33

8/10
County Quarter Sessions   11 Jan. 1775
New brick building in Mill Lane
Reg. by Benjamin King, Gideon Costin, William Belsham, Richard Leach, Thomas
Askew Leach
BRO, QSP43/14
There are two copies of the certificate

8/11   Independent
County Quarter Sessions   12/12 Jan. 1791
**Building commonly called Mr Hill's barn in his orchard in St Peters parish,
fronting Queens-head Lane, for dissenters usually denominated Independents**
Reg. by William Baker, minister, William Hill, William Smith, John Corley, Joseph
Whitehouse, John Simmons (inhabitants)
BRO, QSR 1791, 68; QSM, vol. 18, p. 240. PRO, RG 31/6, 12

8/12   Baptist
County Quarter Sessions   11 Aug. 1792
**Building commonly called the Old Chapell in George Yard belonging to Mr
Blackwell in St. Paul's par., for dissenters usually denominated Baptists**
Reg. by William Negus, John Woodham, Joseph Whitehouse, Nathaniel Woodham,
Ebenezer Cavit, William Smith (inhabitants)
BRO, QSR 1792, 57; QSM, vol. 19, p. 12

8/13   Baptist
County Quarter Sessions   16/16 Jan. 1793
**Mr Leach's Forge Shop in Mill Lane in St Paul's par., for congregation usually
denominated Baptist**
Reg. by William Rush, John Corley, William Smith, John Lilley, John Emery, Ebenezer
Cavit
BRO, QSR 1793, 53; QSM, vol. 19, p. 25. PRO, RG 31/6, 17

8/14
Borough Quarter Sessions   4 Apr. 1796
Building in High Street, late a Cooper's shop (St Paul's par.)
Bedford Borough Records, F3/2

Plate 5: Bedford: The Methodist chapel in Harpur Street (then known as Angel Street) built in 1804. No licence is recorded. (*Watercolour: Thomas Fisher, c.1820*)

8/15
Archdeaconry   **26 Apr. 1806**
Sessions House (County Hall) at Bedford, granted by the magistrates for the temporary convenience of the Old Meeting now being repaired
Reg. by S. Hillyard, William Smith, T. Kilpin
BRO, ABN 1/1; ABN 2/131. PRO, RG 31/2, 128

8/16
Archdeaconry   **30 Apr. 1808**
House of William Rush
BRO, ABN 1/1

8/17
Archdeaconry   **25 July 1812**
Building in occ. of William Sargeant
Reg. by William Sargeant, Joseph Dicker, John Hulat, Nathan Huelat, William Brooks Wright, E.H. Barringer
BRO, ABN 1/1; ABN 2/146. PRO, RG 31/2, 144

8/18
Archdeaconry   **24/24 Oct. 1821**
Building in a yard on the premises of Daniel Attack in Castle Street, St. Cuthbert's par.
Reg. by William Peet (Peck)
ABN 1/2; ABN 2/184; ABN 3/3, 31. PRO, RG 31/2, 202

8/19
Archdeaconry   10/10 Nov. 1821
House in occ. of Isaac Anthony in St. John's par.
Reg. by Isaac Anthony
BRO, ABN 1/2; ABN 2/185; ABN 3/3, 32

8/20
Archdeaconry   17/17 June 1830
Newly erected chapel in St. Paul's par.
Reg. by William Sargeant of St Cuthberts, George Stocker, John Green (both of St Pauls)
BRO, ABN 1/2; ABN 2/240; ABN 3/3, 97. PRO, RG 31/2, 269

8/21
Archdeaconry   23/23 Apr. 1831
Dwelling house of Timothy Richard Matthews of Bedford, clerk
Reg. by T.R. Matthews
BRO, ABN 1/2; ABN 2/256; ABN 3/3, 105. PRO, RG 31/2, 277

8/22
Archdeaconry   2/16 May 1831
House of Benjamin Norman of St Paul's par.
Reg. by Benjamin Norman
BRO, ABN 1/2; ABN 2/258; ABN 3/3, 107
Certificate addressed to the Bishop of Lincoln

8/23
Archdeaconry   11/11 July 1831
House of William Bettle in St. Paul's par.
Reg. by William Bettle
BRO, ABN 1/2; ABN 2/260; ABN 3/3, 109. PRO, RG 31/2, 281
Certificate addressed to the Bishop of Lincoln

8/24
Archdeaconry   30 June/1 July 1834
House of Mrs Blackwell in Wells Street (printed form)
Reg. by Thomas Clements, minister
BRO, ABN 1/2; ABN 2. PRO, RG 31/2, 313
Certificate addressed to the Bishop of Lincoln

8/25
Archdeaconry   27/27 Aug. 1836
Dwelling house of Leonora Russell in the Crescent
Reg. by Leonora Russell, spinster
BRO, ABN 1/2; ABN 2/313. PRO, RG 31/2, 337

8/26
Archdeaconry   10/10 Sept. 1836
Priory Chapel in St Paul's par.
Reg. by Timothy Richard Matthews of St Paul's par.
BRO, ABN 1/2; ABN 2. PRO, RG 31/2, 338
Certificate addressed to the Bishop of Lincoln

8/27   **Independent**
Marriages   **22 May 1837**
The Old Meeting in Mill Street
3159 substituted on 11 Apr. 1850
OPCS, RG(M) 10

8/28   **Independent**
Marriages   **24 May 1837**
Howard Chapel in Mill Street [United Reformed Church]
OPCS, RG(M) 11

8/29
Archdeaconry   **12/12 Sept. 1837**
Howard Chapel in Mill Street
Reg. by Jacob Anthony of Bedford
BRO, ABN 1/2; ABN 2/318. PRO, RG 31/2, 341

8/30
Archdeaconry   **30 Nov. 1838**
House in occ. of Leonora Russell in the Crescent
Reg. by William Hannum, Mrs Barber, Mrs Wilmott, Miss (L.) Russell
BRO, ABN 1/2; ABN 2/333. PRO, RG 31/2, 355

8/31   **Proprietary Church of England**
Marriages   **4 May 1839**
Christ's Church, Bedford
Cancelled 7 Oct. 1856
OPCS, RG(M) 1455
See 8/26 for original registration

8/32   **Primitive Methodist**
Archdeaconry   **23/23 May 1840**
Building (house) of Thomas Clements in Hassock Street
Reg. by Thomas Clements, minister, George Rowles, Samuel Francis
BRO, ABN 1/2; ABN 2/347. PRO, RG 31/2, 370
Certificate originally addressed to the Bishop of Lincoln and altered to Ely

8/33
Archdeaconry. Borough Quarter Sessions   **5/5 Mar. 1841**
House of John Garner Sheffield in St. Paul's par.
Reg. by J.G. Sheffield of St Paul's par.
BRO, ABN 1/2; ABN 2/360. PRO, RG 31/2, 375; RG 31/8, 1
No entry in Borough Quarter Sessions records

8/34
Archdeaconry. Borough Quarter Sessions   **28/28 Dec. 1844**
Large room in occ. of John Mayle
Reg. by Robert Martin of St. Paul's par. [George Osborn and William Smith [*deleted*]
BRO, ABN 1/2; ABN 2/373. PRO, RG 31/2, 399; RG 31/3, 2
Certificate addressed to the Bishop of Ely. No entry in Borough Quarter Sessions records

8/35
County Quarter Sessions   1 Dec. 1849/1 Jan. 1850
Mr Sheppard's New Room, Market Hill, Bedford (temporary place)
Reg. by T.T. Crybace, A.M.
BRO, QSR 50/1. PRO, RG 31/6, 41

8/36   Congregational
Marriages   11 Apr. 1850
Bunyan Meeting House in Mill Lane
Substituted for RG(M) 10
OPCS, RG (M) 3159

8/37   Baptist
Archdeaconry. Borough Quarter Sessions   29/29 May 1851
Baptist Chapel in Mill Lane, St Paul's par. (printed form)
Reg. by Hugh Killen of St Peter's par., minister
BRO, ABN 1/2; ABN 2/428 & 429 (2 copies). PRO, RG 31/2, 454; RG 31/8, 3
Certificate addressed to the Bishop of Ely. No entry in Borough Quarter Sessions records

8/38
Archdeaconry. Borough Quarter Sessions   16/16 Aug. 1851
House of William Preston in Cauldwell Street, St. Mary's par.
Reg. by James Costin Stewart (baker), William Swithin, butcher, Nathaniel Sturges
BRO, ABN 1/2; ABN 2/431. PRO, RG 31/2, 455; RG 31/8, 4
Certificate addressed to the Bishop of Ely. No entry in Borough Quarter Sessions records

8/39
Archdeaconry. Borough Quarter Sessions   30/30 Aug. 1851
Room in occ. of Joseph Hornsey in Castle Lane, St. Paul's par.
Reg. by Samuel Bell, builder (bricklayer), Charles Wootton, builder, Thomas Linford of
St Paul's, James Costin Stewart of St Peter's
BRO, ABN 1/2; ABN 2/430. PRO, RG 31/2, 456; RG 31/8, 5
Certificate addressed to the Bishop of Ely. No entry in Borough Quarter Sessions records

8/40   Free Gospel
Archdeaconry. Borough Quarter Sessions   13/15 May 1852
Free Gospel Chapel in Grey Friars' Walk in occ. of Society
Reg. by Charles Catlin, William Stacey, George Lane, Joseph Frazer, John William
Miller, William Frazer
BRO, ABN 1/2; ABN 2/437. PRO RG 31/2, 463; ABN 31/8, 6
Certificate addressed to the Bishop of Ely. No entry in Borough Quarter Sessions records

8/41   Primitive Methodist
Worship   8 Oct. 1852
Primitive Methodist Chapel in Hassett Street
Reg. by John Deighton, Beauchamp Row, Bedford, labourer (trustee)
Cancelled 27 July 1959
OPCS, RG(W) 271

8/42   Independents
Worship   8 Oct. 1853
Howard Chapel in Mill Street
Reg. by Jacob Anthony of Bedford, chemist (trustee)
62526 substituted on 8 Dec. 1949
OPCS, RG(W) 1256

8/43 **Baptist**
Worship **6 Dec. 1853**
Victoria Rooms
Reg. by James Shepherd of Bedford, tailor & draper (proprietor)
Cancelled 31 Dec. 1866
OPCS, RG(W) 1360

8/44 **Wesleyan**
Worship **9 Feb. 1854**
Wesleyan Methodist Chapel in Harpur St
Reg. by William Henry Clarkson, Harpur St., Bedford, superintendent minister
Cancelled 20 Feb. 1869
OPCS, RG(W) 1864
Clarkson registered Wesleyan chapels at Cardington, Clapham, Kempston, Milton Ernest,
Pavenham, Turvey, Wilshamstead & Wootton on the same day

8/45 **Primitive Methodist**
Marriages **17 Nov. 1854**
Primitive Methodist Chapel, Hassett Street
Cancelled 27 July 1959
OPCS, RG(M) 3733

8/46 **Wesleyan**
Marriages **9 Dec. 1859**
Wesleyan Chapel in Harpur Street
Cancelled 20 Feb. 1969
OPCS, RG(M) 4520

8/47 **Congregational**
Worship **7 July 1860**
Bunyan Meeting in Mill Street
Reg. by Benjamin Prole sen., 36 Mill St., Bedford, maltster (senior trustee)
OPCS, RG(W) 9403
'Independent' in 1954

8/48 **Berean**
Worship **16 Apr. 1861**
Berean Chapel in occ. of Thomas Swanson in Thurlow Street
Reg. by Thomas Swanson, Thurlow St., Bedford (occupier)
Cancelled 31 Dec. 1866
OPCS, RG(W) 14181
Described as 'No relevant appellation'

8/49 **Particular Baptist**
Worship **8 Nov. 1862**
St Mary's Baptist Chapel in Caudwell Street, St Mary's par.
Reg. by Jabez Carter of St John's par., Bedford, surgeon (attendant)
Cancelled 19 July 1897
OPCS, RG(W) 15376

Plate 6: Bedford: Plan of the new Baptist Chapel in Mill Street, Bedford. The building was licensed in 1866.   (*Architect's drawing: John Usher, 1862*)

8/50   **Wesleyan**
Worship   **4 June 1866**
Wesleyan Chapel in Caudwell Street
Reg. by Thomas Alexander Rayner, Westbourne Villas, Bedford, minister
Cancelled 13 Sept. 1954
OPCS, RG(W) 17292

8/51   **Baptist**
Worship   **30 Oct. 1866**
Baptist Chapel in Mill Street
Reg. by Samuel Wainwright Jarvis, Hasset St, Bedford, builder & stonemason (deacon)
Cancelled 9 Feb. 1870
OPCS, RG(W) 17519

8/52   **Baptist**
Marriages   **31 Oct. 1866**
Baptist Chapel in Mill Street
7054 substituted on 9 Feb. 1870
OPCS, RG(M) 6143

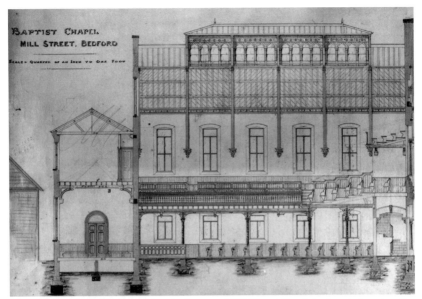

Plate 7: Bedford: Section through the new Mill Street Baptist chapel showing the galleries and seating.   (*Architect's drawing: John Usher, 1862*)

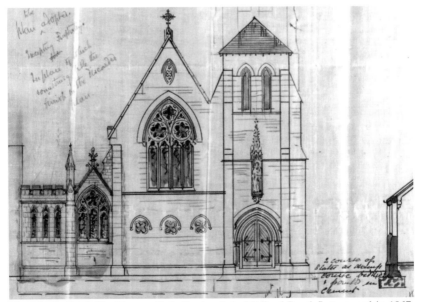

Plate 8: Bedford: The Roman Catholic church in Midland Road first opened in 1867. This drawing shows the main front as completed in 1912 to designs first proposed in 1877.   (*Architect's drawing: A. Edward Purdie, 1911*)

8/53   Independent
Worship   15 Dec. 1866
Zion Chapel, Larke Lane
Reg. by Luke Cherry of Bedford, draper (proprietor)
Cancelled 3 June 1907
OPCS, RG(W) 17622

8/54   Roman Catholic
Worship   26 Apr. 1867
A building adjoining the dwelling house of John P. Warmoll in New Street, running out of Midland Road
Reg. by John Priestley Warmoll of Bedford, Catholic priest
Cancelled 8 May 1895
OPCS, RG(W) 17905

8/55   Wesleyan
Marriages   11 July 1867
Wesleyan Methodist Chapel in St. Mary's
Cancelled 13 Sept. 1954
OPCS, RG(M) 6322

8/56   Moravian
Worship   25 Sept. 1867
The Moravian Chapel in St. Peter's Street (St Luke's United Church)
Reg. by John Lang of St Peter's par., Bedford, minister
OPCS, RG(W) 18104
Noted that the 'old chapel was demolished and a new chapel built on the site'

8/57   Moravian
Marriages   5 Oct. 1867
Moravian Chapel in St Peter's Street (St Luke's Church)
OPCS, RG(M) 6387

8/58   Particular Baptist
Worship   19 Aug. 1869
Providence Chapel in Castle Lane
Reg. by John Thornber of Bedford, minister (proprietor)
Substituted 34613 on 16 Nov. 1894
OPCS, RG(W) 19208

8/59   Particular Baptist
Marriages   20 Aug. 1869
Providence Chapel in Castle Lane
13803 substituted on 29 Nov. [1894]
OPCS, RG(M) 6908

8/60   Baptist
Worship   8 Feb. 1870
Baptist Chapel in Mill Street
Reg. by Samuel W. Jarvis, Brereton Rd., Bedford, deacon
Cancelled 23 Jan. 1964
OPCS, RG(W) 19488

8/61
Marriages
Baptist Chapel in Mill Street
Substituted for RG(M) 6143. Cancelled 23 Jan. 1964
OPCS, RG(M) 7054

Baptist
9 Feb. 1870

8/62
Marriages
Catholic School Room in Midland Road
9434 substituted on 8 Apr. 1878
OPCS, RG(M) 7569

Roman Catholic
19 Jan. 1872

8/63
Marriages
Zion Chapel, Larke Lane
Cancelled 3 June 1907
OPCS, RG(M) 7989

Independent
11 July 1873

8/64
Worship
Wesleyan Chapel, Ampthill Road
Reg. by Thomas L. Gray of Bedford, wine merchant (trustee)
OPCS, RG(W) 21527

Wesleyan
6 Nov. 1873

8/65
Worship
Church of the Holy Child in Midland Road
Reg. by John Priestley Wormall of Bedford, R.C. priest
OPCS, RG(W) 21723

Roman Catholic
30 Mar. 1874

8/66
Marriages
Southend Wesleyan Chapel in Ampthill Road
OPCS, RG(M) 9261

Wesleyan
5 Sept. 1877

8/67
Worship
Bromham Road Wesleyan Methodist Chapel in Conduit Road
Reg. by John Clulow, 60 Midland Rd., Bedford, Wesleyan minister
Cancelled 5 Oct. 1955
OPCS, RG(W) 23777

Wesleyan
20 Nov. 1877

8/68
Marriages
Church of the Holy Child & St. Joseph in Midland Road
Substituted for 7569
OPCS, RG(M) 9434

Roman Catholic
8 Apr. 1878

8/69
Marriages
Wesleyan Methodist Chapel, Conduit Street, Bromham Road
Cancelled 5 Oct. 1955
OPCS, RG(M) 9843

Wesleyan
23 Oct. 1879

8/70   Salvation Army
Worship   24 Mar. 1888
Salvation Army Barracks in Rutland Street, Midland Road
Reg. by Harriet Lawrence, 75 Harpur St., Bedford, Staff Captain, S.A.
Cancelled on revision, 8 May 1895
OPCS, RG(W) 30750

8/71   Salvation Army
Worship   28 Mar. 1888
The Skating Rink in Duck Mill Lane
Reg. by Harriet Lawrence, 75 Harpur St., Bedford, Staff Captain, S.A.
Cancelled 28 Feb. 1889   `
OPCS, RG(W) 30771

8/72   Salvation Army
Worship   28 Feb. 1889
Congress Hall in River Street
Reg. by Hannah Leedham, 6 Peel St., Bedford, minister, S.A.
Substituted 74630 on 1 June 1977
OPCS, RG(W) 31399

8/73   Catholic Apostolic
Worship   20 Feb. 1891
Catholic Apostolic Church in Gwyn Street
Reg. by Edward Stuart, 22 Rutland Rd., Bedford, minister
Cancelled on revision, 5 July 1954
OPCS, RG(W) 32586

8/74   Catholic Apostolic
Marriages   13 Oct. 1891
Catholic Apostolic Church in Gwyn Street
Cancelled on revision, 5 July 1954
OPCS, RG(M) 12912

8/75   Unsectarian
Worship   5 Oct. 1893
Iron Hall in Park Road
Reg. by C. Elliott Smith, 150 Foster Hill Rd., Bedford, trustee
Cancelled 27 Mar. 1906
OPCS, RG(W) 34045

8/76   Baptist
Worship   16 Nov. 1894
Providence Baptist Chapel in Rothsay Road
Reg. by William Thomas Lansbury, High St., Bedford, straw merchant (trustee)
Substituted for 19208
OPCS, RG(W) 34613

8/77   Unsectarian
Worship   23 Nov. 1894
Bedford United Mission in Costin Street
Reg. by Azor Savage, 13 Beaconsfield St., Bedford, banker (trustee)
Cancelled on revision, 5 July 1954
OPCS, RG(W) 34616

8/78   **Baptist**
Marriages   **29 Nov. 1894**
Providence Baptist Chapel in Rothsay Road
Substituted for 6908
OPCS, RG(M) 13803

8/79   **Primitive Methodist**
Worship   **21 Oct. 1895**
Primitive Methodist Chapel in Park Road (West)
Reg. by John Savage, 11 Park Rd., Bedford, trustee
OPCS, RG(W) 35052

8/80   **Primitive Methodist**
Marriages   **25 Oct. 1895**
Primitive Methodist Chapel in Park Road (West)
OPCS, RG(M) 14085

8/81   **Primitive Methodist**
Marriages   **6 Aug. 1897**
Primitive Methodist Chapel in Cauldwell Street
Cancelled 6 July 1946
OPCS, RG(M) 14729

8/82   **Unsectarian**
Marriages   **7 July 1899**
Iron Hall in Park Road
Cancelled 27 Mar. 1906
OPCS, RG(M) 15443

8/83   **Primitive Methodist**
Worship   **19 July 1899**
Primitive Methodist Chapel in Cauldwell Street
Reg. by Richard Newman Wycherley, 15 Western St., Bedford, minister
Cancelled 6 July 1946
OPCS, RG(W) 36120

9. BIDDENHAM

9/1
Archdeaconry   **12/17 Dec. 1832**
Dwelling house of Uriah Johnson of Biddenham
Reg. by Uriah Johnson
BRO, ABN 1/2; ABN 2/275; ABN 3/3, 124. PRO, RG 31/2, 296
Certificate addressed to the Bishop of Lincoln

10. BIGGLESWADE

10/1   **Congregational**
House of John Ward   **22 July 1672**
O.R., p. 858

10/2   **Baptist**
Quarter Sessions   **11 Jan. 1786**
Newly erected building in Langford Street
BRO, QSM 18, p. 42. PRO, RG 31/6, 8

10/3
Archdeaconry   **5/7 Nov. 1794**
Barn late in occ. of Richard Mantle, carpenter, and now of John Freeman, gent.
Reg. by John Freeman, Samuel Bennett, John Hickling
BRO, ABN 1/1; ABN 2/74. PRO, RG 31/2, 74
Certificate addressed to the Bishop of Lincoln

10/4
Peculiar Jurisdiction   **4 Nov. 1795**
A chapel on Cowfair Lands, the property of Miss Elizabeth Harvey of Hinxworth (Herts.)
Reg. by John Freeman, William Francis, Thomas [Linay], Stephen Wilson
BRO, PB/S6/1

10/5   **Wesleyan**
Peculiar Jurisdiction   **6/9 Apr. 1836**
Wesleyan Chapel
Reg. by Jonathan Turner of Biggleswade (printed form)
CRO, A277/250
The certificate was originally addressed to the Bishop of Lincoln, amended first to the Bishop of Ely, then to the Peculiar Jurisdiction, and finally to the Registrar of Huntingdon Archdeaconry. The licence was probably issued by the Peculiar Jurisdiction

Plate 9: Biggleswade: The Wesleyan chapel built in 1834 and licensed in 1836.
(*Postcard: c.1910*)

10/6   **Baptist**
Marriages   **7 July 1837**
Baptist Meeting
Cancelled 31 Jan. 1968
OPCS, RG(M) 173

10/7   **Wesleyan**
Marriages   **10 July 1837**
Wesleyan Chapel
OPCS, RG(M) 191

10/8   **Baptist**
Quarter Sessions   **8 Apr. 1845**
Building in poss. or occ. of John Corbitt
Reg. by John Corbitt, Charles Sloper, Edmund Powers, John Green, Samuel Peacock, John Simms
BRO, QSR 15/2. PRO, RG 31/6, 37

10/9
Peculiar Jurisdiction   **4 Apr. 1848**
Dwelling house in occ. of John Rawlings (printed form)
Reg. by John Guy of Baldock (Herts.)
CRO, A277, 323
Although the certificate is addressed to the Bishop of Lincoln or his registrar, it is amongst the records of the Peculiar Jurisdiction

10/10   **Primitive Methodist**
Archdeaconry   **18 Nov. 1848**
Room in late dwelling house of John Guy held in trust for Primitive Methodists (printed form)
Reg. by John Parrott of St. Paul's par., Bedford
BRO, ABN 1/2; ABN 2/403. PRO, RG 31/2, 426
Certificate addressed to the Bishop of Ely

10/11   **Mormon**
Archdeaconry   **10/10 Mar. 1849**
Latter Day Saints Meeting Room (House) in Palace Street
Reg. by Thomas Smith of Bedford
BRO, ABN 1/2; ABN 2/407. PRO, RG 31/2, 434

10/12   **Primitive Methodist**
Worship   **24 Dec. 1853**
Primitive Methodist Chapel in Short Mead Street
Reg. by Edward Powell, 1 Pembroke Rd., Baldock (Herts.), minister (trustee)
Cancelled 31 Dec. 1866
OPCS, RG(W) 1388

10/13   **Wesleyan**
Worship   **9 Feb. 1854**
Wesleyan Chapel
Reg. by Robert Maxwell of Biggleswade, Wesleyan minister
OPCS, RG(W) 1877
Maxwell registered Wesleyan chapels at Langford, Sandy, Shefford & Stotfold on the same day

10/14   Primitive Methodist
Worship   29 Nov. 1860
Primitive Methodist Chapel in Shortmead Street
Reg. by James Young, Sun St., Biggleswade, Primitive Methodist minister
Cancelled 6 Mar. 1876
OPCS, RG(W) 9837
Young registered Primitive Methodist chapels at Arlesey, Stotfold & Wrestlingworth on
the same day

10/15   Baptist
Worship   5 Mar. 1861
Baptist Meeting House in Langford Street
Reg. by Philip Griffiths, Langford St., Biggleswade, Baptist minister
Substituted 71252 on 31 Jan. 1968
OPCS, RG(W) 13264

10/16   Strict Baptist
Marriages   26 Oct. 1874
Providence Chapel
Cancelled 8 June 1988
OPCS, RG(M) 8367

10/17   Primitive Methodist
Worship   8 Mar. 1875
Primitive Methodist Chapel in Shortmead Street
Reg. by William Sidebottom, Hitchin St., Biggleswade, Primitive Methodist minister
Cancelled 13 Sept. 1939
OPCS, RG(W) 22156

10/18   Salvationists
Worship   2 June 1887
Wesleyan Branch School in Cowfair Lands
Reg. by Polly Young of Biggleswade, Captain, S.A.
Cancelled 10 Sept. 1887
OPCS, RG(W) 30174

10/19   Salvationists
Worship   6 Sept. 1887
Jubilee Hall in Shortmead Street
Reg. by James Townson of Biggleswade, Adjutant, S.A.
Cancelled 3 Sept. 1907
OPCS, RG(W) 30325
Title later amended to Salvation Army

10/20   Brethren
Worship   25 July 1893
Gospel Room in Back Street
Reg. by Samuel Peacock of Biggleswade, coach fitter (trustee)
Cancelled on revision, 26 June 1925
OPCS, RG(W) 33948

10/21
Marriages
Primitive Methodist Chapel in Shortmead Street
Cancelled 13 July 1939
OPCS, RG(M) 14583

Primitive Methodist
20 Mar. 1897

11. BILLINGTON

11/1
Archdeaconry
Dwelling house in occ. of Zachary Whitehead at Great Billington (Leighton Buzzard)
Reg. by Thomas Wake, teacher, Zachary Whitehead, John Craggs
BRO, ABN 1/1; ABN 2/97

21 Aug. 1798/2 Apr. 1799

11/2
Archdeaconry
Room in dwelling house of James Leach
Reg. by James Leach, William Garrett, William Johnson, Thomas Newens
BRO, ABN 1/1; ABN 2/110. PRO, RG 31/2, 111

11/13 May 1803

11/3
Peculiar Jurisdiction of Leighton Buzzard
Messuage or tenement in occ. of Thomas Stevens
Reg. by Thomas Stevens of Billington, farmer
BRO, RI 6824

15/15 Jan. 1828

11/4
Peculiar Jurisdiction of Leighton Buzzard
Dwelling house in occ. of James Pain of Billington
Reg. by William Piggott of Leighton Buzzard
BRO, RI 6824

Wesleyan
19 Oct. 1823

11/5
Archdeaconry
Dwelling house in occ. of John Read Badrick (printed form)
Reg. by J.R. Badrick of Great Billington
BRO, ABN 2
Certificate addressed to the Bishop of Ely

25/29 Mar. 1850

11/6
Worship
Wesleyan Methodist Chapel
Reg. by Joshua Mottram of Leighton Buzzard, minister
Cancelled 11 Jan. 1980 (advertised 11 Jan.)
OPCS, RG(W) 14203
Mottram registered Wesleyan chapels at Eggington & Leighton Buzzard; Mentmore, Stoke Hammond & Soulbury (Bucks.) on the same day

Wesleyan
19 Apr. 1861

11/7   **Primitive Methodist**
Worship   **29 Apr. 1864**
Bethesda Primitive Methodist Chapel
Reg. by William Birks of Leighton Buzzard, minister
Cancelled on revision, 5 Aug. 1954
OPCS, RG(W) 16169
Birks registered Primitive Methodist chapels at Heath & Lidlington on the same day

12. BLETSOE

12/1
Archdeaconry   **19/20 Sept. 1815**
Dwelling house in occ. of Elizabeth Markham (printed form)
Reg. by John Dean of Bedford, minister
BRO, ABN 1/1, ABN 2/170. PRO, RG 31/2, 169

12/2
Archdeaconry   **8/8 Dec. 1832**
House of Charles Partridge
Reg. by Charles Partridge of Bletsoe
BRO, ABN 1/2; ABN 2/274; ABN 3/3, 123. PRO, RG 31/2, 295

12/3
Archdeaconry   **29/29 Mar. 1843**
Dwelling house of Thomas Brown
Reg. by Thomas Brown of Bletsoe
BRO, ABN 1/2; ABN 2/372. PRO, RG 31/2, 394
Certificate addressed to the Bishop of Ely

12/4   **Primitive Methodist**
Worship   **12 Mar. 1860**
Dwelling house in occ. of Harry Brown
Reg. by Henry Brown of Bletsoe, labourer (occupier)
Cancelled on revision, 8 May 1895
OPCS, RG(W) 9175

13. BLUNHAM

13/1   **Congregational**
Lake House Barn   **1 May 1672**
O.R., p. 856

13/2
Archdeaconry   **n.d. (c. 1710)**
Houses of Mary Ravens, widow, & William Dix, husbandman, both of Blunham
Reg. by Joseph Ravens of Blunham & Samuel Henshman of Bedford, grocers
BRO, ABC 24, f. 116

81/1. The house registered at Blunham, 17 Nov. 1753 in RG 31/2 is for Roxton

13/3
Archdeaconry   **13/13 Mar. 1753**
Barn of Thomas Craner of Blunham, gent., in his yard
Reg. by Thomas Craner, Samuel Butler of Bedford, wheelwright
BRO, ABN 1/1, ABN 2/2. PRO, RG 31/2, 3
Certificate addressed to the Commissary & Official of Bedford

13/4
Archdeaconry   **27/27 Jan. 1759**
House of John Rutt of Blunham, baker
Reg. by John Rutt [Anthony Crawley of Blunham, farmer, *deleted*, and John Keeling of
Bedford, woolstapler *substituted*]
BRO, ABN 1/1; ABN 2/15
Certificate addressed to the Commissary & Official of Bedford

13/5   **Baptist**
Marriages   **28 Sept. 1837**
Baptist Meeting House
OPCS, RG(M) 609

13/6
Archdeaconry   **9/9 June 1842**
Building in occ. of John Howe
Reg. by John Howe (his mark)
BRO, ABN 1/2; ABN 2/303. PRO, RG 31/2, 391
Certificate addressed to the Bishop of Ely

13/7
Archdeaconry   **13/13 Dec. 1842**
Building in occ. of William Judd of Blunham
Reg. by William Judd, Thomas Bath
BRO, ABN 1/2, ABN 2/361. PRO, RG 31/2, 393
Certificate addressed to the Bishop of Ely

13/8   **Baptist**
Worship   **26 Mar. 1861**
Baptist Old Meeting House
Reg. by William Abbott of Blunham, Baptist minister
OPCS, RG(W) 13845

14. BOLNHURST

14/1   **Congregational**
House of Simon Haynes   **10 June 1672**
O.R., p. 856

14/2
Archdeaconry   **28/28 Dec. 1765**
Dwelling house of John Emery of Bolnhurst, husbandman
Reg. by John Emery, William Bond of Pavenham
BRO, ABN 1/1, ABN 2/21. PRO, RG 31/2, 26
Certificate addressed to the Commissary & Official of Bedford. RG31/2 dates this 8 Dec.
1768

14/3
Archdeaconry   19 Dec. 1818
House of Joseph Edrop
Reg. by William Green and others
BRO, ABN 1/2; ABN 3/3, 8; DDWG 1502 & 3. PRO, RG 31/2, 179
DDWG 1502 is the undated petition for the licence & 1503 is the original licence

14/4
Archdeaconry   19 Dec. 1818
House of Samuel White
Reg. by R.F. Horne and others
BRO, ABN 1/2; ABN 3/3, 9. PRO, RG 31/2, 180

14/5
Archdeaconry   2/2 May 1838
Dwelling house of James Wiles of Bolnhurst
Reg. by James Wiles
BRO, ABN 1/2, ABN 2/325. PRO, RG 31/2, 348
Certificate addressed to the Bishop of Ely

15. BROMHAM

15/1
Archdeaconry   15 Sept. 1832
House of Samuel Hall
Reg. by Thomas Middleditch
BRO, ABN 1/2; ABN 3/3, 122

15/2   Wesleyan
Worship   17 Apr. 1889
A building in occ. of - Odell
Reg. by John Maydew Wambley of Bedford, Wesleyan minister
Cancelled on revision, 13 July 1925
OPCS, RG(W) 31514

16. CADDINGTON

16/1
Archdeaconry   27 Apr./3 May 1811
House of William Plummer at Woodside
Reg. by John Rossell, minister, Joseph Gostick, William Underwood, William Jackson
BRO, ABN 1/1; ABN 2/140. PRO, RG 31/2, 139

16/2
Archdeaconry   22 Apr./8 May 1813
Dwelling house in occ. of George Evans
Reg. by Ebenezer Daniel, William Rudd, Thomas Mead, William Bolton, James Smith
BRO, ABN 1/1; ABN 2/152. PRO, RG 31/2, 151

16/3
Archdeaconry   22/24 Dec. 1824
Dwelling house in occ. of James Bingham
Reg. by Ebenezer Daniel, David Barber, Francis Harrison, Samuel Davison
BRO, ABN 1/2; ABN 2/216; ABN 3/3, 66. PRO, RG 31/2, 236

16/4
Archdeaconry   26 Dec. 1827/2 Feb. 1828
Dwelling house in occ. of William Bigg at Woodside
Reg. by Ebenezer Daniel, William Bigg, William Clark, Francis Harrison
BRO, ABN 1/2; ABN 2/238; ABN 3/3, 85. PRO, RG 31/2, 257

16/5   Wesleyan
Worship   6 Feb. 1854
Wesleyan Methodist Chapel in Markyate Street
Reg. by Wright Shovelton, Chapel St., Luton, superintendent minister
Cancelled 18 Mar. 1876
OPCS, RG(W) 1752
Shovelton registered Wesleyan chapels at Barton & Luton on the same day

16/6   Wesleyan
Worship   6 Feb. 1854
Wesleyan Methodist Chapel at Aley Green
Reg. by Wright Shovelton, Chapel St., Luton, superintendent minister
OPCS, RG(W) 1755

16/7   Wesleyan
Worship   6 Feb. 1854
Wesleyan Methodist Chapel at Chaul End
Reg. by Wright Shovelton, Chapel St., Luton, superintendent minister
Cancelled on revision, 12 May 1896
OPCS, RG(W) 1757

16/8   Baptist
Worship   15 Nov. 1862
Woodside Baptist Chapel at Woodside
Reg. by William Dancer of Luton, manufacturer (trustee)
OPCS, RG(W) 15389

16/9   Salvation Army
Worship   21 Oct. 1884
Salvation Army Warehouse in Main Street, Market Street
Reg. by John Edward Margetts, 43 Kings Rd., Reading (Berks.), A.D.C., S.A.
Cancelled on revision, 12 May 1896
OPCS, RG(W) 28178

16/10   Union
Worship   12 Nov. 1897
Union Chapel (Baptists & Independents) [Caddington Baptist Chapel]
Reg. by William Mayles, Ivy House, Union St., Luton (trustee)
OPCS, RG(W) 36280

16/11   **Union**
Marriages   **21 Nov. 1897**
Union Chapel (Baptists & Independents) [Caddington Baptist Chapel]
OPCS, RG(M) 14807

17. CAMPTON

17/1
Archdeaconry   **11/14 Dec. 1841**
A tenement in occ. of Francis Clark
Reg. by William King, Francis Clark
BRO, ABN 1/2; ABN 2/237. PRO, RG 31/2, 383

18. CARDINGTON

18/1
Archdeaconry   **19/19 Feb. 1775**
House of Robert Huckle
Reg. by Joseph Smith of Cardington, John Whitemore of Cardington, Joshua Symonds of Bedford
BRO, ABN 1/1, ABN 2/35. PRO, RG 31/2, 35
A copy of the licence was sent to Symonds by the Deputy Registrar on 9 Mar. 1775. As Symonds, the minister of Bunyan Meeting in Bedford, had become a Baptist, this was either a Baptist or Union chapel

Plate 10: Cardington: The Wesleyan chapel, described as "newly erected" in the licence issued in 1824, has a date-stone of 1823 over the entrance. (*Photograph: c.1910*)

18/2
Archdeaconry   **23/27 Dec. 1777**
Newly built Meeting House at Cotton End
Reg. by Phillip Thompson, John Quenby, both of Cotton End
BRO, ABN 1/1; ABN 2/45. PRO, RG 31/2, 45
Thompson was the Independent minister at Cotton End

18/3   **Methodist**
Archdeaconry   **7 Feb./7 Apr. 1824**
Newly erected Methodist Chapel (printed form)
Reg. by John H. Rowe, minister
BRO, ABN 1/2; ABN 2/207; ABN 3/3, 58. PRO, RG 31/2, 229
Probably Wesleyan as the form was printed by T. Cordeux, 14 City Rd., London

18/4
Archdeaconry   **7/7 Mar. 1835**
House of William Rudd at Cotton End
Reg. by William Rudd, Edward Tomlinson, William Taylor
BRO, ABN 1/2; ABN 2/297. PRO, RG 31/2, 320
Certificate addressed to the Bishop of Lincoln

18/5   **Union**
Marriages   **23 Sept. 1837**
Cotton End Meeting (Independents & Baptists)
OPCS, RG(M) 586

Plate 11: Cardington: The Union chapel as it was from 1838 until 1908 when it was replaced by the present Howard Congregational church.   (*Photograph: c.1900*)

18/6
Archdeaconry   14/14 Oct. 1839
A Chapel, building in poss. of Benjamin Blabey
Reg. by Benjamin Prole, William Wootton, John Edward Bodger, Ebenezer Malden
BRO, ABN 1/2; ABN 2/343. PRO, RG 31/2, 365
'Inhabitants of the said parish' added to the certificate in pencil

18/7
Archdeaconry   21 Oct. 1848
House of Samuel Lawrence Taylor at Cotton End
Reg. by S.L. Taylor
BRO, ABN 1/2. PRO, RG 31/2, 429

18/8   Wesleyan
Worship   9 Feb. 1854
Wesleyan Methodist Chapel
Reg. by William Henry Clarkson, Harpur St., Bedford, superintendent minister
OPCS, RG(W) 1868
Clarkson registered Wesleyan chapels at Bedford, Clapham, Kempston, Milton Ernest,
Pavenham, Turvey, Wilshamstead & Wootton on the same day

18/9   Congregational
Worship   12 July 1860
Fenlake Chapel in Eastcotts (attached to Bunyan Meeting, Bedford)
Reg. by John Jukes, Dame Alice St., Bedford, Congregational minister (senior minister)
54416 substituted on 27 Apr. 1933
OPCS, RG(W) 9417

18/10   Congregational
Worship   12 July 1860
**Congregational Chapel at Cotton End (connected with the Bunyan Meeting,
Bedford)**
Reg. by John Jukes, Dame Alice St., Bedford, Congregational minister (senior minister)
Substituted 45643 on 19 Mar. 1913
OPCS, RG(W) 9422
Jukes registered Congregational chapels at Elstow, Goldington, Kempston, Oakley &
Stagsden on the same day

18/11   Wesleyan
Marriages   11 Jan. 1898
Wesleyan Methodist Chapel
OPCS, RG(M) 14868

19. CARLTON

19/1
Archdeaconry   19/19 Apr. 1760
Dwelling house & barn of Thomas Hull of Carlton, minister
Reg. by William Wharton jun. of Carlton, cordwainer; William Wilshire of Bedford,
victualler
BRO, ABN 1/1; ABN 2/16. PRO, RG 31/2, 15
Certificate addressed to the Commissary & Official of Bedford

Plate 12: Carlton: The Baptist meeting, built and licensed in 1760 (not in 1860 as printed on this view). (*Postcard: Blake & Edgar, c.1905*)

19/2
Archdeaconry **19/19 July 1760**
Newly erected building in Carlton Street abutting W on house of John Reynholds & S on house of Thomas Mardling
Reg. by William Wharton jun. of Carlton, cordwainer; William Wilshire of Bedford, victualler
BRO, ABN 1/1; ABN 2/17. PRO, RG 31/2, 16
Certificate addressed to the Vicar-general of Lincoln

19/3
Archdeaconry **16/23 Nov. 1783**
House & premises of William Wharton
Reg. by Walter Clark, James Pratt, William Pendred, William Wharton
BRO, ABN 1/1; ABN 2/53. PRO, RG 31/2, 53
Year altered from 1782 on dorse of certificate

19/4 **Baptist**
Marriages **14 Apr. 1838**
Baptist Meeting House
OPCS, RG(M) 1143

20. CHALGRAVE

20/1
Archdeaconry   1 May 1800
House of John Branson in Tebworth
BRO, ABN 1/1

20/2   Methodist
Archdeaconry   26/30 Aug. 1813
Methodists' Chapel in Tebworth (printed form)
Reg. by John Crosby Leppington of Luton, minister
BRO, ABN 1/1; ABN 2/155. PRO, RG 31/2, 154
Certificate addressed to the Bishop of Lincoln. Form printed by T. Cordeux, 14 City Rd.,
London

20/3
Archdeaconry   29 May/2 June 1823
Dwelling house of John Groom, labourer, in Wingfield
Reg. by John Groom (Godson)
BRO, ABN 1/2; ABN 2/204; ABN 3/3, 52. PRO, RG 31/2, 224
Certificate addressed to the Bishop of Lincoln

20/4
Archdeaconry   14/14 May 1833
House in occ. of Abraham Day in Wingfield
Reg. by Robert Peet of Bedford
BRO, ABN 1/2; ABN 2/278. PRO, RG 31/2, 299
Possibly Wesleyan, see *Dunstable Methodist Circuit, p. 185*

20/5   Wesleyan
Archdeaconry   19 May 1835
Wesleyan Chapel in Tebworth (printed form)
Reg. by Thomas Rogerson of Luton
BRO, ABN 1/2; ABN 2/304. PRO, RG 31/2, 324
Certificate addressed to the Bishop of Lincoln. Rogerson registered Wesleyan chapels at
Barton, Houghton Regis, Leagrave, Luton, Toddington & Whipsnade on the same day

20/6
Archdeaconry   17/21 Feb. 1839
House & premises of William Hide in Tebworth (printed form)
Reg. by William Hide
BRO, ABN 1/2; ABN 2/338. PRO, RG 31/2, 360

20/7   Wesleyan
Archdeaconry   4/5 May 1846
Wesleyan Chapel in Tebworth (printed form)
Reg. by Wright Shovelton of Dunstable
BRO, ABN 1/2; ABN 2/384. PRO, RG 31/2, 407
Certificate addressed to the Bishop of Ely

20/8   Wesleyan
Worship   9 Feb. 1854
Wesleyan Methodist Chapel in Tebworth

Reg. by Matthew Trevan Male of Dunstable, superintendent minister
Cancelled 24 Apr. 1892
OPCS, RG(W) 1855
Male registered Wesleyan chapels at Harlington, Hockliffe & Toddington on the same day

21. CLAPHAM

21/1
Archdeaconry   **12/12 June 1815**
House in occ. of Thomas East (printed form)
Reg. by John Dean of Bedford
BRO, ABN 1/1; ABN 2/169. PRO, RG 31/2, 168
Probably Wesleyan because the form was printed by T. Cordeux, 14 City Rd., London.
Certificate addressed to the Bishop of Lincoln

21/2
Archdeaconry   **20/20 Apr. 1833**
Dwelling house of James Cowley
Reg. by James Cowley
BRO, ABN 1/2; ABN 2/280A. PRO, RG 31/2, 305
Certificate addressed to the Bishop of Lincoln

21/3   **Wesleyan**
Worship   **9 Feb. 1854**
Wesleyan Methodist Chapel
Reg. by William Henry Clarkson, Harpur St., Bedford, superintendent minister
Cancelled 5 Dec. 1876
OPCS, RG(W) 1872
Clarkson registered Wesleyan chapels at Bedford, Cardington, Kempston, Milton Ernest, Pavenham, Turvey, Wilshamstead & Wootton on the same day

21/4   **Primitive Methodists**
Worship   **28 Dec. 1860**
Dwelling house of Thomas Shepherd
Reg. by Edward Bishop, 6 Adelaide Sq., Bedford, occasionally minister
Cancelled 3 Mar. 1876
OPCS, RG(W) 10906
Bishop registered a Primitive Methodist chapel at Stevington on the same day

21/5   **Primitive Methodist**
Worship   **27 Aug. 1868**
A building in occ. of Samuel Crosby
Reg. by William Birks, 50 Commercial Rd., Bedford, minister
Cancelled 3 Mar. 1876
OPCS, RG (W) 18668

21/6   **Wesleyan**
Worship   **9 Nov. 1876**
Wesleyan Chapel
Reg. by John Clulow of Bedford, Wesleyan minister
OPCS, RG(W) 23077

21/7   **Wesleyan**
Marriages   **22 Oct. 1880**
Wesleyan Chapel
OPCS, RG(M) 10072

22. CLIFTON

22/1   **Congregational**
House of Isaac Bedford   **16 May 1672**
O.R., p. 858

22/2
Archdeaconry   **27/27 Apr. 1761**
House of Edward Burridge
Reg. by Edward Burridge of Clifton, labourer (his mark); William Parker of Bedford, grocer
BRO, ABN 1/1; ABN 2/18. PRO, RG 31/2, 17

22/3
Archdeaconry   **17/19 Nov. 1776**
Dwelling house of William Albone
Reg. by William Tansley, John Harrison
BRO, ABN 1/1; ABN 2/40. PRO, 31/2, 41
Certificate addressed to the Commissary & Official of Bedford

22/4
Archdeaconry   **27 Mar./28 Apr. 1802**
The Meeting House
Reg. by Joseph Fisher, Richard Armour, William Green (inhabitants)
BRO, ABN 1/1; ABN 2/107. PRO, RG 31/2, 109

22/5
Archdeaconry   **2 Nov. 1807**
Clifton New Meeting House
BRO, ABN 1/1

22/6
Archdeaconry   **30/30 June 1841**
A building (Chapel) in occ. of George Kempson
Reg. by George Millard, Thomas Fane, Thomas Kent, Thomas Pope, Thomas Arnold, James Young, George Thompson, James Roberts, Thomas Rainden
BRO, ABN 1/2; ABN 2/355. PRO, RG 31/2, 379
Certificate addressed to the J.P.s in Quarter Sessions. Particular Baptist (*Memoir of Septimus Sears*, London, 1880)

22/7
Archdeaconry   **8/14 Nov. 1848**
House in occ. of Elizabeth West
Reg. by Wright Shovelton of Biggleswade
BRO, ABN 1/2; ABN 2/402. PRO, RG 31/2, 425

Plate 13: Clifton: The Baptist chapel of 1853, registered by the Rev. Septimus Sears in 1854. (*Postcard: Blake & Edgar, c.1905*)

Plate 14: The Rev. Septimus Sears (1819-1877), for 35 years pastor of the Particular Baptist church at Clifton. (*Oil painting: unsigned, c.1870*)

22/8
Worship
Clifton Chapel

Particular Baptist
26 June 1854

Reg. by Septimus Sears of Clifton, dissenting minister
OPCS, RG(W) 5455

22/9
Marriages
Clifton Chapel
OPCS, RG(M) 3684

Particular Baptist
8 July 1854

23. CLOPHILL

23/1
Archdeaconry
21/21 Dec. 1812
A certain building adjoining the premises of Thomas Parrish of Clophill, draper
Reg. by Thomas Parrish, John Butcher, James Bedford, John Chapman, all parishioners
BRO, ABN 1/1; ABN 2/148. PRO, RG 31/2, 147

23/2
Archdeaconry
29/29 June 1848
A building in occ. of Caroline Upton (printed form)
Reg. by Samuel Sexton
BRO, ABN 1/2; ABN 2/395. PRO, RG 31/2, 418
Certificate addressed to the J.P.s in Quarter Sessions

23/3
Worship
Primitive Methodist Chapel in Luton Road

Primitive Methodist
1 Feb. 1853

Reg. by John Symonds Gostling of St Paul's par., Bedford, upholsterer (trustee)
Substituted 47895 on 29 Sept. 1920 (advertised 30 Sept. 1920)
OPCS, RG(W) 758

24. COLMWORTH

24/1
Quarter Sessions
House in Colmworth

- July (1725)

BRO, QSR 1725, 76
This document is damaged

24/2
Archdeaconry
19 Dec. 1766
Dwelling house of Mary Fisher, widow
Reg. by Russell Chapman of Colmworth, husbandman, (his mark); Thomas Lee of Great
Barford, husbandman
BRO, ABN 1/1; ABN 2/23. PRO, RG 31/2, 22
Certificate addressed to the Commissary & Official of Bedford

24/3
Archdeaconry   **3 Apr. 1810**
Dwelling house & premises in occ. of William Wagstaff
Reg. by William Wagstaff (his mark), Thomas Calvert, William Calvert
BRO, ABN 1/1; ABN 2/137. PRO, RG 31/2, 136

24/4
Archdeaconry   **27/27 Nov. 1830**
Dwelling house of Robert Shimmon (Skinner)
Reg. by Robert Shimmon (his mark). Witnesses Samuel Barley, John Fielding
BRO, ABN 1/2; ABN 2/248; ABN 3/3, 100. PRO, RG 31/2, 272
Certificate addressed to the Bishop of Lincoln

24/5
Archdeaconry   **2/2 Jan. 1841**
Dwelling house of George Creamer
Reg. by George Creamer of Colmworth
BRO, ABN 1/2; ABN 2/351. PRO, RG 31/2, 374
Certificate addressed to the Bishop of Ely

24/6
Archdeaconry   **12/12 Apr. 1841**
Dwelling house of Charles Crowsley
Reg. by Charles Crowsley, George Cornish
BRO, ABN 1/2; ABN 2/354. PRO, RG 31/2, 377

24/7
Archdeaconry   **14/14 May 1842**
Building of Henry Shimmon
Reg. by Charles Parker
BRO, ABN 1/1; ABN 2/364. PRO, RG 31/2, 390

24/8
Archdeaconry   **7/6 Jan. 1844**
A building in occ. of James Ashwell
Reg. by William Youle (Gould)
BRO, ABN 1/2, ABN 2/375. PRO, RG 31/2, 397
Certificate addressed to the Bishop of Ely

24/9   **Primitive Methodist**
Worship   **28 Feb. 1854**
Primitive Methodist Chapel
Reg. by Henry Kent of Bedford, baker (trustee)
Cancelled on revision, 13 July 1925
OPCS, RG(W) 2510

25. COPLE

25/1
Archdeaconry   **23 Mar. 1791**
House of John March of Cople
BRO, ABN 1/1

25/2
Archdeaconry   15/21 Nov. 1814
Dwelling house in occ. of William Jordan (printed form)
Reg. by John Dean of Bedford, minister
BRO, ABN 1/1, ABN 2/165. PRO, RG 31/2, 164
Probably Wesleyan as the form was printed in City Rd., London. Certificate addressed to
the Bishop of Lincoln

25/3
Archdeaconry   5 Dec. 1818
House of Thomas Jordan
Reg. by Richard Gower
BRO, ABN 1/2; ABN 3/3, 7. PRO, RG 31/2, 178

25/4
Archdeaconry   23 Sept. 1820
House of William Rutland
Reg. by William Rutland and others
BRO, ABN 1/2; ABN 3/3, 19. PRO, RG 31/2, 190

25/5
Archdeaconry   3/4 Jan. 1844
House in occ. of John Nicholson
Reg. by Edward C. Thomlinson, Thomas Minney, Richard Barcock, John Nicholson
BRO, ABN 1/2; ABN 2/376, 377 (2 copies). PRO, RG 31/2, 396
Certificate addressed to the Bishop of Ely

26. CRANFIELD

26/1   Congregational
House of William Arm   1 May 1672
O.R., p. 857

26/2   Congregational
House of George Palmer   1 May 1672
O.R., p. 857

26/3
Quarter Sessions   13 Dec. 1772
Meeting House at East End, the property of Ebenezer Keech
Reg. by William Buckell, Joel Bass, John Butterfield (Basterfield)
BRO, QSP43/10
Original certificate & draft licence (written on parchment)

26/4
Archdeaconry   21/23 May 1804
Dwelling house of Thomas Perry, labourer
Reg. by Thomas Perry (his mark), William Page, Thomas Smith, John Humphrey,
Thomas Bigg (Edward Banke *deleted*)
BRO, ABN 1/1; ABN 2/115. PRO, RG 31/2, 114
Certificate addressed to the Bishop of Lincoln

26/5
Archdeaconry   21 Apr. 1806
House of William Lord
BRO, ABN 1/1

26/6
Archdeaconry   9/10 Mar. 1827
Dwelling house of Thomas Savage (printed form)
Reg. by John Stevens of Newport Pagnell (Bucks.), minister
BRO, ABN 1/2, ABN 2/227; ABN 3/3, 76. PRO, RG 31/2, 248
Probably Wesleyan as the form was printed in City Rd., London

26/7
Archdeaconry   26/21 Mar. 1828 *(sic)*
House of Mr Joseph Robinson, in occ. of Paul Derby
Reg. by William Early, T. Marshall, Joseph Lilley, Edward Phillips
BRO, ABN 1/2; ABN 2/237; ABN 3/3, 86. PRO, RG 31/2, 258

26/8   **Baptist**
Marriages   **2 Sept. 1837**
Baptist Chapel [Bedford Road]
OPCS, RG(M) 885

26/9
Archdeaconry   5 May 1849
House of William Goodman
Reg. by Hillyard Nicholls of Bedford
BRO, ABN 1/2. PRO, RG 31/2, 436

26/10
Archdeaconry   24/24 Dec. 1851
Separate building in occ. of Robert Tutt (printed form)
Reg. by Robert Tutt of Cranfield, Thomas Pedder
BRO, ABN 1/2; ABN 2/434. PRO, RG 31/2, 459
The form is one intended for Quarter Sessions with the heading cut off. Certificate
addressed to the Bishop of Ely

26/11   **Particular Baptist**
Worship   **17 Dec. 1860**
Old Baptist Meeting House at East End (Bedford Road)
Reg. by Thomas Owen of Cranfield, Baptist minister
OPCS, RG(W) 10242

26/12   **Wesleyan**
Worship   **19 Feb. 1861**
Wesleyan Chapel
Reg. by Thomas White Smith of Newport Pagnell (Bucks.), Wesleyan minister
OPCS, RG(W) 12870

26/13   **Particular Baptist**
Worship   **13 Apr. 1868**
Mount Zion Chapel
Reg. by John Augustus Dean of Cranfield, Baptist minister
Cancelled 20 Sept. 1920
OPCS, RG(W) 18467

26/14
Marriages
Mount Zion Chapel
Cancelled 20 Sept. 1920
OPCS, RG(M) 6538

Particular Baptist
16 Apr. 1868

27. DEAN

27/1
House of James Mees
O.R., p. 852

Congregational
22 July 1672

27/2
House of Peter Yorke
O.R., p. 852

Congregational
22 July 1672

27/3
Archdeaconry
Dwelling house of Robert Corby at Upper Dean
Reg. by Robert Corby (his mark), John White, Thomas Palmer
BRO, ABN 1/1; ABN 2/55. PRO, RG 31/2, 55

12/17 Dec. 1785

27/4
Archdeaconry
House of William Burgess
BRO, ABN 1/1

13 Apr. 1811

27/5
Archdeaconry
Chapel
Reg. by James Sherriff
BRO, ABN 1/2; ABN 3/3, 2. PRO, RG 31/2, 173

9 Apr. 1818

27/6
Worship
Wesleyan Methodist Chapel at Nether Dean
Reg. by Thomas Jeffery of Higham Ferrers (Northants.), Wesleyan minister
Cancelled on revision, 18 Mar. 1971
OPCS, RG(W) 4687

Wesleyan
3 May 1854

27/7
Worship
Congregational Chapel at Upper Dean [United Reformed Church]
Reg. by Joseph Allison Rendon Skinner of Upper Dean, Independent minister
OPCS, RG(W) 23745

Congregational
26 Oct. 1877

27/8
Marriages
Congregational Chapel at Upper Dean [United Reformed Church]
OPCS, RG(M) 9322

Congregational
26 Nov. 1877

27/9
Marriages
Wesleyan Methodist Chapel at Nether Dean
Cancelled 18 Mar. 1971
OPCS, RG(M) 15643

Wesleyan
10 Mar. 1900

28. DUNSTABLE

28/1
Archdeaconry   11 Jan. 1779
House of Richard Gutteridge in occ. of Mary Parken (tenant)
Reg. by Mary Parken, Richard Gutteridge of Dunstable
BRO, ABN 1/1; ABN 2/49. PRO, RG 31/2, 49

28/2
Archdeaconry   5/8 Oct. 1790
House in tenure of Thomas Holland in Church Street
Reg. by William Jenkins, Thomas Holland, Charles Evans
BRO, ABN 1/1; ABN 2/64. PRO, RG 31/2, 66

28/3
Quarter Sessions   24 Apr./4 Oct. 1797
House of Mr Joseph Elliott of Dunstable
Reg. by John Darley, James Ellis, Charles Evans, William Prior, Thomas Sum[mer]field,
Thomas Hodson
BRO, QSR 1797, 68; QSM 20, p. 34. PRO, RG 31/6, 22

Plate 15: Dunstable: The first Methodist meeting house in Dunstable was licensed in 1797. This chapel (built in 1845 to replace a building of 1831 which burnt down) was destroyed by fire on 14th September 1908.   (*Photograph: c.1900*)

28/4
Archdeaconry   **11/12 Sept. 1797**
House in occ. of Thomas Summerfield
Reg. by John Darley, Thomas Summerfield, Sarah Summerfield (her mark), Dorcas Summerfield, Sarah Horrley, Richard Underwood, Thomas Warr, John Purton, Ann Underwood, William Elliott, Rebecah Elliott, Alice Fowler
BRO, ABN 1/1; ABN 2/82. PRO, RG 31/2, 81
Certificate addressed to the Bishop of Lincoln. Identified as Wesleyan in *Dunstable Methodist Circuit, p.35*

28/5
Archdeaconry   **18/23 Mar. 1799**
House in occ. of John Darley at Church End
Reg. by Joseph Harper, John Darley, Dorcas Darley, Richard Underwood, Thomas Warr
BRO, ABN 1/1; ABN 2/101. PRO, RG 31/2, 100
Certificate addressed to the Bishop of Lincoln. Identified as Wesleyan (see 28/4)

28/6
Quarter Sessions   **11 Apr. 1809**
Dwelling house of Thomas Hallifax at West End of Dunstable
Reg. by Joseph Squire, Thomas Scott, George Hall, William Christmas, Richard Underwood, Samuel Guttiridge, William Garrett, Samuel Shattock [Shabbot], John Purton [Ricton] (householders)
BRO, QSR 1809, 86; QSM 23, 77. PRO, RG 31/2, 31

28/7
Archdeaconry   **30 Oct./5 Nov. 1812**
Dwelling house of Daniel Liberty, gent.
Reg. by Daniel Liberty, Ann Fossey, Isabel Phenix, Lancelot Copleston, F.P. Hewes
BRO, ABN 1/1; ABN 2/147. PRO, RG 31/2, 146
Certificate addressed to the Bishop of Lincoln

28/8   **Calvinist Baptist**
Archdeaconry   **5 Nov. 1817**
Dwelling house late in occ. of Mr Crawley, but now unoccupied
Reg. by Thomas Kimpton of Luton, baker, William Henly, B. Burrows, John Day, John Darley, Francis Hews
BRO, ABN 1/2; ABN 2/174; ABN 3/3, 5. PRO, RG 31/2, 176
Both ABN 1/2 & RG 31/2 date this 11 Oct. 1818, but the certificate & letter in ABN 2 are dated 5 & 8 Nov. 1817, indicating a delay of almost a year in issuing the licence. The attached letter from Kimpton at Luton to Mr Bailey asks him to complete the heading (which he did not do) and file it in the bishop's or archdeacon's court. It adds that this was a separation from 'the old Baptist Calvinist interest'

28/9   **Wesleyan**
Archdeaconry   **5 Aug./24 Sept. 1831**
Newly erected Chapel called the Wesleyan Chapel
Reg. by William Pollard of Luton, minister
BRO, ABN 1/2; ABN 2/261; ABN 3/3, 110. PRO, RG 31/2, 282
Certificate addressed to the Bishop of Lincoln

28/10   **Wesleyan**
Archdeaconry   **19/21 June 1834**
Wesleyan Chapel
Reg. by Isaac Wale of Bedford (printed form)
BRO, ABN 1/2; ABN 2/287. PRO, RG 31/2, 308
Certificate addressed to the Bishop of Lincoln. Wale registered Wesleyan chapels at
Barton & Hockliffe on the same day

28/11
Archdeaconry   **2/3 Sept. 1834**
Barn on premises of William Partridge in Church Street
Reg. by William Partridge, Richard Walton, William Groom, John Fowler, housekeepers
in Dunstable
BRO, ABN 1/2; ABN 2/295. PRO, RG 31/2, 315
Identified as Wesleyan, This licence reproduced in *Dunstable Methodist Circuit, p.37*

28/12   **Baptist**
Marriages   **28 Apr. 1838**
Baptist Meeting House in West Street
Cancelled 10 Oct. 1849 [*but see 28/15 below*]
OPCS, RG(M) 1130

28/13   **Wesleyan**
Marriages   **28 Nov. 1845**
Wesleyan Chapel
Substituted 19477 on 17 Feb. 1910
OPCS, RG(M) 2510

28/14   **Wesleyan**
Archdeaconry   **6/6 Dec. 1845**
Wesleyan Chapel (printed form)
Reg. by Wright Shovelton of Dunstable
BRO, ABN 1/2; ABN 2/381. PRO, RG 31/2, 404
Certificate addressed to the Bishop of Lincoln

28/15   **Baptist**
Marriages   **10 Oct. 1849**
West Street Baptist Chapel, West Street (West Street Christian Centre)
Substituted for 1130
OPCS, RG(M) 3080

28/16   **Baptist**
Worship   **26 July 1852**
West Street Baptist Church [West Street Christian Centre/ New Covenant Church]
Reg. by Daniel Gould of Dunstable, dissenting minister
OPCS, RG(W) 21

28/17   **Independent**
Worship   **1 Sept. 1852**
A building in Edward Street
Reg. by Joseph Osborn of Dunstable, trustee
Cancelled 18 Mar. 1876
OPCS, RG(W) 99

NEW   BAPTIST   CHAPEL.   DUNSTABLE.

Plate 16: Dunstable: The Baptist chapel in West Street was built in 1847-8.
(Engraving from a photograph: c.1859)

28/18   **Primitive Methodist**
Worship   **18 Sept. 1852**
Primitive Methodist Chapel in Mount Street
Reg. by Richard Tearle of Houghton Regis, plait dealer (trustee)
Cancelled on revision, 12 May 1896
OPCS, RG(W) 127

28/19   **Mormon**
Worship   **13 June 1853**
Building in occ. of Frederick Bird in Mount Street for Latter Day Saints
Reg. by Frederick Bird, Mount St., Dunstable, straw bonnet manufacturer (occupier)
Cancelled 31 Dec. 1866
OPCS, RG(W) 1004

28/20   **Wesleyan**
Worship   **9 Feb. 1854**
Wesleyan Methodist Chapel in High Street
Reg. by Matthew Trevan Male of Dunstable, superintendent minister
Substituted 44005 on 17 Feb. 1910
OPCS, RG(W) 1896
Male registered Wesleyan chapels at Houghton Regis, Kensworth, Leagrave & Sundon
on the same day

28/21
Worship
The Tabernacle in Edward Street
Reg. by James Lyon of Dunstable, minister
Substituted 73678 on 2 May 1974
OPCS, RG(W) 6488

Congregational
12 June 1855

28/22
Marriages
The Tabernacle in Edward Street (United Reformed Church)
Substituted 37862 on 2 May 1974
OPCS, RG(M) 4264

Congregational
8 July 1858

28/23
Worship
Primitive Methodist Chapel
Reg. by Edwin Johnson of Dunstable, hat manufacturer (attendant)
Cancelled on revision, 12 May 1896
OPCS, RG(W) 11635

Primitive Methodist
3 Jan. 1861

28/24
Worship
Primitive Methodist Chapel in Victoria Street
Reg. by Thomas Huckle of Luton, bonnet manufacturer (trustee)
Cancelled 16 Nov. 1965
OPCS, RG(W) 15620
Huckle registered a Primitive Methodist chapel at Houghton Regis on the same day

Primitive Methodist
28 Mar. 1863

28/25
Marriages
Primitive Methodist Chapel in Victoria Street
Cancelled 16 Nov. 1965
OPCS, RG(M) 6074

Primitive Methodist
13 Aug. 1866

28/26
Worship
The Mission Hall in King Street, by those who object to be designated
Reg. by Robert Pickering of Dunstable, bonnet blocker (an attendant)
68771 substituted on 15 Aug. 1962
OPCS, RG(W) 20886

Objectors
26 Aug. 1872

28/27
Worship
Assembly Rooms in Church Street
Reg. by Alexander Mathew Nicol, 14 Aldershot Rd., Kilborn, London, Colonel, S.A.
Cancelled on revision, 12 May 1896
OPCS, RG(W) 29042

Salvation Army
7 Dec. 1885

28/28
Worship
Salvation Army Barracks in Matthew Street
Reg. by Charles Taylor, 1 Matthew St., Dunstable, Serjeant major, S.A.
36179 substituted on 7 Sept. 1897
OPCS, RG(W) 32459

Salvationists
24 Nov. 1890

28/29 Salvation Army
Worship 7 Sept. 1897
Salvation Army Citadel in the Market Place
Reg. by Joshua Spooner, 35 Brook St., Luton, Major, S.A. (occupier)
Substituted for 32459
OPCS, RG(W) 36179

28/30 Salvation Army
Worship 3 Sept. 1900
Salvation Army Hall in High Street North
Reg. by Mary Jackson of Dunstable, Captain, S.A.
57636 substituted on 30 Sept. 1937
OPCS, RG(W) 37899

29. DUNTON

29/1
Archdeaconry 12/12 Mar. 1756
Dwelling house of William Winters
Reg. by William Winters of Dunton (his mark), William Wilsher of Bedford
BRO, ABN 1/1; ABN 2/8. PRO, RG 31/2, 9
Certificate addressed to the Commissary & Official of Bedford. 'Exhibited same day. D. Gregory, Deputy Registrar'

29/2
Archdeaconry 17/17 Oct. 1770
Barn of Edward Baulk
Reg. by Henry Baulk, yeoman (his mark), Edward Munsen (his mark), yeoman, of Dunton
BRO, ABN 1/1; ABN 2/28. PRO, RG 31/2, 28
RG 31/2 dates this 27 Oct. 1768. Certificate addressed to the Commissary & Official of Bedford. 'Lycence went out the same day. John Impey, Deputy Registrar'

29/3
Archdeaconry 17/17 Oct. 1770
Barn late in poss. of Henry Baulk, and now of Edward Muncon, shoemaker of Dunton
Reg. by William Winters (his mark), Benjamin Harper, John Simpson (his mark), Edward Muncon (his mark), Henry Baulk, Robert Brunt (his mark)
BRO, ABN 1/1; ABN 2/29. PRO, RG 31/2, 29
RG 31/2 dates this 27 Oct. 1768. Certificate addressed to the Commissary & Official of Bedford

29/4
Archdeaconry 17/19 Nov. 1776
House of John Peppercorn of Newton Berry in Dunton for occasional public worship
Reg. by Joseph King, Thomas Wattes
BRO, ABN 1/1; ABN 2/41. PRO, RG 31/2, 40
Endorsed - '19th Nov. 1776. Copy and Certificate . . . was delivered to the House of John Peppercorn, Newton Berry, Dunton'

29/5   **Baptist**
Worship   **28 Mar. 1861**
Baptist Chapel
Reg. by Philip Griffiths, Langford St., Biggleswade, Baptist minister
OPCS, RG(W) 13907

30. EATON BRAY

30/1
Archdeaconry   **29/30 June 1795**
Dwelling house and premises of John Rawlins, higler
Reg. by John Rawlins, John Hickling, Jeffery Gadsden
BRO, ABN 1/1; ABN 2/75. PRO, RG 31/2, 75
Certificate addressed to the Bishop of Lincoln

Plate 17: Eaton Bray: The interior of the Wesleyan chapel built in 1795 and enlarged in 1829.   (*Postcard: Kay, c.1910*)

30/2
Archdeaconry   **21/24 Nov. 1795**
Chapel
Reg. by Richard Partridge, Jeffery Gadsden, Byron Mouse, Curtes Travell
BRO, ABN 1/1; ABN 2/77. PRO, RG 31/2, 77

30/3
Archdeaconry   **8 May 1806**
Building adjoining the dwelling house of Jeffery Gadsden
BRO, ABN 1/1

30/4
Archdeaconry   **31 Dec. 1813/3 Jan. 1814**
School in occ. of John King
Reg. by John King, William Wotts, John James (his mark)
BRO, ABN 1/1; ABN 2/159. PRO, RG 31/2, 158

30/5
Archdeaconry   **8 Nov. 1817**
House in occ. of George Burrows
Reg. by John Brandon, John Gurney, Jeremiah Bird, Richard Moss
BRO, ABN 2/128
Certificate endorsed '8 Nov.'

30/6
Archdeaconry   **24/28 Sept. 1825**
House in occ. of John Brandon
Reg. by William Southam, Richard Moss, Henry Perton
BRO, ABN 1/2; ABN 2/220A; ABN 3/3, 70. PRO, RG 31/2, 241

30/7
Archdeaconry   **13/13 June 1829**
A building or edifice in occ. of William Sear of Eaton Bray
Reg. by William Sear
BRO, ABN 1/2; ABN 2/244; ABN 3/3, 93. PRO, RG 31/2, 265
Certificate addressed to the Commissary & Official of Bedford

30/8
Archdeaconry   **2/3 Sept. 1834**
A barn on premises of John Stratford
Reg. by John Stratford, Samuel Hawkins, William Bless jun., John Bless, Thomas Room
(housekeepers)
BRO, ABN 1/2; ABN 2/294. PRO, RG 31/2, 316

30/9   **Wesleyan**
Archdeaconry   **29/31 Dec. 1838**
Wesleyan Methodist Chapel
Reg. by William Sear, Joseph Eustace, Thomas Gadsden (substantial householders)
BRO, ABN 1/2; ABN 2/335. PRO, RG 31/2, 358
Certificate addressed to the Registrar of the County of Bedford

30/10
Archdeaconry   **4/8 July 1848**
House and premises in occ. of John Mead
Reg. by Robert Hodgert of Billington (Leighton Buzzard)
BRO, ABN 1/2; ABN 2/396. PRO, RG 31/2, 419
Certificate addressed to the Bishop of Ely

30/11
Archdeaconry   **17/18 Sept. 1849**
House in occ. of John Fenn
Reg. by Richard Hodgert of Billington (Leighton Buzzard), John Mead, Samuel Impey
(witnesses)
BRO, ABN 1/2; ABN 2/414. PRO, RG 31/2, 442
Certificate addressed to the Bishop of Ely

30/12
Archdeaconry   **29 Oct./7 Nov. 1849**
House & premises in occ. of George Dickenson of Eaton Bray
Reg. by George Dickenson, Jeremiah Stanbridge, John Mead
BRO, ABN 1/2; ABN 2/415. PRO, RG 31/2, 443
Certificate addressed to the Bishop of Ely. A note attached to the certificate promises to
send a Post Office order for the fee when the licence is received

30/13   **Baptist**
Worship   **28 Oct. 1852**
Baptist Chapel at Moor End
Reg. by William Janes, Moor End, Eaton Bray (trustee)
OPCS, RG(W) 380

30/14   **Wesleyan**
Worship   **15 Mar. 1861**
Wesleyan Methodist Chapel
Reg. by James S. Haigh of Leighton Buzzard, Wesleyan minister
OPCS, RG(W) 13534
Haigh registered Wesleyan chapels at Heath & Stanbridge; Ivinghoe & Wing (Bucks.) on
the same day

30/15   **Wesleyan**
Marriages   **19 Mar. 1872**
Wesleyan Chapel
OPCS, RG(M) 7617

30/16   **Salvationists**
Worship   **8 Feb. 1888**
A building in Bower Lane
Reg. by Annie Ingram of Eaton Bray, Captain, S.A.
Cancelled on revision, 16 Apr. 1896
OPCS, RG(W) 30656

31. EATON SOCON

31/1
Archdeaconry   **8 June 1754**
Dwelling house of Thomas Palmer
Reg. by Thomas Palmer (his mark) of Eaton Socon, John Queenby (Quenby) of
Cardington
BRO, ABN 1/1; ABN 2/5. PRO, RG 31/2
Certificate addressed to the Commissary & Official of Bedford

31/2   **Presbyterian**
Quarter Sessions   **11/11 Jan. 1769**
House with appurtenances in occ. of James Crow
Reg. by James Crow, yeoman (proprietor), John Savill, Henry Davis
BRO, QSM 15, 9; QSP43/8 PRO, RG 31/6, 6
Original certificate, draft licence & licence. Henry Davis' name not in licence

31/3
Archdeaconry   **29/29 Sept. 1770**
House of Mr Emery, for occasional worship
Reg. by Thomas Coley, Thomas Paine
BRO, ABN 1/1; ABN 2/27

31/4   **General Baptists**
Archdeaconry   **7/7 Oct. 1778**
House with appurtenances in occ. of Edward Mayson
Reg. by William Smith, George Knightley, Thomas Hutchinson
BRO, ABN 1/1; ABN 2/47. PRO, RG 31/2, 47
Certificate addressed to the J.P.s, but altered to Rev. Hadley Cox, Commissary of Bedford

31/5
Quarter Sessions   **26 Apr. 1786**
House in occ. of Mrs Jane Hicks in Eaton
Reg. by Jane Hicks, William Day, William Stocks
BRO, QSR 1786, 15; QSM 18, p. 56. PRO, RG 31/6, 9

31/6
Archdeaconry   **21/22 Oct. 1789**
House of John Livett
Reg. by James Crow, William Law, Richard Blowfield, John Gray, Gervas Hutchinson
BRO, ABN 1/1; ABN 2/62. PRO, RG 31/2, 62

31/7
Archdeaconry   **11/11 Oct. 1790**
Outbuilding of Richard Blofield of Eaton Socon
Reg. by Richard Blofield, W. Jenkins, Joseph Fairey 'and others'
BRO, ABN 1/1; ABN 2/67. PRO, RG 31/2, 67

31/8
Archdeaconry   **2/8 Nov. 1798**
Dwelling house of Richard Fisher of Wyboston
Reg. by Richard Fisher (his mark), Francis West, Samuel Bennett
BRO, ABN 2/100. PRO, RG 31/2, 99

31/9
Archdeaconry   **10 Dec. 1808**
Dwelling house of Thomas Howkins in Wyboston for occasional public worship
Reg. by Thomas Howkins 'and others'
BRO, ABN 1/1; Z 133/1
Original licence is sewn into a terrier of the Thurleigh Estate, 1771

31/10
Archdeaconry   **5 Dec. 1810**
House of Mary Lee of Eaton Socon
BRO, ABN 1/1

31/11
Archdeaconry   **6 Mar. 1821**
House of John Pratt in Wyboston
Reg. by Thomas Howkins, John Howkins, Thomas Emery, John Pratt, James Knight
(residents)
BRO, ABN 1/2; ABN 2/179; ABN 3/3, 24. PRO, RG 31/2, 195
Certificate not dated - 'per Rev. Thomas King'

31/12
Archdeaconry   **30 Apr. 1821**
House of Samuel Hodby in Wyboston
Reg. by Samuel Hodby of Wyboston, William Law, T. Hewitt, James King, William Hall
BRO, ABN 1/2; ABN 2/177A ; ABN 3/3, 27. PRO, RG 31/2, 198

31/13
Archdeaconry   **6/6 June 1832**
Brick & tiled barn in occ. of Joseph Allison
Reg. by William Abbott
BRO, ABN 1/2; ABN 2/271; ABN 3/3, 120. PRO, RG 31/2, 292

31/14
Archdeaconry   **26 June/1 July 1835**
A place of worship on premises of John Emery
Reg. by John Emery, John Brown, Joseph Neall, Joseph Topham
BRO, ABN 1/2; ABN 2/306. PRO, RG 31/2, 331
Certificate addressed to the Surrogate

31/15
Archdeaconry   **13/13 Mar. 1841**
Building in poss. of John Mariott in Honeydon
Reg. by Reg. by John Mariott
BRO, ABN 1/2; ABN 2/353. PRO, RG 31/2, 376

31/16
Archdeaconry   **15 Oct./2 Dec. 1841**
Building in occ. of Joseph Clerk in Wyboston
Reg. by Joseph Clerk
BRO, ABN 1/2; ABN 2/356. PRO, RG 31/2, 382

31/17
Archdeaconry   **14/15 Jan. 1842**
Building in Wyboston in poss. of Thomas Hewit
Reg. by John Hewitt
BRO, ABN 1/2; ABN 2/368. PRO, RG 31/2, 385
Date altered from 15 Oct. in ABN 2

31/18
Archdeaconry   **30 Apr. 1842**
Building in Wyboston
Reg. by John Hewitt
BRO, ABN 1/2

31/19
Archdeaconry   **20 Dec. 1848/10 Jan. 1849**
Dwelling house of Thomas Joice in Wyboston
Reg. by Thomas Smith of Bedford
BRO, ABN 1/2; ABN 2/404. PRO, RG 31/2, 430

31/20
Archdeaconry   **22/25 Oct. 1851**
A separate building (printed form)
Reg. by John D. Julian of St Neots (Hunts.)
BRO, ABN 1/2; ABN 2/432. PRO, RG 31/2, 458

31/21   **Wesleyan**
Worship   **2 Mar. 1854**
Wesleyan Chapel
Reg. by Adam Fletcher of St Neots (Hunts.), Wesleyan minister
Cancelled 20 May 1971
OPCS, RG(W) 2636

31/22   **Primitive Methodist**
Worship   **4 Apr. 1859**
A building
Reg. by John Blackburn of Eynsbury, St Neots (Hunts.), Primitive Methodist minister
OPCS, RG(W) 8755

31/23   **Primitive Methodist**
Worship   **6 Oct. 1870**
Primitive Methodist Chapel at Wyboston [53 Great North Road]
Reg. by Oliver Jackson of Eynsbury (Hunts.), Primitive Methodist minister
OPCS, RG(W) 19829

31/24   **Primitive Methodist**
Worship   **18 May 1871**
Primitive Methodist Chapel
Reg. by Oliver Jackson of Eynsbury (Hunts.), Primitive Methodist minister
OPCS, RG(W) 20167

31/25   **Wesleyan**
Worship   **16 July 1872**
Honeydon Wesleyan Chapel [now Staploe]
Reg. by Thomas Baine of St Neots (Hunts.), superintendent minister
OPCS, RG(W) 20836

31/26   **Wesleyan**
Marriages   **15 Jan. 1895**
Wesleyan Chapel
Cancelled 20 May 1871
OPCS, RG(M) 13839

32. EDWORTH

32/1   **Congregational**
House of George Pridden   **1 May 1672**
OR, p. 858

33. EGGINGTON

33/1
Archdeaconry   **2 Apr. 1799**
House of William Scroggs
BRO, ABN 1/1

33/2
Archdeaconry   **29 Aug/6 Sept. 1821**
House in occ. of William Pantlin of Eggington in Leighton Buzzard
Reg. by William Pantlin
BRO, ABN 1/2; ABN 2/183; ABN 3/3, 30. PRO, RG 31/2, 201

33/3
Peculiar Jurisdiction   **12 Jan. 1843**
Chapel & premises in occ. of John Reed and others
Reg. by John Reed of Eggington
BRO, RI 3/6824d
Certificate addressed to the Bishop of Ely

33/4   **Wesleyan**
Worship   **19 Apr. 1861**
Wesleyan Methodist Chapel
Reg. by Joshua Mottram of Leighton Buzzard, minister
OPCS, RG(W) 14204
Mottram registered Wesleyan chapels at Billington & Leighton Buzzard; Mentmore, Stoke Hammond & Soulbury (Bucks.) on the same day

34. ELSTOW

34/1
Archdeaconry   **18 Dec. 1754 (1756)**
Dwelling house of William Maulden of Elstow, wheelwright
Reg. by Joseph Freelove, John Mays, both of Bedford
BRO, ABN 1/1; ABN 2/7. PRO, RG 31/2, 6
A later endorsement on certificate gives 18 Dec. 1756

34/2
Archdeaconry   **10 Nov./4 Dec. 1792**
House of Samuel Goodman
Reg. by William Berrill, Samuel Goodman, Jonathan Negus, John Risley
BRO, ABN 1/1; ABN 2/70. PRO, RG 31/2, 70

34/3
Archdeaconry   **7 Nov. 1812**
Green House
BRO, ABN 1/1

34/4
Archdeaconry   **12/12 Nov. 1814**
Dwelling house in occ. of John Goodman (printed form)
Reg. by John Dean of Bedford, minister

BRO, ABN 1/1; ABN 2/164. PRO, RG 31/2, 162
Probably Wesleyan as the form was printed by T. Cordeux, 14 City Rd., London.
Certificate addressed to the Bishop of Lincoln

34/5
Archdeaconry   **17/20 Feb. 1836**
House in occ. of George Smith
Reg. by George Smith, William Ansell, George Goddard, Edward Thomlinson, Ann
Noraway, Samuel Smith, Ann Halyer
BRO, ABN 1/2; ABN 2/311. PRO, RG 31/2, 335
Certificate addressed to the Bishop of Lincoln

34/6
Archdeaconry   **5/5 Aug. 1850**
House & premises in occ. of William Ansill
Reg. by Samuel Smith, George Smith, householder, Thomas Pointer, householder
BRO, ABN 1/2; ABN 2/419. PRO, RG 31/2, 449
Certificate addressed to the Bishop of Ely

34/7   **Congregational**
Worship   **12 July 1860**
Elstow Chapel (connected with Bunyan Meeting, Bedford)
Reg. by John Jukes, Dame Alice St., Bedford, Congregational minister (senior minister)
Cancelled on revision, 13 July 1925
OPCS, RG(W) 9418
Jukes registered Congregational chapels at Cardington, Goldington, Kempston, Oakley &
Stagsden on the same day

35. EVERSHOLT

35/1
Archdeaconry   **27 Mar./20 Apr. 1798**
Building in occ. of Thomas Perry with house of - Childs on one side, high road on
other
Reg. by Charles Collier, G. Breadsell, Thomas Perry (his mark)
BRO, ABN 1/1; ABN 2/90. PRO, RG 31/2, 86

35/2
Archdeaconry   **18 Dec. 1799/31 Jan. 1800**
Dwelling house & premises in occ. of Ann Stevens, between house in occ. of William
Vice & close of pasture belonging to Sir Phillip Monox, bart.
Reg. by Ann Stevens (her mark), Charles Collier
BRO, ABN 1/1; ABN 2/103. PRO, RG 31/2, 103

35/3
Archdeaconry   **22 Nov. 1815**
House of John Perry of Eversholt
BRO, ABN 1/1

35/4
Archdeaconry   **22 Oct. 1822**
Barn in occ. of James Large, cordwainer at Brook End
Reg. by James Large. Witnesses - W. Millard, John Robarts
BRO, ABN 2/199; ABN 3/3, 45. PRO, RG 31/2, 216

35/5
Archdeaconry   27 Oct./4 Dec. 1823
House in occ. of William Southam at Brook End
Reg. by William Southam, James Fanch, William Millard
BRO, ABN 1/2; ABN 2/205; ABN 3/3, 55. PRO, RG 31/2, 226

35/6
Archdeaconry   28/30 Oct. 1824
House in occ. of Thomas Chew at Rands End
Reg. by Thomas Chew, William Thackray, James Smith
BRO, ABN 1/2; ABN 2/210; ABN 3/3, 61. PRO, RG 31/2, 232

35/7
Archdeaconry   16/23 Apr. 1827
House of Richard Boughton, in occ. of John Roberts (printed form)
Reg. by Richard Boughton, Thomas Roberts, both of Ridgmont
BRO, ABN 1/2; ABN 2/234; ABN 3/3, 77. PRO, RG 31/2, 249
Probably Wesleyan as the form was printed by T. Cordeux, City Rd., London.

35/8
Archdeaconry   13 Oct./17 Nov. 1835
Room in occ. of Thomas Smart, labourer
Reg. by William Wood of Toddington, minister, Thomas Smart, Daniel Howe, both of
Eversholt
BRO, ABN 1/2; ABN 2/309. PRO, RG 31/2, 322, 332
Certificate addressed to the Bishop of Lincoln. This entry appears as Toddington in ABN
1/2 by mistake

35/9
Archdeaconry   4/4 Apr. 1842
Building in occ. of John Holmes of Eversholt
Reg. by John Holmes
BRO, ABN 1/2; ABN 2/366. PRO, RG 31/2, 389

35/10   **Wesleyan**
Worship   **11 Feb. 1854**
Wesleyan Methodist Chapel
Reg. by William Henry Clarkson, 4 Harpur St., Bedford, superintendent minister
Cancelled on revision, 9 Jan. 1880
OPCS, RG(W) 1969
Clarkson registered a Wesleyan chapel at Ridgmont on the same day

36. EVERTON

36/1   **Methodist**
Archdeaconry   **30/31 July 1824**
House of John Smith (printed form)
Reg. by Aquila Barber, Methodist minister
BRO, ABN 1/2; ABN 2/209; ABN 3/3, 60. PRO, RG 31/2, 231
Form printed by T. Cordeux, 14 City Rd., London

36/2
Archdeaconry   10/15 Jan. 1825
House in occ. of John Smith (printed form)
Reg. by William Brocklehurst of St Neots (Hunts.), minister, James Golding
BRO, ABN 1/2; ABN 2/218; ABN 3/3, 68. PRO, RG 31/2, 239
Probably Wesleyan as the form was printed by T. Cordeux, City Rd., London. Certificate
addressed to the Bishop of Lincoln

36/3
Archdeaconry   15 Mar. 1838
House of Christopher Bone
Reg. by Christopher Bone, Samuel Sage, James Wagstaff, John Leonard, James Oakey
(residents)
BRO, ABN 1/2; ABN 2/323. PRO, RG 31/2, 346
Certificate undated

37. EYWORTH

37/1
Archdeaconry   7/19 May 1822
House in poss. of Samuel Sole (printed form)
Reg. by Richard Farr of Wrestlingworth
BRO, ABN 1/2; ABN 2/192; ABN 3/3, 39. PRO, RG 31/2, 210
Probably Wesleyan as the form was printed by T. Cordeux, 14 City Rd., London

37/2
Archdeaconry   8/8 May 1849
House of David Humbersdone (Humberstone) of Eyworth
Reg. by David Humbersdone
BRO, ABN 1/2; ABN 2/410. PRO, RG 31/2, 437

38. FELMERSHAM

38/1
Archdeaconry   1 Aug./6 Oct. 1781
House of Thomas Rootham of Radwell (Meeting House)
Reg. by William Swannell sen., William Swannell jun., John Sharman, Samuel Wright,
Edward Swannell, Thomas Rootham, John Rootham, Thomas Rootham jun., Robert
Rootham
BRO, ABN 1/1; ABN 2/52. PRO, RG 31/2, 52

38/2
Archdeaconry   2 Oct. 1790
House of William Curtis
BRO, ABN 1/1

38/3
Archdeaconry   17/18 Oct. 1806
Dwelling house of John Partridge in Radwell hamlet
Reg. by John Partridge, William Joice, William Law, Ann Luck, Francis Hullot
BRO, ABN 1/1; ABN 2/124. PRO, RG 31/2, 123

38/4
Archdeaconry   **22/31 Oct. 1807**
Chapel in Radwell
Reg. by John Ward, Joseph Swannell, Samuel Swannell, William Leighton, John Bell
BRO, ABN 1/1; ABN 2/130. PRO, RG 31/2, 132
Certificate addressed to the Bishop of Lincoln

38/5
Archdeaconry   **3/23 Jan. 1813**
Dwelling house of William Swannell sen., in occ. of William Drage (printed form)
Reg. by Samuel Wright of Felmersham
BRO, ABN 1/1; ABN 2/149. PRO, RG 31/2, 148
Probably Wesleyan as the form was printed by T. Cordeux, 14 City Rd., London.
Certificate addressed to the bishop of Lincoln

38/6
Archdeaconry   **10/19 Jan. 1815**
Dwelling house in occ. of Joseph Swannell (printed form)
Reg. by John Fordred of Bedford, minister
BRO, ABN 1/1; ABN 2/166. PRO, RG 31/2
Probably Wesleyan as the form was printed by T. Cordeux, 14 City Rd., London.
Certificate addressed to the Bishop of Lincoln

38/7
Archdeaconry   **7/12 Feb. 1840**
Building to be used as a chapel in poss. of James Ward
Reg. by John Single, William Trivit (his mark), James Ward
BRO, ABN 2/346. PRO, RG 31/2, 369
'Thomas Lovelidge acting for the Deputy Registrar, Samuel Bailey'

38/8   **Wesleyan**
Worship   **27 Feb. 1854**
Wesleyan Methodist Chapel at Radwell
Reg. by William Henry Clarkson, Harpur St., Bedford, superintendent minister
Cancelled on revision, 18 Mar. 1971
OPCS, RG(W) 2463

38/9   **Primitive Methodist**
Worship   **2 Mar. 1860**
Room belonging to George Whitworth
Reg. by George Whitworth of Felmersham, shoemaker (proprietor)
Cancelled on revision, 8 May 1895
OPCS, RG(W) 9176

39. FLITTON

39/1   **Congregational**
House of Elizabeth Hawkins at Fleethaven   **22 July 1672**
OR, p. 858
Flitton is called Fleethaven in the Ampthill parish records (BRO, DDP 30/8/1). The
Hawkins family lived at Flitton in 1671 (B.H.R.S., vol. 16, p. 32)

39/2
Archdeaconry   **23/23 Apr. 1775**
House of Thomas Sharp in occ. of William Harrington at Greenfield
Reg. by William Harrington, William Clark, William Langford (both of Flitton)
BRO, ABN 1/1; ABN 2/36. PRO, RG 31/2, 36

39/3
Archdeaconry   **24 Oct. 1799**
House of John Brightman
BRO, ABN 1/1

39/4
Archdeaconry   **24 July 1818**
House of William Row
Reg. by Thomas Row
BRO, ABN 1/1; ABN 3/3, 4. PRO, RG 31/2, 175

39/5
Archdeaconry   **17 Nov. 1821**
House of John Thompson
Reg. by John (James) Thompson, Joseph Clark, William Row
BRO, ABN 1/2; ABN 2/187; ABN 3/3. PRO, RG 31/2, 205
Certificate addressed to the Bishop of Lincoln, undated

39/6
Archdeaconry   **11/11 Mar. 1832**
House in occ. of William Clark in Greenfield (Cranfield)
Reg. by William Clark
BRO, ABN 1/2; ABN 2/266; ABN 3/3, 115. PRO, RG 31/2, 287

39/7   **Wesleyan**
Archdeaconry   **6/6 Dec. 1845**
Building or chapel in Greenfield called the Wesleyan Chapel (printed form)
Reg. by Wright Shovelton of Dunstable
BRO, ABN 1/2; ABN 2/382. PRO, RG 31/2, 403
Certificate addressed to the Bishop of Lincoln

39/8   **Wesleyan**
Worship   **9 Feb. 1854**
Wesleyan Methodist Chapel in Greenfield
Reg. by Matthew Trevan Male, Harpur St., Bedford, superintendent minister
OPCS, RG(W) 1905

39/9   **Primitive Methodist**
Worship   **27 Feb. 1861**
Dwelling house in occ. of George Downing
Reg. by Edward Bishop, 6 Adelaide Sq., Bedford, minister
Cancelled 31 Dec. 1866
OPCS, RG(W) 13135
Bishop registered Primitive Methodist chapels at Marston Morteyne, Maulden & Silsoe
on the same day

40. FLITWICK

40/1
Archdeaconry   **15/20 Apr. 1798**
Dwelling house of John Potter at East End
Reg. by John Potter, James Oliver
BRO, ABN 1/1; ABN 2/85. PRO, RG 31/2, 87

40/2
Archdeaconry   **26/29 Oct. 1813**
Dwelling house in occ. of Joseph Dillingham at Daniel End
Reg. by Samuel Hobson of Maulden, minister, Richard Goodman, William Howson of Flitwick
BRO, ABN 1/1; ABN 2/157. PRO, RG 31/2, 156
Samuel Hobson was a Congregational minister trained at Newport Pagnell Academy. Certificate addressed to the Registrar

40/3
Archdeaconry   **20/24 Mar. 1821**
House of James Jellious (Jellis)
Reg. by James Jellious, Thomas Hobbs, William Howson, Je[remiah] James
BRO, ABN 1/2; ABN 2/181; ABN 3/3, 26. PRO, RG 31/2, 197
Certificate addressed to the Bishop of Lincoln

40/4
Archdeaconry   **6/10 Feb. 1827**
House of Jeremiah James of Denal End
Reg. by Jeremiah James, William Housand [*sic*], Richard Goodman
BRO, ABN 1/2; ABN 2/226; ABN 3/3, 75. PRO, RG 31/2, 247

40/5   **Wesleyan**
Worship   **18 Nov. 1873**
Flitwick Wesleyan Methodist Chapel in Chapel Road
Reg. by Francis Hewitt of Ampthill, Methodist minister
OPCS, RG(W) 21546

41. GOLDINGTON

41/1   **Congregational**
House of Gilbert Ashley   **1 May 1672**
OR, p. 856

41/2
Archdeaconry   **30/13 May 1772** *(sic)*
House in poss. of True Emery
Reg. by George Palmer of Goldington, yeoman, William Sherman of Goldington, farmer
BRO, ABN 1/1; ABN 2/32. PRO, RG 31/2, 32
Certificate addressed to the Commissary & Official of Bedford

41/3
Archdeaconry   **18/18 May 1775**
House of Mr Watford in poss. of John Marshall
Reg. by G. Palmer, Mahanaim Abbott
BRO, ABN 1/1; ABN 2/38. PRO, RG 31/2, 38

41/4
Archdeaconry 27 Mar. 1805
Dwelling house of Elizabeth Williamson
BRO, ABN 1/1

41/5
Archdeaconry 17/19 Apr. 1813
Messuage belonging to George Palmer, yeoman, in occ. of Mahanaim Abbott (printed form)
Reg. by George Palmer, William Mayle
BRO, ABN 1/1; ABN 2/151. PRO, RG 31/2, 150
Probably Wesleyan as the form was printed by T. Cordeux, 14 City Rd., London

41/6 **Congregational**
Worship **12 July 1860**
Goldington Meeting (connected with Bunyan Meeting, Bedford)
Reg. by John Jukes, Dame Alice St., Bedford, Congregational minister (senior minister)
54415 substituted on 27 Apr. 1933
OPCS, RG(W) 9416
Jukes registered Congregational chapels at Cardington, Elstow, Kempston, Oakley & Stagsden on the same day

42. GRAVENHURST

42/1 **Wesleyan**
Archdeaconry **18/23 Sept. 1846**
Wesleyan Methodist Chapel in Upper Gravenhurst (printed form)
Reg. by John Crofts
BRO, ABN 1/2; ABN 2/388. PRO, RG 31/2, 414
Certificate addressed to the Bishop of Lincoln and altered to Ely. Crofts registered Wesleyan chapels at Luton & Shillington on the same day

42/2 **Wesleyan Methodist**
Worship **9 Feb. 1854**
Wesleyan Methodist Chapel at Upper Gravenhurst
Reg. by Wright Shovelton, Chapel St., Luton, superintendent minister
OPCS, RG(W), 1904

42/3 **Wesleyan**
Marriages **27 May 1898**
Wesleyan Methodist Chapel in Upper Gravenhurst
OPCS, RG(M) 15028

43. HARLINGTON

43/1
Archdeaconry 3 May 1811
House of Henry Humphries
BRO, ABN 1/1

43/2
Archdeaconry   **17 June 1816**
House of Edward Wilson
BRO, ABN 1/1

43/3
Archdeaconry   **20/23 Jan. 1821 (1820)**
House of William Huckle
Reg. by William Huckle, John Stonebridge, Thomas Perry
BRO, ABN 1/2; ABN 2/175; ABN 3/3, 22. PRO, RG 31/2, 193
Certificate addressed to the Bishop of Lincoln, dated 1820

43/4
Archdeaconry   **4/5 Apr. 1828**
Tenement of John Cotching of Toddington in his own occ.
Reg. by John Cotching
BRO, ABN 1/2; ABN 2/239; ABN 3/3, 88. PRO, RG 31/2, 260

43/5
Archdeaconry   **16 Oct. 1835/9 Jan. 1836**
Cottage in occ. of Philip Ellis
Reg. by Phillip [*sic*] Ellis
BRO, ABN 1/2; ABN 2/308. PRO, RG 31/2, 334

43/6   **Wesleyan**
Archdeaconry   **8/11 May 1839**
Wesleyan Chapel
Reg. by Samuel Hope of Luton
BRO, ABN 1/2; ABN 2/340. PRO, RG 31/2, 363
This is registered as Luton in ABN 1/2 by mistake

43/7   **Wesleyan**
Worship   **9 Feb. 1854**
Wesleyan Methodist Chapel
Reg. by Matthew Trevan Male of Dunstable, superintendent minister
OPCS, RG(W) 1856
Male registered Wesleyan chapels at Chalgrave, Hockliffe & Toddington on the same day

44. HARROLD

44/1
Quarter Sessions   **12/12 Jan. 1774**
House of John Boddington
Reg. by William Pendred, William Sharton, Walter Clark, John Boddington
BRO, QSP43/12
Original certificate & draft licence

44/2
Archdeaconry   **17/17 Oct. 1791**
House of William Faulkner for occasional use
Reg. by Eaton Jeffery, Ephram Smith (his mark)
BRO, ABN 1/1; ABN 2/69. PRO, RG 31/2, 69

Plate 18: Harrold: The Congregational church and schoolroom. The church was founded in 1808 and the present chapel dates from 1863.   (*Postcard: c.1910*)

44/3
Archdeaconry   **8 Aug. 1807**
House of John Mardling
BRO, ABN 1/1

44/4
Archdeaconry   **12/12 Sept. 1809**
New-built Chapel
Reg. by Thomas Kilpin, Richard Hensman, Benjamin Allen
BRO, ABN 1/1; ABN 2/134. PRO, RG 31/2, 135
ABN 1/1 gives the year as 1808

44/5
Archdeaconry   **23 Jan. 1812**
Dwelling house of Knightley Smith of Harrold
BRO, ABN 1/1

44/6   **Independent**
Marriages   **29 June 1840**
Harrold Chapel (United Reformed Church)
OPCS, RG(M) 1667
This number is duplicated in the register

44/7   **Unsectarian**
Worship   **16 Apr. 1884**
Mission Hall [Harrold Evangelical Church in High Street]
Reg. by Miss M. St Quintain of Harrold, proprietor
OPCS, RG(W) 27845

44/8   Unsectarian
Marriages   **11 May 1889**
Mission Hall in High Street [Harrold Evangelical Church]
OPCS, RG(M) 12216

45. HAYNES

45/1
Archdeaconry   **30/30 Jan. 1766**
Dwelling house of Thomas Randall
Reg. by Richard Wheeler, William Tansley
BRO, ABN 1/1; ABN 2/22A. PRO, RG 31/2, 20
Certificate addressed to the Commissary & Official of Bedford

45/2
Quarter Sessions   **12 July 1775**
House of Elizabeth Arms, widow
Reg. by Elizabeth Arms, Simon Tansley, Thomas Farviel, James Andrew (his mark),
James Brashier
BRO, QSP43/15
Original certificate & draft licence. Only day of the month given on licence

45/3
Archdeaconry   **11/11 June 1807**
Dwelling house of Thomas Taylor for occasional worship
Reg. by Thomas Taylor, Thomas King, John Whitridge
BRO, ABN 1/1; ABN 2/129. PRO, RG 31/2, 129

45/4
Archdeaconry   **26/27 Aug. 1816**
Tenement of Stephen Beale in his own occ.
Reg. by Stephen Beale (his mark), Samuel Beard, William Green, John Cox
BRO, ABN 1/1; ABN 2/172. PRO, RG 31/2, 171

45/5
Archdeaconry   **14/18 Dec. 1824**
Newly erected Chapel (Building)
Reg. by William Whitteridge, John Cox, Thomas Allen
BRO, ABN 1/2; ABN 2/217; ABN 3/3, 64. PRO, RG 31/2, 237

45/6   Wesleyan
Worship   **17 Feb. 1854**
Wesleyan Methodist Chapel
Reg. by William Henry Clarkson, 4 Harpur St., Bedford, superintendent minister
Cancelled 29 Aug. 1894
OPCS, RG(W) 2129
Clarkson registered Wesleyan chapels at Ampthill, Houghton Conquest, Lidlington,
Marstom Morteyne & Maulden on the same day

45/7   Wesleyan
Worship   **30 Mar. 1875**
Wesleyan Methodist Chapel in Silver End Road
Reg. by Hugh Jones of Bedford, Wesleyan minister
OPCS, RG(W) 22183

45/8   Calvinistic Baptist
Worship   8 Sept. 1894
Baptist Chapel
Reg. by William Rudd Green, Cotton End, Eastcotts, butcher (trustee)
61395 substituted on 14 June 1946
OPCS, RG(W) 34508

46. HEATH & REACH

46/1
Archdeaconry   2 Apr. 1799
House of John Tompkins
BRO, ABN 1/1

46/2
Archdeaconry   7/24 Mar. 1801
**House & premises of Thomas Cox & William Yerby at Heath and Reach in
Leighton Buzzard**
Reg. by Thomas Cox, William Yerby, James Attwell, William Attwell, Thomas Stevens
BRO, ABN 1/1; ABN 2/106. PRO, RG 31/2, 106

46/3
Archdeaconry   24 Sept. 1822
A Chapel (Building)
Reg. by Thomas Wake, minister, Thomas Matthews, John Matthews, William Paragreen,
Joseph Carpender
BRO, ABN 1/2; ABN 2/190, 195 (two copies); ABN 3/3, 42. PRO, RG 31/2, 213
Certificate undated

46/4   Wesleyan
Peculiar Jurisdiction   10 Nov. 1823
Wesleyan Methodist Chapel
Reg. by Jonathan Williams of Leighton Buzzard, Wesleyan minister
BRO, RI 3/6824a

46/5   Wesleyan
Worship   15 Mar. 1861
Wesleyan Methodist Chapel
Reg. by James S. Haigh of Leighton Buzzard, Wesleyan minister
Cancelled 27 June 1878
OPCS, RG(W) 13535
Haigh registered Wesleyan chapels at Eaton Bray & Stanbridge on the same day

46/6   Primitive Methodist
Worship   19 May 1862
**A building, the property of Mr Robert Belgrave, in occ. of James Northwood in
Reach**
Reg. by Samuel Turner of Aylesbury (Bucks.), minister
Cancelled 31 Dec. 1866
OPCS, RG(W) 15160

46/7   Primitive Methodist
Worship   27 Apr. 1864

Ebenezer Primitive Methodist Chapel
Reg. by William Birks of Leighton Buzzard, minister
Cancelled 23 Mar. 1906
OPCS, RG(W) 16160
Birks registered Primitive Methodist chapels at Billington & Lidlington on the same day

46/8   **Wesleyan**
Worship   **1 June 1878**
Wesleyan Methodist Chapel in Heath
Reg. by Abraham S. White, 1 Wesley Villas, Leighton Buzzard, Wesleyan minister
Cancelled on revision, 16 Apr. 1896
OPCS, RG(W) 24061

46/9   **Salvation Army**
Worship   **18 Aug. 1888**
The Barracks in Woburn Road
Reg. by William Brandon, 3 North St., Leighton Buzzard, general merchant (proprietor)
Cancelled on revision, 16 Apr. 1896
OPCS, RG(W) 31047

46/10   **Wesleyan**
Worship   **30 Aug. 1892**
Wesleyan Methodist Chapel
Reg. by John Wallace of Leighton Buzzard, tailor (attendant)
OPCS, RG(W) 33438

46/11   **Wesleyan**
Marriages   **3 Sept. 1892**
Wesleyan Methodist Chapel
OPCS, RG(M) 13165

47. HENLOW

47/1
Archdeaconry   **15 Jan. 1716/7**
House of Samuell Sandon
Reg. by John Johnson, John Underwood, John Hearst, Samuel Sandon
BRO, ABC 24, f. 115

47/2
Quarter Sessions   **20 Apr. 1737**
Dwelling house of Thomas Willson, wheelwright
Reg. by William Willsher, witness Thomas Barker
BRO, QSR 1737, 60
Not entered in QSM 6, unlike 48/1, but see 48/1 which uses the same wording for the
certificate

47/3
Archdeaconry   **16/18 Sept. 1786**
House of Thomas Tansley
Reg. by Thomas Tansley (his mark), William Tansley
BRO, ABN 1/1; ABN 2/56. PRO, RG 31/2, 57

47/4
Archdeaconry   9 Apr.1810/3 May 1811
Dwelling house of Barzilla Seymour
Reg. by Joseph Patrick, Barzilla Seymour, Elizabeth Seymour, Thomas Armour, Sarah Cowlan
BRO, ABN 1/1; ABN 2/139. PRO, RG 31/2, 138

47/5
Archdeaconry   18/18 Jan. 1844
House of Thomas Gentle, in occ. of Edward Gentle (printed form)
Reg. by Edward Gentle
BRO, ABN 1/2; ABN 2/374. PRO, RG 31/2, 398
Certificate addressed to the Bishop of Ely

47/6   Salvationists
Worship   9 Nov. 1887
Salvation Army Barracks
Reg. by Henry Coote, Mount Pleasant Cottage, Langford, Captain, S.A.
Cancelled on revision, 19 Apr. 1895
OPCS, RG(W) 30480

48. HOCKLIFFE

48/1
Quarter Sessions   12 Jan. 1736/7
The now dwelling house with the appurtenances thereunto belonging to William Gould of Hockliff in the parish of Chalgrave, scrivner
Reg. by William Willsher, John Fanch
BRO, QSR 1737, 57; QSM 6, p. 112. PRO, RG 31/6, 2
See 47/2 for same wording

48/2
Archdeaconry   27 Jan. 1806
House of William Read
BRO, ABN 1/1

48/3
Archdeaconry   15 Aug. 1807
Meeting House
BRO, ABN 1/1

48/4
Archdeaconry   10 Aug. 1809
Building near the dwelling house of Thomas Smith & John Adams
Reg. by William Downing, John Stevenson
BRO, ABN 2/127. PRO, RG 31/2, 134

48/5
Archdeaconry   6/9 Feb. 1813
Messuage or dwelling house in occ. of Thomas Smith (printed form)
Reg. by Thomas Smith (his mark), Richard Labrum
BRO, ABN 1/1; ABN 2/150. PRO, RG 31/2, 149
Probably Wesleyan as the form was printed by T. Cordeux, 14 City Rd., London

48/6
Archdeaconry   **7 June 1815**
Dwelling house of James Roberts
BRO, ABN 1/1

48/7   **Wesleyan**
Archdeaconry   **19/21 June 1834**
Wesleyan Chapel (printed form)
Reg. by Isaac Wale of Bedford
BRO, ABN 1/2; ABN 2/280. PRO, RG 31/2, 309
Certificate addressed to the Bishop of Lincoln. Wale registered Wesleyan chapels at
Barton & Dunstable on the same day

48/8
Archdeaconry   **17/21 Feb. 1839**
House & premises in occ. of Samuel Wells (printed form)
Reg. by Samuel Wells
BRO, ABN 2/337. PRO, RG 31/2, 361

48/9   **Independent**
Marriages   **11 Nov. 1843**
Independent Chapel
OPCS, RG(M) 2169

48/10   **Wesleyan**
Worship   **9 Feb. 1854**
Wesleyan Methodist Chapel
Reg. by Matthew Trevan Male of Dunstable, superintendent minister
Cancelled 15 Feb. 1922
OPCS, RG(W) 1857
Male registered Wesleyan chapels at Chalgrave, Harlington & Toddington on the same day

48/11   **Primitive Methodist**
Worship   **28 Aug. 1862**
Primitive Methodist Chapel
Reg. by William Beckitt of Woburn Sands, minister
Cancelled on revision, 4 Apr. 1935
OPCS, RG(W) 15281

49. HOLWELL

49/1
Archdeaconry   **11/11 Oct. 1774**
House & barn of John Foster at Cadwell
Reg. by Samuel Bradly, Robert Thomas, Thomas Ward
BRO, ABN 1/1; ABN 2/34. PRO, RG 31/2, 34

49/2
Archdeaconry   **14/16 Mar. 1776**
House of William Honour
Reg. by William Thomas, Robert Thomas
BRO, ABN 1/1; ABN 2/39. PRO, RG 31/2, 39

50. HOUGHTON CONQUEST

50/1
Quarter Sessions   **20 June 1774**
House of Thomas Potter, esq., in poss. of John Arms in Bedford Houghton
Reg. by John Arms, Richard Whiteman, James Betts
BRO, QSP43/13
Original certificate

50/2
Archdeaconry   **5 Feb. 1796**
House of William Baker
BRO, ABN 1/1

50/3
Archdeaconry   **24 Oct. 1798**
House of Matthew Goss
BRO, ABN 1/1

50/4   **Methodist**
Archdeaconry   **18 July/18 Oct. 1805**
Methodist Chapel, property of John Armstrong
Reg. by John Armstrong, William Baker, James Kent
BRO, ABN 1/1; ABN 2/119. PRO, RG 31/2, 120

50/5   **Wesleyan**
Archdeaconry   **28/30 Mar. 1834**
Wesleyan Chapel (printed form)
Reg. by Isaac Wale, trustee
BRO, ABN 1/2; ABN 2/284. PRO, RG 31/2, 319

50/6   **Wesleyan**
Worship   **17 Feb. 1854**
Wesleyan Methodist Chapel at Houghton *[sic]*
Reg. by William Henry Clarkson, 4 Harpur St., Bedford, superintendent minister
Cancelled 29 Aug. 1894
OPCS, RG(W) 2130
Clarkson registered Wesleyan chapels at Ampthill, Haynes, Lidlington, Marston
Morteyne & Maulden on the same day

50/7   **Primitive Methodist**
Worship   **16 May 1861**
Primitive Methodist Chapel
Reg. by Edward Bishop, 6 Adelaide Sq., Bedford, minister
Cancelled 27 July 1946
OPCS, RG(W) 14318
Bishop registered a Primitive Methodist chapel at Millbrook on the same day

50/8   **Wesleyan**
Worship   **30 Oct. 1878**
Wesleyan Methodist Chapel
Reg. by George Henry Bellamy, Woburn St., Ampthill, Wesleyan minister
OPCS, RG(W) 24257

51. HOUGHTON REGIS

51/1
Quarter Sessions   **10 July 1740**
Newly erected house at Thorne in Kings Houghton, near the messuage or tenement of John Bunker, wherein he now dwells
Reg. by Samuel Ch[*illeg.*], John Cooper, S. Mason, Thomas Cooper
BRO, QSR 1740, 111

51/2
Archdeaconry   **14/15 May 1790**
House of Thomas Wilstead at Bakers Corner
Reg. by Thomas Wilstead (his mark), Robert Fawkner, Daniel Queneborough, Thomas Poulter, John Cotchins
BRO, ABN 1/1; ABN 2/65. PRO, RG 31/2, 122

51/3
Archdeaconry   **29 Nov. 1806**
House of Mr George Scroggs in Sewell for occasional worship
Reg. by Fisher Scroggs, Daniel Queenbury, James Buttfield, Richard Gutteridge jun., George Scroggs
BRO, ABN2/123

51/4
Archdeaconry   **13 Jan./15 Mar. 1822**
House of Elizabeth Cook in Sewell
Reg. by Elizabeth Cook
BRO, ABN 1/2; ABN 2/188; ABN 3/3, 36. PRO, RG 31/2, 207

51/5
Archdeaconry   **18/29 Dec. 1827**
Dwelling house of Edward Messenger at Chalk Hill
Reg. by Francis Brooke Potts of Luton
BRO, ABN 1/2; ABN 2/235; ABN 3/3, 84. PRO, RG 31/2, 256
Certificate originally addressed to the Clerk of the Peace and altered to the Archdeacon

51/6
Archdeaconry   **2/3 Sept. 1834**
A room in house in occ. of William Scrivener at Houghton Turn
Reg. by William Scrivener, Richard Birt, William Groom, Benjamin Billington (housekeepers)
BRO, ABN 1/2; ABN 2/293. PRO, RG 31/2

51/7   **Wesleyan**
Archdeaconry   **19/19 May 1835**
Wesleyan Chapel (printed form, two copies)
Reg. by Thomas Rogerson of Luton
BRO, ABN 1/2, ABN 2/300, 302. PRO, RG 31/2, 326
Rogerson registered Wesleyan chapels at Barton, Leagrave, Luton, Tebworth, Toddington & Whipsnade on the same day

51/8   **Wesleyan**
Archdeaconry   **19 May 1835**

Wesleyan Chapel at Puddle Hill
Reg. by Thomas Rogerson of Luton
BRO, ABN 1/2. PRO, RG 31/2, 328

51/9
Quarter Sessions   **19/19 Oct. 1847**
A building (printed form)
Reg. by Thomas Hobson, minister
BRO, QSR 47/4. PRO, RG 31/6, 38
Hobson registered a building at Toddington on the same day

51/10   **Wesleyan**
Worship   **9 Feb. 1854**
Wesleyan Methodist Chapel
Reg. by Matthew Trevan Male of Dunstable, superintendent minister
62423 substituted on 28 Aug. 1949 (advertised 23 Aug. 1949)
OPCS, RG(W) 1899
Male registered Wesleyan chapels at Dunstable, Kensworth, Leagrave & Sundon on the
same day

51/11   **Wesleyan**
Worship   **9 Feb. 1854**
Wesleyan Methodist Chapel at Chalkhill
Reg. by Matthew Trevan Male of Dunstable, superintendent minister
Cancelled 4 Nov. 1936
OPCS, RG(W) 1900

51/12   **Baptist**
Marriages   **13 Apr. 1860**
Baptist Chapel in Five Bells Yard
5549 substituted on 15 July 1864
OPCS, RG(M) 4586

51/13   **Baptist**
Worship   **5 May 1860**
Baptist Chapel
Reg. by Michael Cook jun. of Houghton Regis, grocer (trustee)
Cancelled 15 July 1864, but 16289 (51/15) substituted
OPCS, RG(W) 9249
The clerk made several errors with this registration giving different dates and using the
Marriages registration (5549)

51/14   **Primitive Methodist**
Worship   **3 Jan. 1861**
Primitive Methodist Chapel
Reg. by Richard Tearle of Houghton Regis, plait dealer (Society Steward)
Cancelled on revision, 12 May 1896
OPCS, RG(W) 11636
'Society Steward' altered to 'attendant' by Registrar

51/15   **Primitive Methodist**
Worship   **28 Mar. 1863**
Primitive Methodist Chapel

Reg. by Thomas Huckle of Luton, bonnet manufacturer (trustee)
Cancelled on revision, 4 Sept. 1935
OPCS, RG(W) 15621
Huckle registered a Primitive Methodist chapel at Dunstable on the same day

51/16   **Baptist**
Worship   **9 July 1864**
Baptist Chapel in High Street
Reg. by George Hicks Davies of Houghton Regis, dissenting minister
Substituted for 9249. Cancelled 8 Jan. 1973
OPCS, RG(W) 16289

Plate 19: Houghton Regis: The new Baptist chapel built in 1863-4 and licensed in 1864.
It was demolished in 1972-3.   (*Photograph: Bedfordshire County Council, 1972*)

51/17   **Baptist**
Marriages   **15 July 1864**
Baptist Chapel in High Street
Substituted for 4586. Cancelled 8 Jan. 1973
OPCS, RG(M) 5549

51/18   **Salvation Army**
Worship   **18 Oct. 1884**
Salvation Army Barn in High Street
Reg. by John Edward Margetts, 43 King St., Reading (Berks.), A.D.C., S.A.
36178 substituted on 7 Sept. 1897
OPCS, RG(W) 28172

Plate 20: Houghton Regis: The Salvation Army Hall behind the Unicorn Inn in the High
Street.   (*Photograph: c.1906*)

51/19   **Salvation Army**
Worship   **7 Sept. 1894**
Salvation Army Barracks in High Street
Reg. by Joshua Spooner, 35 Brook St., Luton, Major S.A. (occupier)
Substituted for 28172. Cancelled in 1964
OPCS, RG(W) 36178

52. HUSBORNE CRAWLEY

52/1
Quarter Sessions   **4 July 1792**
Dwelling house in occ. of Joseph Harris, glaisher (glazier)
Reg. by Joseph Harris, glaisher, John Keech, labourer, John Turney, butcher, John
Gurney, miller
BRO, QSR 1792, 56; QSM 19, p. 12. PRO, RG 31/6, 14
Christian name & occupation of Harris added later in QSR

52 / 2
Archdeaconry   13 Jan / 24 Mar. 1801
Premises of Samuel Harris near the Swan, in occ. of John Barrel, on other side of house in tenure of Jeffery Hart
Reg. by Samuel Harris, Francis Beall
BRO, ABN 1/1; ABN 2/105. PRO, RG 31/2, 105

52 / 3
Archdeaconry   5 / 12 Mar. 1805
House of Thomas Bennet
Reg. by Thomas Bennet, Samuel Harris, Francis Beall
BRO, ABN 1/1; ABN 2/116. PRO, RG 31/2, 119

52 / 4
Archdeaconry   10 / 23 Apr. 1827
Dwelling house of Joseph Higgens (printed form)
Reg. by Joseph Higgens (his mark), William Cuttriss, Felix Higgins
BRO, ABN 1/2; ABN 2/228; ABN 3/3, 78; X347/42. PRO, RG 31/2, 250
Although the form was printed by T. Cordeux, the original licence is with the Ridgmont Baptist Church records

52 / 5
Archdeaconry   27 Mar. 1830
House in occ. of William Fossey
Reg. by Willam Fossey, Joseph Bowler, Thomas Herbert
BRO, ABN 1/2; ABN 2/246; ABN 3/3, 94. PRO, RG 31/2, 266
Certificate undated

Plate 21: Husborne Crawley: Crow Lane Primitive Methodist chapel built in 1867 and licensed in 1870.   (*Postcard: c.1910*)

52/6
Archdeaconry   **22/26 Oct. 1845**
Building (Chapel) in occ. of John Sibley
Reg. by Joseph Brooks, Richard Boughton, Thomas Francis (householders)
BRO, ABN 1/2; ABN 2/379; X347/43. PRO, RG 31/2, 402
Original licence with Ridgmont Baptist Church records. X 347/44 is a note by John
Sibley that he was licenced to preach at Husborne Crawley by Rev. J.H. Brooks, and that
the forms & candlesticks of the church are in his possession

52/7   **Primitive Methodist**
Worship   **24 June 1870**
Primitive Methodist Chapel
Reg. by Thomas Penroe of Linslade (Bucks.), Primitive Methodist minister
Cancelled on revision, 31 Oct. 1935
OPCS, RG(W) 19720

53. KEMPSTON

53/1   Congregational
House of John Baxter   1 May 1672
OR, p. 854

53/2
Archdeaconry   **10 Dec. 1799**
House & premises of John Burr
BRO, ABN 1/1
53/3
Archdeaconry   **26 Oct. 1804**
Dwelling house of Ann Burridge
BRO, ABN 1/1

53/4
Archdeaconry   **18 Oct. 1805**
House of James Ames
BRO, ABN 1/1

53/5
Archdeaconry   **21 Apr. 1807**
House of Samuel Favell of Kempston
BRO, ABN 1/1

53/6
Archdeaconry   **22 July/6 Aug. 1812**
Newly erected building in Giles Close belonging to John Joice of Kempston
Reg. by James Smith, John Joice, William Dugliss
BRO, ABN 1/1; ABN 2/145. PRO, RG 31/2, 145

53/7
Archdeaconry   **20 Nov./6 Dec. 1821**
Dwelling house of George Lumbis (Lumbus) in own occ.
Reg. by George Lumbis
BRO, ABN 1/2; ABN 2/186; ABN 3/3, 35. PRO, RG 31/2, 206
Certificate addressed to the Bishop of Lincoln

53/8
Archdeaconry   **16/16 Nov. 1831**
House & barn of Joseph Saville
Reg. by Joseph Saville
BRO, ABN 1/2; ABN 2/262; ABN 3/3, 111. PRO, RG 31/2, 283
Certificate addressed to the Bishop of Lincoln

53/9
Archdeaconry   **3/4 Jan. 1833**
House of William Cooper
Reg. by William Cooper (his mark), William Carter, William Robinson, James
Musgraves (his mark)
BRO, ABN 1/2; ABN 2/276. PRO, RG 31/2, 297

53/10
Archdeaconry   **17/17 Dec. 1835**
Dwelling house of Isaac Barratt of Kempston
Reg. by Isaac Barratt
BRO, ABN 1/2; ABN 2/310. PRO, RG 31/2, 333
Certificate addressed to the Bishop of Lincoln

53/11
Archdeaconry   **1/1 Apr. 1842**
Building in poss. of William Smith
Reg. by William Smith
BRO, ABN 1/2; ABN 2/365. PRO, RG 31/2, 388

53/12   **Wesleyan**
Worship   **9 Feb. 1854**
Wesleyan Methodist Chapel
Reg. by William Henry Clarkson, Harpur St., Bedford, superintendent minister
Cancelled 31 Oct. 1904
OPCS, RG(W) 1869
Clarkson registered Wesleyan chapels at Bedford, Cardington, Clapham, Milton Ernest,
Pavenham, Turvey, Wilshamstead & Wootton on the same day

53/13   **Congregational**
Worship   **12 July 1860**
Kempston Chapel (connected with Bunyan Meeting, Bedford)
Reg. by John Jukes, Dame Alice St., Bedford, Congregational minister (senior minister)
Cancelled 26 Aug. 1892
OPCS, RG(W) 9419
Jukes registered Congregational chapels at Cardington, Elstow, Goldington, Oakley &
Stagsden on the same day

53/14   **Wesleyan**
Worship   **30 Jan. 1861**
Wesleyan Methodist Chapel
Reg. by Charles Carter, Harpur St., Bedford, minister
Cancelled 31 Dec. 1866
OPCS, RG(W) 12243
Carter registered a Wesleyan chapel at Pavenham on the same day

53/15   Wesleyan
Marriages   10 Mar. 1890
Wesleyan Methodist Chapel
Substituted 17492 on 31 Oct. 1904
OPCS, RG(M) 12445

53/16   Congregational
Worship   22 Aug. 1892
Bunyan Chapel
Reg. by James Coombs of Bedford, M.D. (trustee)
Substituted 54418 on 27 Apr. 1933
OPCS, RG(W) 33432

53/17   Union
Marriages   23 Aug. 1892
Bunyan Chapel - Congregational & Baptist (Baptist & Independent)
OPCS, RG(M) 13156

53/18   Primitive Methodist
Worship   10 Aug. 1898
Primitive Methodist Chapel in Bedford Road
Reg. by Richard Newman Wycherley, 20 Ampthill Rd., Bedford, Primitive Methodist
minister
OPCS, RG(W) 36727

53/19   Unsectarian
Worship   1 May 1899
Mission Hall in Duncombe Street
Reg. by Arthur William Panter, Bedford Rd., Kempston, builder (proprietor)
Cancelled 17 Dec. 1914
OPCS, RG(W) 37160

54. KENSWORTH

Kensworth parish was transferred from Herts. to Beds. in 1897

54/1   Quaker
Herts. Quarter Sessions   7 Oct. 1689
A house
HRO, QS misc. 1471

54/2   Baptist
Herts. Quarter Sessions   14 July 1690
House of Thomas Hayward
HRO, QS misc. 1471

54/3
Archdeaconry   17 Nov. 1807
Dwelling house of John Frost
Reg. by John Frost, John Read, Francis Emerston, William Iredale, James Wright,
George Bingham
Urwick, *Nonconformity in Hertfordshire* (London, 1884), p. 447

54/4
Archdeaconry   **10 Apr. 1810**
Dwelling house of David Taylor
Reg. by David Talor [*sic*], John Coates, William Iredale, John Read, Henry Bradshaw,
James Wright, George Bingham
HRO, 63721/1

54/5   **Wesleyan**
Archdeaconry   **4 Dec. 1830**
Wesleyan Chapel
Reg. by William Pollard
Urwick, *op. cit.*, p. 447
Identified as Wesleyan. Transcript in *Dunstable Methodist Circuit*, pp. 94 & 95

54/6   **Wesleyan**
Archdeaconry   **14 July 1847**
Wesleyan Chapel
Reg. by Wright Shovelton, minister
HRO, AHH 18/1

54/7   **Wesleyan**
Worship   **9 Feb. 1854**
Wesleyan Methodist Chapel
Reg. by Matthew Trevan Male of Dunstable, superintendent minister
OPCS, RG(W) 1897
Male registered Wesleyan chapels at Dunstable, Houghton Regis, Leagrave & Sundon on
the same day

54/8   **Mormon**
Worship   **12 June 1855**
A Building, the property of Daniel Evans, for Latter Day Saints
Reg. by Daniel Evans of Kensworth, straw plait dealer (proprietor)
Cancelled 31 Dec. 1866
OPCS, RG(W) 6487

55. KEYSOE

55/1   **Congregational**
House of George Fowler   **8 May 1672**
OR, p. 852

55/2   **Congregational**
House of John Donne   **10 May 1672**
OR, p. 852

55/3   **Congregational**
House of Thomas Richards   **22 May 1672**
OR, p. 852

55/4
Archdeaconry   **21 Mar. 1808**
Building of Joel Miles
BRO, ABN 1/1

Plate 22: Keysoe: Brook End Baptist church (originally Independent) was established in 1652, and the church book (now lost) commenced in 1658.

(Postcard: Blake & Edgar, c.1905)

55 / 5	**Baptist**
Archdeaconry	**21 / 22 Oct. 1825**

Building in occ. of Richard Barnet to be used as a Chapel
Reg. by William Cunnington, Stephen Dickins, William Crockford
BRO, ABN 1/2; ABN 2/222; ABN 3/3, 71. PRO, RG 31/2, 242

55 / 6	**Particular Baptist**
Marriages	**22 June 1838**

Brook End Meeting
OPCS, RG(M) 1179

55 / 7	
Archdeaconry	**21 / 21 Dec. 1838**

House of Mr Samuel Whitmee of Kesoe Row
Reg. by Samuel Whitmee, Eli Shelford (his mark), William Packwood
BRO, ABN 1/2; ABN 2/334. PRO, RG 31/2, 357

56. KNOTTING

56 / 1	**Wesleyan**
Worship	**13 Apr. 1889**

Wesleyan Methodist Chapel, Knotting Green
Reg. by Arthur James Pickworth of Higham Ferrers (Northants.), Wesleyan minister
OPCS, RG(W) 31500

57. LANGFORD

57/1
Archdeaconry   **27/27 Mar. 1780**
House of Thomas Roberson for public occasional worship
Reg. by William Tansley, Robert Douglass
BRO, ABN 1/1; ABN 2/50. PRO, RG 31/2, 50

57/2
Archdeaconry   **17/17 Sept. 1788**
House of Thomas Robinson
Reg. by Henry Finch, Anthony Thody, Thomas Robinson (parishioners)
BRO, ABN 1/1; ABN 2/59. PRO, RG 31/2, 59
The three parishioners were agreeable for Robinson to have a licence

57/3
Archdeaconry   **13/15 Jan. 1807**
Farm house & barn in occ. of Henry Bean for occasional public worship
Reg. by E. Ell, William Lyles, Henry Bean
BRO, ABN 1/1; ABN 2/126. PRO, RG 31/2, 126

57/4
Archdeaconry   **2 June 1807**
House of William West
BRO, ABN 1/1

57/5
Archdeaconry   **28 Aug. 1815**
House of John Wright
BRO, ABN 1/1

57/6
Archdeaconry   **7/8 May 1822**
Building on premises of William Edwards
Reg. by Thomas Spencer, John Pryor, William Edwards
BRO, ABN 1/2; ABN 2/191; ABN 3/3, 38. PRO, RG 31/2, 209

57/7
Archdeaconry   **24 Nov./1 Dec. 1827**
Building of John Foster to be used as a chapel
Reg. by John Foster, William Kent, Caleb Evans, Blyth Foster, Thomas Middleditch
BRO, ABN 1/2; ABN 2/233; ABN 3/3, 83. PRO, RG 31/2, 255

57/8
Archdeaconry   **28 May/17 June 1838**
House of Hugh Kilby
Reg. by Joseph Bailey, Edmund Thody, John Street
BRO, ABN 1/2; ABN 2/328. PRO, RG 31/2, 352
Certificate received by Thomas Lovelidge acting for the Deputy Registrar

57/9
Archdeaconry   **7/7 Nov. 1840**
House of William Timpson
Reg. by William Timpson, John Searl (his mark), William Seal (his mark)
BRO, ABN 1/2; ABN 2/350. PRO, RG 31/2, 373

57/10   Wesleyan
Worship   9 Feb. 1854
Wesleyan Chapel
Reg. by Robert Maxwell of Biggleswade, Wesleyan minister
Cancelled 31 Dec. 1866
OPCS, RG(W) 1873
Maxwell registered Wesleyan chapels at Biggleswade, Sandy, Shefford & Stotfold on the
same day

57/11   Wesleyan
Worship   5 Oct. 1861
Wesleyan Chapel
Reg. by Henry Wilkinson Williams of Biggleswade, Wesleyan minister
OPCS, RG(W) 14615

57/12   Wesleyan
Marriages   30 Sept. 1870
Wesleyan Chapel
OPCS, RG(M) 7228

57/13   Salvationists
Worship   26 Nov. 1887
Salvation Army Barracks
Reg. by Henry Coote of Langford, Captain, S.A.
Substituted 45385 on 20 Sept. 1912
OPCS, RG(W) 30518

58. LEAGRAVE

58/1
Archdeaconry   12/14 June 1798
House in occ. of Edward Pain
Reg. by Edward Pain, Elizabeth Pain, Richard Patridge, Joseph Harper
BRO, ABN 1/1; ABN 2/87. PRO, RG 31/2, 94

58/2
Archdeaconry   3 June 1807
House of Richard Partridge
BRO, ABN 1/1

58/3
Archdeaconry   28 Sept./4 Oct. 1822
House of William Haydon
Reg. by James Cream, William Haydon, Edward East
BRO, ABN 1/2; ABN 2/189; ABN 3/3. PRO, RG 31/2, 214
Certificate addressed to the Bishop of Lincoln

58/4
Archdeaconry   29 May/15 July 1824
Newly erected brick Chapel (printed form)
Reg. by William Brocklehurst of Luton, minister
BRO, ABN 1/2; ABN 2/213; ABN 3/3, 59.
Probably Wesleyan as the form was printed by T. Cordeux

58/5   **Wesleyan**
Archdeaconry   **19/19 May 1835**
Wesleyan Chapel
Reg. by Thomas Rogerson of Luton
BRO, ABN 1/2; ABN 2/303. PRO, RG 31/2, 325
Rogerson registered Wesleyan chapels at Barton, Houghton Regis, Luton, Tebworth, Toddington & Whipsnade on the same day

58/6   **Wesleyan**
Worship   **9 Feb. 1854**
Wesleyan Methodist Chapel in High Street
Reg. by Matthew Trevan Male of Dunstable, superintendent minister
OPCS, RG(W) 1901
Male registered Wesleyan chapels at Dunstable, Houghton Regis, Kensworth & Sundon on the same day

58/7   **Primitive Methodist**
Worship   **24 Nov. 1890**
Primitive Methodist Chapel
Reg. by Joseph Harding, 74 Wenlock St., High Town, Luton, Primitive Methodist minister
Substituted 77873 on 6 Apr. 1989
OPCS, RG(W) 32458
Number duplicated in register

59. LEIGHTON BUZZARD

59/1   **Presbyterian**
House of Thomas Bryan   **17 Apr. 1672**
OR, p. 851

59/2
Quarter Sessions   **4 Feb. 1721/2**
Newly erected residence of John Edge, locksmith, in the Leakend
BRO, QSR 1721, 17

59/3
Quarter Sessions   **20/20 July 1761**
House of Joseph Brooks
Reg. by William Brown, John Morris, John Bennell, Michael Morris
BRO, QSP 43/3
Original certificate & draft licence

59/4
Quarter Sessions   **15 Apr. 1789**
Newly erected building called the Meeting House near the Alms Houses at the North End
Reg. by Joseph Brook, Benjamin Reeve, Peter Bassett, John Grant (householders)
BRO, QSR 1789, 3

59/5
Quarter Sessions   **6 July 1798**
Dwelling house & premises of Thomas Chew
Reg. by Thomas Chew, W. Emerton, John Procter
BRO, QSR 1798, 65

Plate 23: Leighton Buzzard: The Friends' (Quaker) meeting house in North Street, described in the licence as "newly erected" in 1789.

(Photograph: W. & J. Piggott, c.1880)

59/6
Archdeaconry   **2 Apr. 1799**
Dwelling house of Zach. Whitehead, teacher
Reg. by Thomas Wake, Zach. Whitehead, John Craggs
PRO, RG 31/2, 101

59/7
Quarter Sessions   **12 Apr. 1817**
A certain room in dwelling house of John Warner
Reg. by John Hodgson of Leighton Buzzard, preacher
BRO, QSR 1817, 286, 287; QSM 26, p. 20. PRO, RG 31/6, 35

59/8
Archdeaconry   **24 Dec. 1818**
House of Thomas Chew
Reg. by David Lee Willis
BRO, ABN 1/2; ABN 3/3, 10. PRO, RG 31/2, 181

59/9
Peculiar Jurisdiction   **18 Sept. 1819**
Wheeler's shop in yard of Richard Lock, wheelwright
Reg. by Rev. George Row of Leighton Buzzard, minister
BRO, RI 3/6821

59/10
Peculiar Jurisdiction   **15 Jan. 1828**
Messuage at Billington
Reg. by Thomas Stevens of Billington, farmer
BRO, RI 3/6824c

59/11
Archdeaconry   **29/30 Oct. 1830**
House of Thomas Shepherd at North End
Reg. by Thomas Shepherd
BRO, ABN 1/2; ABN 2/251; ABN 3/3, 99. PRO, RG 31/2, 271

59/12
Peculiar Jurisdiction   **7 June 1833**
**Warehouse (formerly a granary) in yard & garden in occ. of Thomas Matthews in
High Street**
Reg. by Thomas Matthews of Leighton Buzzard
BRO, RI 3/ 6823

59/13
Peculiar Jurisdiction   **19 Oct. 1833**
Dwelling house in occ. of John Pain of Billington
Reg. by William Piggott of Leighton Buzzard
BRO, RI 3/6824g

59/14   **Baptist**
Marriages   **25 Aug. 1837**
Baptist Chapel in Lake Street
5686 substituted on 17 Feb. 1865
OPCS, RG(M) 431

59/15   **Wesleyan**
Marriages   **10 Jan. 1838**
Wesleyan Methodist Chapel in Jeff's Lane
Substituted 5710 on 20 Mar. 1865
OPCS, RG(M) 969

59/16   **28/28 Mar. 1848**
Archdeaconry
House of William Stevens at Pleasant Hall (printed form)
Reg. by William Stevens of Heathenreach [Heath & Reach]
BRO, ABN 1/2; ABN 2/393. PRO, RG 31/2, 416
Certificate addressed to the Bishop of Ely

59/17   **Baptist**
Quarter Sessions   **4 July 1849**
**Chapel or meeting house known as Ebenezer Baptist Chapel at back of premises of
Thomas Southam, plait dealer, in Hockliffe Road**
Reg. by Thomas Hedge, printer, George Gamaliel Aveline, cabinet maker
BRO, QSR 49/3. PRO, RG 31/6, 40
Two copies of certificate. Sessions opened on 3 July

59/18
Archdeaconry   29 Mar. 1850
House of John Read Badrick at Great Billington
Reg. by J.R. Badrick
BRO, ABN 1/2. PRO, RG 31/2, 446

59/19
Archdeaconry   25/26 Feb. 1851
House in occ. of John Kitley in Friday Street
Reg. by William Theophilus Cope of Northall in Edlesborough (Bucks.), Benjamin Johnson
BRO, ABN 1/2; ABN 2/425. PRO, RG 31/2, 450
Certificate addressed to the Bishop of Ely

59/20   **Quaker**
Worship   **1 May 1854**
Friends' Meeting House & Burial Ground at North End
Reg. by John Dollin Bassett of Leighton Buzzard (trustee)
OPCS, RG(W) 4638

59/21   **Primitive Methodist**
Worship   **11 Dec. 1860**
Primitive Methodist Chapel
Reg. by Samuel Turner of Aylesbury (Bucks.), Primitive Methodist minister
Cancelled on revision, 30 Oct. 1896
OPCS, RG(W) 10093

59/22   **Wesleyan**
Worship   **19 Apr. 1861**
Wesleyan Methodist Chapel
Reg. by Joshua Mottram of Leighton Buzzard, minister
Cancelled 31 Dec. 1866
OPCS, RG(W) 14206
Mottram registered Wesleyan chapels at Billington & Eggington; Mentmore, Stoke
Hammond & Soulbury (Bucks.) on the same day

59/23   **Protestant Dissenters**
Worship   **7 Feb. 1865**
Lake Street Chapel
Reg. by William Delf Elliston of Leighton Buzzard, dissenting minister
Cancelled 9 Nov. 1979
OPCS, RG(W) 16547

59/24   **Protestant Dissenters**
Marriages   **17 Feb. 1865**
Lake Street Chapel
Substituted for 431. Cancelled 9 Nov. 1979
OPCS, RG(M) 5686

59/25   **Wesleyan**
Worship   **17 Mar. 1865**
Wesleyan Chapel in Hockliffe Street
Reg. by James Sutch of Leighton Buzzard, Wesleyan minister
Cancelled 1 Sept. 1960
OPCS, RG(W) 16619

Plate 24: Leighton Buzzard: The Wesleyan chapel in Hockliffe Street, built in 1864 and licensed in 1865.   (*Photograph: c.1920*)

59/26	**Wesleyan**
Marriages	**20 Mar. 1865**

Wesleyan Methodist Chapel in Hockliffe Street
Substituted for 969. Cancelled 1 Sept. 1960
OPCS, RG(M) 5710

59/27	**Baptist**
Marriages	**17 Dec. 1866**

Hockliffe Road Baptist Chapel
13181 substituted on 28 Sept. 1892
OPCS, RG(M) 6185

59/28	**Primitive Methodist**
Worship	**18 Nov. 1871**

Primitive Methodist Chapel in Mill Road
Reg. by John Robert Swift of Leighton Buzzard, Primitive Methodist minister
32158 substituted on 5 July 1890
OPCS, RG(W) 20387
The date for the substitution is a mistake, being the date of the marriages licence

59/29	**Primitive Methodist**
Marriages	**26 Aug. 1878**

Primitive Methodist Chapel in Mill Road
12541 substituted on 5 July 1890
OPCS, RG(M) 9549

59/30   Salvation Army
Worship   25 Mar. 1886
Salvation Army Barracks in Lake Street
Reg. by Francis Summers, Lake St., Leighton Buzzard, Captain, S.A.
41257 substituted on 24 Aug. 1905
OPCS, RG(W) 29280

59/31   Primitive Methodist
Worship   20 May 1890
Primitive Methodist Chapel in North Street
Reg. by George Mitchell of Leighton Buzzard, minister
Substituted for 20387
OPCS, RG(W) 32158

59/32   Primitive Methodist
Marriages   5 July 1890
Primitive Methodist Chapel in North Street (Trinity Methodist Church)
Substituted for 9549
OPCS, RG(M) 12541

59/33   Baptist
Worship   19 Sept. 1892
Baptist Church in Hockliffe Road
Reg. by George Durrell of Leighton Buzzard, Baptist minister
Substituted for 17005 (*sic*)
OPCS, RG(W) 33470

59/34   Baptist
Marriages   28 Sept. 1892
Baptist Chapel in Hockliffe Road
Substituted for 6185
OPCS, RG(M) 13181

60. LIDLINGTON

60/1
Archdeaconry   3 June 1796
House of William Burgon
BRO, ABN 1/1

60/2
Archdeaconry   26/29 May 1798
House in occ. of Mr Thomas Briggs
Reg. by Thomas Briggs, John Dawsett, William Prior, Charles Evans, Joseph Harper
BRO, ABN 1/1; ABN 2/92. PRO, RG 31/2, 89
Certificate addressed to the Bishop of Lincoln

60/3
Archdeaconry   17 Nov. 1807
Meeting House
BRO, ABN 1/1

60/4   **Wesleyan**
Worship   **17 Feb. 1854**
Wesleyan Methodist Chapel
Reg. by William Henry Clarkson, 4 Harpur St., Bedford, superintendent minister
Cancelled 29 Dec. 1961
OPCS, RG(W) 2131
Clarkson registered Wesleyan chapels at Ampthill, Haynes, Houghton Conquest, Marston Morteyne & Maulden on the same day

60/5   **Primitive Methodist**
Worship   **2 Jan. 1861**
Primitive Methodist Chapel
Reg. by Samuel Turner of Aylesbury (Bucks.), Primitive Methodist minister
Cancelled 18 Jan. 1876
OPCS, RG(W) 11500

60/6   **Primitive Methodist**
Worship   **4 May 1864**
Bethel Primitive Methodist Chapel [in Church Road]
Reg. by William Birks of Leighton Buzzard, minister
OPCS, RG(W) 16180
Birks registered Primitive Methodist chapels at Billington & Heath on the same day

61. LUTON

Plate 25: Luton: A Baptist meeting was established in Luton in 1707. The octagonal chapel - curiously known as the "Round Meeting" - was destroyed in a storm in 1866.
(*Photograph: c.1860*)

61/1
Quarter Sessions   **Quaker**
                                                                          11 Jan. 1748/9
House in edfifice in poss. of Daniel Brown
Reg. by John Freeth, Daniel Brown, Joseph Brown, Richard Brown
BRO, QSR 1748, 40. PRO, RG 31/2, 3

61/2
Archdeaconry   **12/14 June 1798**
Chapel near Church Street built by Esquire Cole of Luton
Reg. by Joseph Harper, Thomas Spilsbury, George Spilsbury, William Davis, James Cowdale
BRO, ABN 1/2; ABN 2/86. PRO, RG 31/2, 92

61/3
Quarter Sessions   **Quaker**
                                                                          11/23 Apr. 1800
New erection or building called the Meeting house in or near Castle Street for
protestant dissenters called Quakers
Reg. by Richard Brown, John Freeth, Daniel Brown, Joseph Brown, Christopher Pryor
BRO, QSR 1800, 105; QSM 20, p. 153. PRO, RG 31/6, 24

61/4
Quarter Sessions   **14 Apr. 1802**
Newly erecting building called the Meeting House in Rosemary Lane
Reg. by F. Hews, minister, James Rushmore, James Field, Joseph Hagger, Samuel Field,
Samuel Field jun.,John Teddey, Stephen Taylor, Samuel Gatward, Samuel Rutt, Caleb
Young, Seabrook Hill
BRO, QSR 1802, 80; QSM 21, p. 108. PRO, RG 31/6, 26
They also registered the next entry and a meeting house in Toddington

61/5
Quarter Sessions   **28/28 Apr. 1802**
Three adjoining tenements & yard, estate of Mr Rushmore
Reg. by F. Hews, minister, James Rushmore, Samuel Gatward, John Teddey, Joseph
Hagger, George Brett, Samuel Rutt, James Field, Samuel Field, Seabrook Hill
BRO, QSR 1802, 89; QSM 21, p.108. PRO, RG 31/6, 25

61/6
Quarter Sessions   **20 Apr. 1803**
The Press House in occ. of Mr Francis Cooper, straw hat manufacturer
Reg. by Francis Cooper, J. Crew, William Butterfield, John Day, Thomas Johnson,
William Cooper
BRO, QSR 1803, 58; QSM 21, p. 153. PRO, RG 31/6, 28

61/7
Quarter Sessions   **20 Apr. 1803**
Dwelling house of Thomas Wingrove, labourer, at Ramridge Edge
Reg. by Thomas Wingrove, John Newman, William Hare, John Abbett, James Pryor jun.,
Joseph Jackson
BRO, QSR 1803, 59; QSM 21, p. 153. PRO, RG 31/6, 29

61/8
Quarter Sessions   **13 July/5 Oct. 1803**
New Meeting House
Reg. by F.S. Coupees, Thomas Coupees, Ann Coupees, Joseph Jackman, Elizabeth
Jackson, William Butterfield, Deb. Butterfield, John Day, Sara Day, James Pryor

61/9 **Baptist**
Archdeaconry 18 Mar./8 Apr. 1815
New Baptist Meeting House
Reg. by Ebenezer Daniel, Daniel Rudd, Joseph Pain, F.S. Coupees
BRO, ABN 2/167
BRO, QSR 1803, 67; QSM 21, p. 166. PRO, RG 31/6, 30

61/10
Archdeaconry 14/18 June 1821
Dwelling house in occ. of Thomas Newman
Reg. by Ebenezer Daniel, Francis Newman, William Bolton, George Day
BRO, ABN 1/2; ABN 2/182; ABN 3/3, 29. PRO, RG 31/2, 200

61/11
Archdeaconry 13/15 Jan. 1823
House of John Squires of Stopsley
Reg. by John Squires, James Quarrie [Cream], James Jarvis
BRO, ABN 1/2; ABN 2/203; ABN 3/3, 48. PRO, RG 31/2, 220
Certificate addressed to the Bishop of Lincoln

61/12
Archdeaconry 15 Jan./17 Feb. 1824
House in occ. of George Worsley (Worley) at East Hyde
Reg. by Francis Harrison, Samuel Davison, David Barber, William Clark
BRO, ABN 1/2; ABN 2/212; ABN 3/3, 56. PRO, RG 31/2, 227

61/13
Archdeaconry 29 May 1824
Chapel
Reg. by William Brocklehurst, minister
PRO, RG 31/2, 230

61/14 **Wesleyan**
Archdeaconry 19/19 May 1835
Wesleyan Chapel (printed form)
Reg. by Thomas Rogerson of Luton
BRO, ABN 1/2; ABN 2/298. PRO, RG 31/2, 321
Certificate addressed to the Bishop of Lincon. Rogerson registered Wesleyan chapels at
Barton, Houghton Regis, Leagrave, Tebworth, Toddington & Whipsnade on the same day

61/15
Archdeaconry 10/13 Dec. 1836
Building in occ. of William Bolton
Reg. by William Bolton, Francis Harrison, [torn] Spencer
BRO, ABN 1/2; ABN 2/316. PRO, RG 31/2, 340

43/6. The Wesleyan chapel registered for Luton, 11 May 1839, is a mistake for Harlington

61/16 **Union**
Archdeaconry 18/19 Sept. 1839
Union Chapel in occ. of William Bolton, Francis Harrison and others
Reg. by John S. Bright, minister, T. Spencer, Edward Woakes, John Jones, Francis
Harrison
BRO, ABN 1/2; ABN 2/341. PRO, RG 31/2, 364

Plate 26: Luton: The Union Chapel in London Road, licensed in 1839.
(Photograph: E. Deacon (Friths), 1897)

61/17
Marriages
Union Chapel (Baptists & Independents)
40581 substituted on 23 Nov. 1986
OPCS, RG(M) 1523

Union
10 Oct. 1839

61/18
Marriages
Baptist Meeting House in Park Street
6308 substituted on 18 June 1867
OPCS, RG(M) 1533

Baptist
30 Oct. 1839

61/19
Archdeaconry
A Chapel
Reg. by William Willis, William Brewer
BRO, ABN 1/2; ABN 2/370. PRO, RG 31/2, 380

22 Oct./2 Nov. 1841

61/20
Marriages
Primitive Methodist Chapel in High Town
6182 substituted on 15 Dec. 1866
OPCS, RG(M) 2398

Primitive Methodist
2 Apr. 1845

61/21
Archdeaconry   **30 Apr. 1845**
House of W. Burgess
Reg. by W. Burgess
BRO, ABN 1/2. PRO, RG 31/2, 405

61/22   **Wesleyan**
Marriages   **29 Nov. 1845**
Wesleyan Chapel
Cancelled 21 July 1852
OPCS, RG(M) 2511

61/23
Archdeaconry   **7/9 Sept. 1846**
Victoria Hall in Wellington Street (printed form)
Reg. by John Crofts, minister
BRO, ABN 1/2; ABN 2/386. PRO RG 31/2, 415
Certificate addressed to the Bishop of Lincoln and amended to Ely

61/24   **Wesleyan**
Archdeaconry   **18/23 Sept. 1846**
Wesleyan Methodist Chapel at Stopsley (printed form)
Reg. by John Crofts of Luton
BRO, ABN 1/2; ABN 2/391. PRO, RG 31/2, 411
Crofts registered Wesleyan chapels at Shillington & Upper Gravenhurst on the same day

61/25   **Wesleyan**
Archdeaconry   **18/23 Sept. 1846**
Wesleyan Methodist Chapel at Limbury cum Biscot (printed form)
Reg. by John Crofts of Luton
BRO, ABN 1/2, ABN 2/392. PRO, RG 31/2, 409
Certificate addressed to the Bishop of Lincoln and amended to Ely

61/26
Archdeaconry   **8/10 Nov. 1848**
Town Hall
Reg. by Richard Vyse, John Jones, Robert How, Edmund Williamson, all of Luton
BRO, ABN 1/2; ABN 2/401. PRO, RG 31/2, 424

61/27
Archdeaconry   **15/17 Feb. 1849**
House of William Brown in New Town
Reg. by Robert Hodgert of Billington
BRO, ABN 1/2; ABN 2/406. PRO, RG 31/2, 433

61/28   **Baptist**
Archdeaconry   **24/26 May 1849**
Baptist Chapel in Wellington Street
Reg. by James Waller, William Bolton, Samuel Toyer, Joseph Anstee
BRO, ABN 1/2; ABN 2/409, 411. PRO, RG 31/2, 439
ABN 2/411 is a copy of the licence by Thomas Lovelidge, Assistant Registrar

61/29
Archdeaconry   22 Oct. 1849
Chapel in occ. of William Willis and others (printed form)
Reg. by William Brewer
BRO, ABN 2

61/30   **Baptist**
Marriages   **9 June 1851**
Ceylon Chapel in Wellington Street
Cancelled 8 Oct. 1985
OPCS, RG(M) 3294

61/31   **Wesleyan**
Archdeaconry   **14/15 May 1852**
Wesleyan Methodist Chapel in Chapel Street (printed form)
Reg. by Wright Shovelton, Thomas B. Goodwin
BRO, ABN 1/2; ABN 2/438. PRO, RG 31/2, 462

61/32   **Wesleyan**
Marriages   **21 July 1852**
Wesleyan Chapel in Chapel Street [Luton Industrial Mission]
38509 substituted on 22 Nov. 1976
OPCS, RG(M) 3457

PRIMITIVE METHODIST CHAPEL LUTON.
BEDS 1852.

Plate 27: Luton: The Primitive Methodist chapel in High Town, built in 1852.
(Engraving: Thomas Corney, c.1852)

61/33   Primitive Methodist
Worship   15 Dec. 1852
Primitive Methodist Chapel in High Town
Reg. by Thomas Bennett of Luton, grocer (trustee)
Cancelled on revision, 12 May 1896
OPCS, RG(W) 581

61/34   Independents
Worship   4 Oct. 1853
New Hall in Wellington Street
Reg. by Matthew Thomson, College House, Southgate (Middx), schoolmaster
(proprietor)
Cancelled 31 Dec. 1866
OPCS, RG(W) 1247

61/35   Wesleyan
Worship   6 Feb. 1854
Wesleyan Methodist Chapel in Church Street
Reg. by Wright Shovelton, Chapel St., Luton, superintendent minister
Cancelled on revision, 4 Nov. 1935
OPCS, RG(W) 1751
Shovelton registered Wesleyan chapels at Barton & Caddington on the same day

61/36   Wesleyan
Worship   6 Feb. 1854
Wesleyan Methodist Chapel in Limbury
Reg. by Wright Shovelton, Chapel St., Luton, superintendent minister
Cancelled 12 Mar. 1913
OPCS, RG(W) 1754

61/37   Wesleyan
Worship   6 Feb. 1854
Wesleyan Methodist Chapel at Stopsley
Reg. by Wright Shovelton, Chapel St., Luton, superintendent minister
34536 substituted on 3 Oct. 1894
OPCS, RG(W) 1756

61/38   Wesleyan
Worship   6 Feb. 1854
**Wesleyan Methodist Chapel in Chapel Street, erected 1852 [Luton Industrial
Mission]**
Reg. by Wright Shovelton, Chapel St., Luton, superintendent minister
74470 substituted on 22 Nov. 1976
OPCS, RG(W) 1758

61/39   Wesleyan
Worship   6 Feb. 1854
Methodist Chapel in Chapel Street
Reg. by Wright Shovelton, Chapel St., Luton, superintendent minister
Cancelled on revision, 12 May 1896
OPCS, RG(W) 1759

61/40   **Quakers**
Worship   **5 May 1854**
Friends' Meeting House in Castle Street
Reg. by Richard Brown of Luton, timber merchant (trustee)
Cancelled on revision, 1 June 1964
OPCS, RG(W) 4740. BRO, FR2/9/17/1
Original licence in Society of Friends records

61/41   **Wesleyan**
Worship   **19 Nov. 1860**
Wesleyan Chapel in Markyate [Albert] Street
Reg. by Charles Trafford, Markyate St., Bedford, straw hat manufacturer (trustee)
OPCS, RG(W) 9773
This entry is mistakenly attributed to Bedford in the register. It closed between 1932 &
1949

61/42   **Protestant Dissenters**
Worship   **20 Dec. 1860**
Union Branch Chapel in Chase Street, Newtown for Protestant Dissenters
Reg. by Charles Robinson, Market Hill, Luton, manufacturer (trustee)
Cancelled on revision, 12 May 1896
OPCS, RG(W) 10369

61/43   **Baptist**
Worship   **28 Dec. 1860**
Old Baptist Meeting House in Park Street
Reg. by Thomas Hands, Lea Villa, Luton, minister
Cancelled 18 June 1867
OPCS, RG(W) 10901

61/44   **Baptist**
Worship   **3 Jan. 1861**
Ceylon Chapel in Wellington Street
Reg. by James Waller of Luton, gent. (trustee)
Cancelled 8 Oct. 1985
OPCS, RG(W) 11637

61/45   **Unsectarian**
Worship   **2 Dec. 1863**
The New Room in the Old Brewery in Park Street
Reg. by William Gowin Ogborne of St Albans (Herts.), dissenting minister
Cancelled on revision, 12 May 1896
OPCS, RG(W) 15950

61/46   **Wesleyan**
Worship   **6 May 1864**
Wesleyan Chapel in Waller Street
Reg. by James Little, Chapel St., Luton, dissenting minister
Cancelled 26 July 1954
OPCS, RG(W) 16186

61/47   Independent
Worship   16 Aug. 1866
Congregational Church in King Street
Reg. by Arthur Thomas Webster of Luton, straw hat manufacturer (trustee)
Cancelled 31 July 1901
OPCS, RG(W) 17404

61/48   Primitive Methodist
Worship   28 Nov. 1866
Primitive Methodist Chapel in Park Road, Park Street
Reg. by Murray Wilson, Chapel House, Hightown, Luton, minister
Substituted 73272 on 2 Jan. 1973
OPCS, RG(W) 17568

61/49   Primitive Methodist
Worship   14 Dec. 1866
Primitive Methodist Chapel in Hightown Road
Reg. by William Kitchen, Hightown, Luton, minister
Cancelled on revision, 4 Nov. 1935
OPCS, RG(W) 17617

61/50   Primitive Methodist
Marriages   15 Dec. 1866
Primitive Methodist Chapel in Hightown Road
Substituted for 2398. 15011 substituted on 17 May 1898
OPCS, RG(M) 6182

61/51   Objectors
Worship   12 Feb. 1867
**Building in occ. of William Read in Chale Street, Newtown, for those who object to
being designated**
Reg. by William Read, Brighton Terrace, Luton, straw hat manufacturer (occupier)
Cancelled on revision, 12 May 1896
OPCS, RG(W) 17762

61/52   Congregational
Marriages   12 Apr. 1867
Congregational Church in King Street
Cancelled 19 May 1967
OPCS, RG(M) 6261

61/53   Baptists
Worship   7 June 1867
Baptist Meeting House in Park Street
Reg. by Thomas Hands of Luton, Baptist minister
Cancelled 9 Dec. 1974
OPCS, RG(W) 17960

61/54   Baptist
Worship   16 June 1871
Ebenezer Baptist Chapel in Hastings Street
Reg. by Joseph Booth, Cumberland St., Luton, grocer (trustee)
OPCS, RG(W) 20197

61/55   **Baptist**
Marriages   **18 June 1867**
Baptist Meeting House in Park Street
Substituted for 1533. Cancelled 9 Dec. 1974
OPCS, RG(M) 6308

61/56   **Particular Baptist**
Marriages   **19 June 1871**
Ebenezer Baptist Chapel in Hastings Street
OPCS, RG(M) 7434

61/57   **Wesleyan**
Worship   **12 Sept. 1872**
Albert Road Wesleyan Chapel in New Town
Reg. by Richard Eland, Church St., Luton, Wesleyan minister
Cancelled on revision, 4 Nov. 1931
OPCS, RG(W) 20910

61/58   **Wesleyan**
Marriages   **21 May 1877**
Wesleyan Methodist Chapel in Waller Street
Cancelled 26 July 1954
OPCS, RG(M) 9164

61/59   **Primitive Methodist**
Worship   **3 Feb. 1880**
Primitive Methodist Chapel in Church Street
Reg. by Robert Ducker, 16 Victoria St., Luton, Primitive Methodist minister
Cancelled 2 Jan. 1974
OPCS, RG(W) 24913

61/60   **Primitive Methodist**
Worship   **4 June 1881**
Primitive Methodist Chapel in Cardigan Street
Reg. by Murray Wilson, Park Villa, Wenlock St., Luton, superintendent minister
Cancelled 8 Jan. 1951
OPCS, RG(W) 25612

61/61   **Salvation Army**
Worship   **29 Nov. 1882**
Salvation Army Barracks in Park Street
Reg. by William S. Stitt, 101 Queen Victoria St., London, EC, Staff Officer, S.A.
Cancelled on revision, 12 May 1896
OPCS, RG(W) 26662

61/62   **Salvation Army**
Worship   **25 Jan. 1883**
Alexandra Theatre in Manchester Street
Reg. by James Harris, 7 Chobham St., Luton, Captain, S.A.
Cancelled on revision, 12 May 1896
OPCS, RG(W) 26805

61/63   Wesleyan
Worship   20 Sept. 1883
Wesleyan Methodist Mission Chapel in Ashton Street
Reg. by William Kimber Harvey, Napier Rd., Luton, minister
Cancelled 12 Mar. 1913
OPCS, RG(W) 27316

61/64   Primitive Methodist
Marriages   3 Dec. 1884
Primitive Methodist Chapel in Brache Street
Substituted 37512 on 2 Jan. 1973
OPCS RG(M) 11119

61/65   Roman Catholic
Worship   5 Jan. 1886
Little Oratory of our Lady Help of Christians at 23 Rothesay Road
Reg. by Joseph A. O'Connor of Luton, Catholic priest
Cancelled 17 Jan. 1887
OPCS, RG(W) 29095

61/66   Roman Catholic
Worship   17 Jan. 1887
The Little Oratory in Castle Street
Reg. by Joseph A. O'Connor of Luton, Catholic priest
34530 substituted on 22 Sept. 1894
OPCS, RG(W) 29853

61/67   Salvationists
Worship   28 Apr. 1888
Salvation Army Barracks in Manchester Street
Reg. by Martha Jack, 17 Inkerman St., Luton, Captain, S.A.
56923 substituted on 21 Sept. 1936
OPCS, RG(W) 30842

61/68   Salvation Army
Worship   13 Dec. 1890
Salvation Army Temple in Park Street
Reg. by William Winfield, 13 Alfred St., Luton, Captain, S.A.
OPCS, RG(W) 32493

61/69   Wesleyan
Worship   14 Oct. 1893
Wesleyan Chapel at Chaul End near Luton
Reg. by Robert Bentley of Luton, Wesleyan minister
Cancelled on revision, 1 June 1964
OPCS, RG(W) 34063

61/70   Primitive Methodist
Marriages   29 Nov. 1893
Primitive Methodist Chapel in Church Street
Cancelled 2 Jan. 1947
OPCS, RG(M) 13542

61/71   Roman Catholic
Marriages   22 Sept. 1894
St Mary Help of Christians Chapel in Castle Street
19797 substituted on 25 Jan. 1911
OPCS, RG(M) 13760

61/72   Roman Catholic
Worship   22 Sept. 1894
St Mary Help of Christians Chapel in Castle Street
Reg. by John Henry Ashmole of Luton, Roman Catholic priest
44630 substituted on 25 Jan. 1911
OPCS, RG(W) 34530

61/73   Wesleyan
Worship   3 Oct. 1894
Wesleyan Chapel at Stopsley
Reg. by George Dimmock of Luton, straw merchant (trustee)
Substituted for 1756. Cancelled 22 July 1974
OPCS, RG(W) 34536

61/74   Primitive Methodist
Marriages   12 Aug. 1897
Primitive Methodist Chapel in Cardigan Street
Cancelled 8 Jan. 1951
OPCS, RG(M) 14734

61/75   Primitive Methodist
Worship   7 Apr. 1898
Mount Tabor Primitive Methodist Church in Castle Street
Reg. by John Leach, 8 Stockwood Cresc., Luton, minister
Cancelled 22 Oct. 1969
OPCS, RG(W) 36531

61/76   Primitive Methodist
Marriages   17 May 1898
Primitive Methodist Church in High Town
Substituted for 6182
OPCS, RG(M) 15011

61/77   Primitive Methodist
Worship   17 May 1898
Primitive Methodist Church in Hightown Road
Reg. by Thomas Humphries, 74 Wenlock St., Luton, superintendent minister
OPCS, RG(W) 36607

61/78   Wesleyan
Worship   4 Oct. 1898
Wesleyan Methodist Church in Baker Street, Bailey Hill
Reg. by John Joseph Ingram, 43 Stockwood Cresc., Luton, superintendent minister
Cancelled 11 July 1960
OPCS, RG(W) 36799

61/79   Salvation Army
Marriages   21 Oct. 1898
Salvation Army Temple in Park Street
OPCS, RG(M) 15168

61/80   Salvation Army
Worship   21 Jan. 1899
Junior Salvation Army Barracks in Lea Road
Reg. by William Broughton, 35 Brook St., Bedford Rd., Luton (trustee)
Cancelled 21 Dec. 1903
OPCS, RG(W) 36984

61/81   Primitive Methodist
Marriages   18 Mar. 1899
Mount Tabor Church in Castle Street
Cancelled 22 Oct. 1969
OPCS, RG(M) 15323

61/82   Baptist
Worship   30 Jan. 1900
Guildford Hall in Guildford Street
Reg. by William Powell, Rosemary Villa, Harcourt St., Luton, minister
40149 substituted on 19 Jan. 1904
OPCS, RG(W) 37547

61/83   Railway Mission
Worship   14 Jan. 1900
Railway Mission Hall in Bridge Street
Reg. by James Neal, 79 Burry Park Rd., Luton (treasurer)
39302 substituted on 10 Nov. 1902
OPCS, RG(W) 37744

62. MARSTON MORTEYNE

62/1
Archdeaconry   5/5 May 1775
House of John Nichols, esq., in poss. of Joseph Batchelder
Reg. by [Tiso Rose *deleted*], Edward Biggs, Joseph Batchelder
ABN 1/1; ABN 2/37. PRO, RG 31/2, 37

62/2
Quarter Sessions   15 Jan. 1794
Dwelling house of Mr Vincent Millard
BRO, QSM 19, 71. PRO, RG 31/6, 21

62/3
Archdeaconry   2 Feb. 1804
Dwelling house of James Two
BRO, ABN 1/1

62/4
Archdeaconry   15 Jan. 1805
Dwelling house of Samuel Atterbury
BRO, ABN 1/1

62/5
Archdeaconry   **16 Dec. 1806**
House of George Mann
BRO, ABN 1/1

62/6
Archdeaconry   **23/26 Oct. 1833**
House in occ. of Joseph Allen, property of Mr Chapman
Reg. by Joseph Allen, Thomas Braddock, Thomas Odell, James Beesley, Thomas Miller
BRO, ABN 1/2; ABN 2/280. PRO, RG 31/2, 302
Certificate addressed to the Bishop of Lincoln

62/7   **Wesleyan**
Worship   **17 Feb. 1854**
Wesleyan Methodist Chapel
Reg. by William Henry Clarkson, 4 Harpur St., Bedford, superintendent minister
Cancelled 18 Jan. 1876
OPCS, RG(W) 2132
Clarkson registered Wesleyan chapels at Ampthill, Haynes, Houghton Conquest,
Lidlington & Maulden on the same day

62/8   **Wesleyan**
Worship   **5 Feb. 1861**
Wesleyan Methodist Chapel
Reg. by Charles Carter, Harpur St., Bedford, minister
OPCS, RG(W) 12469
Carter registered Wesleyan chapels at Millbrook & Steppingley on the same day

62/9   **Primitive Methodist**
Worship   **27 Feb. 1861**
Primitive Methodist Chapel
Reg. by Edward Bishop, 6 Adelaide Sq., Bedford, minister
Cancelled 5 July 1901
OPCS, RG(W) 13132
Bishop registered Primitive Methodist chapels at Flitton, Maulden & Silsoe on the same
day

62/10   **Salvation Army**
Worship   **25 Mar. 1890**
Salvation Army Barracks in Upper Shelton
Reg. by Daniel Salisbury of Cranfield, labourer (occupier)
Cancelled on revision, 29 June 1954
OPCS, RG(W) 32086

62/11   **Primitive Methodist**
Worship   **8 Mar. 1901**
Primitive Methodist Chapel at Church End
Reg. by Richard Newman Wycherley, Ampthill Rd., Bedford, Primitive Methodist
minister
OPCS, RG(W) 38244

63. MAULDEN

63/1
House of Widow Sarah Tomkins
OR, p. 857

Congregational
1 May 1672

63/2
Archdeaconry
Dwelling house of William Barns
Reg. by Thomas Arnold, John Hawkins sen., John Hawkins jun.
BRO, ABN 1/1; ABN 2/93. PRO, RG 31/2, 96

8/27 June 1798

63/3
Archdeaconry
Meeting House
BRO, ABN 1/1

7 Apr. 1807

63/4
Archdeaconry
Chapel
Reg. by Francis Read & others
BRO, ABN 1/2; ABN 3/3, 1. PRO, RG 31/2, 172

16 Feb. 1818

63/5
Archdeaconry
Dwelling house of George Carter
Reg. by George Carter
BRO, ABN 1/2; ABN 2/317

27/28 Dec. 1834

63/6
Marriages
Maulden Meeting at Duck End [Flitwick Road]
OPCS, RG(M) 991

Baptist
25 Jan. 1838

63/7
Archdeaconry
House of John Richardson
Reg. by John Richardson
BRO, ABN 1/2. PRO, RG 31/2, 431

17 Jan. 1849

63/8
Worship
Wesleyan Methodist Chapel in Bedford Road
Reg. by William Henry Clarkson, 4 Harpur St., Bedford, superintendent minister
57891 substituted on 15 Feb. 1938
OPCS, RG(W) 2133
Clarkson registered Weleyan chapels at Ampthill, Haynes, Houghton Conquest, Lidlington & Marston Morteyne on the same day

Wesleyan
17 Feb. 1854

63/9
Worship
Primitive Methodist Chapel at the Broche
Reg. by Edward Bishop, 6 Adelaide Sq., Bedford, minister
OPCS, RG(W) 13133

Primitive Methodist
27 Feb. 1861

64. MEPPERSHALL

64/1   Salvationists
Worship   29 Dec. 1887
Salvation Army Barracks
Reg. by Edward Batten of Meppershall, Captain, S.A.
Cancelled 19 Apr. 1895
OPCS, RG(W) 30570
Batten registered a barracks at Shefford on the same day

65. MILLBROOK

65/1   Baptist
Quarter Sessions   4 Feb. 1789
House of John Dimmock
Reg. by William Butcher, Thomas Fisher, Parkinton Braysher, Francis Bushby, William
Clark, Thomas Roffe (parishioners)
BRO, QSR 1789, 199

65/2
Archdeaconry   22 May/9 June 1798
Dwelling house of William Roffe in middle of Maulden
Reg. by William Roffe
BRO, ABN 1/1; ABN 2/91. PRO, RG 31/2, 91

65/3
Archdeaconry   27/31 Mar. 1804
Dwelling house of Henry Gee
Reg. by Henry Gee, George Burrows
BRO, ABN 1/1; ABN 2/113. PRO, RG 31/2, 112

65/4
Archdeaconry   4 Apr. 1822
House of William Colbourne
Reg. by Anthony Byrd Seckerson
BRO, ABN 1/2; ABN 3/3, 37. PRO, RG 31/2, 208

65/5   Wesleyan
Worship   5 Feb. 1861
Wesleyan Methodist Chapel
Reg. by Charles Carter, Harpur St., Bedford, minister
Cancelled 22 Sept. 1975
OPCS, RG(W) 12470
Carter registered Wesleyan chapels at Marston Morteyne & Steppingley on the same day

65/6   Primitive Methodist
Worship   16 May 1861
Building in occ. of Charles Gardiner
Reg. by Edward Bishop, 6 Adelaide Sq., Bedford, minister
Cancelled 29 Aug. 1894
OPCS, RG(W) 14319
Bishop registered Primitive Methodist chapels at Flitton, Houghton Conquest, Marston
Morteyne & Silsoe on the same day

66. MILTON BRYAN

66/1
Archdeaconry   30 June 1797/15 Jan. 1798
House in occ. of William Clark near to tenement in occ. of Joseph Tobey on one side
& tenement in occ. of Michael Godfrey on other
Reg. by H. Batchlor, W. Powell, W. Paxton
BRO, ABN 1/1; ABN 2/83. PRO, RG 31/2, 83

66/2
Archdeaconry   14 Nov. 1818
House of William Powell
Reg. by James Fanch & others
BRO, ABN 1/2; ABN 3/3, 6. PRO, RG 31/2, 177

66/3
Archdeaconry   22/22 May 1834
Room in occ. of John Dytum
Reg. by William Wood, John Dytum, Thomas Creamer
BRO, ABN 1/2; ABN 2/286. PRO, RG 31/2, 311
Certificate addressed to the Bishop of Lincoln

Plate 28: Milton Bryan: The chapel on the pond where the Methodists worshipped from 1861 until it closed in 1970. No licence is recorded.

(*Photograph: W. & J. Piggott, c.1875*)

66/4
Archdeaconry   **21 June 1834**
A room
Reg. by William Wood
BRO, ABN 1/2
Although there are two entries in ABN 1/2, this one is out of order and may be a mistake
for the previous entry

66/5
Archdeaconry   **15/15 Nov. 1836**
House in occ. of William Walker
Reg. by William Wood of Toddington, minister, William Walker, Thomas Creamer
BRO, ABN 1/2; ABN 2/315. PRO, RG 31/2, 339
Certificate addressed to the Bishop of Lincoln

66/6
Archdeaconry   **16/16 Nov. 1839**
Room in occ. of John Wright
Reg. by William Wood of Toddington, Joseph Parry of Milton, John Powell of Milton
BRO, ABN 1/2; ABN 2/345. PRO, RG 31/2, 367
Certificate addressed to the Bishop of Lincoln

66/7
Archdeaconry   **4/5 Mar. 1846**
House in occ. of William Ward, labourer
Reg. by Thomas Flower of Dunstable
BRO, ABN 1/2; ABN 2/383. PRO, RG 31/2, 406

67. MILTON ERNEST

67/1
Archdeaconry   **13 Jan. 1798**
House of William Barnett
BRO, ABN 1/1

67/2
Archdeaconry   **26 June 1800**
House of Samuel White
BRO, ABN 1/1

67/3
Archdeaconry   **4 July 1806**
House of James Odell
BRO, ABN 1/1

67/4
Archdeaconry   **5 Aug. 1807**
House of Ruth Hart
BRO, ABN 1/1

67/5
Archdeaconry   **11 Sept. 1819**
A Chapel
Reg. by Richard Gower
BRO, ABN 1/2; ABN 3/3, 15. PRO, RG 31/2, 186

67/6
Archdeaconry   **12/21 Apr. 1838**
Building of James Lamb to be used as a chapel
Reg. by John Turner, John Tuner (*sic*), John Banks
BRO, ABN 1/2; ABN 2/324. PRO, RG 31/2, 347

67/7   **Wesleyan**
Worship   **9 Feb. 1854**
Wesleyan Methodist Chapel
Reg. by William Henry Clarkson, Harpur St., Bedford, superintendent minister
Cancelled 28 June 1973 (advertised 28 June)
OPCS, RG(W) 1871
Clarkson registered Wesleyan chapels at Bedford, Cardington, Clapham, Kempston, Pavenham, Turvey, Wilshamstead & Wootton on the same day

68. MOGGERHANGER

68/1
Archdeaconry   **19/19 May 1832**
House of William Odell in own occ. (printed form)
Reg. by William Odell, Joseph Sims, David Freshwaters
BRO, ABN 1/2; ABN 2/270; ABN 3/3, 119. PRO, RG 31/2, 291
Probably Wesleyan as the form was printed by T. Cordeux, London

68/2   **Wesleyan**
Worship   **11 Feb. 1854**
Wesleyan Methodist Chapel
Reg. by William Henry Clarkson, 4 Harpur St., Bedford, superintendent minister
Cancelled on revision, 19 Apr. 1895
OPCS, RG(W) 1973

69. NORTHILL

69/1   **Congregational**
House of Richard Raven at Thorncott   **22 July 1672**
OR, p. 855

69/2
Archdeaconry   **24 June 1776**
House of Henry Brittain in Lower Caldecote
BRO, ABN 1/1

69/3
Archdeaconry   **22/22 Dec. 1776**
House of Edward Sutton at Beeston
Reg. by Simon Page, Samuel Nicholl
BRO, ABN 1/1; ABN 2/42. PRO, RG 31/2, 42

69/4
Archdeaconry   10 Dec. 1810
House of Robert Inskip
BRO, ABN 1/1

69/5
Archdeaconry   6 Dec. 1819
House of William Bryant in Lower Caldecote
Reg. by Thomas Middleditch
BRO, ABN 1/2; ABN 3/3, 17. PRO, RG 31/2, 188

69/6
Archdeaconry   29/30 June 1831
Barn of Robert Morris
Reg. by Thomas Middleditch of Biggleswade, John Hutchins
BRO, ABN 1/2; ABN 2/259; ABN 3/3, 108. PRO, RG 31/2, 280
In a letter attached to the certificate Middleditch asks C. Bailey, esq., to insert the name of
the archdeacon (which Bailey did not do)

69/7
Archdeaconry   25/29 Sept. 1832
Part of dwelling house of Griffin Cant (printed form)
Reg. by Griffin Cant of Upper Caldecote
BRO, ABN 1/2; ABN 2/273; ABN 3/3, 121. PRO, RG 31/2, 293
Probably Wesleyan as the form was printed by T. Cordeux, London

69/8
Archdeaconry   29/29 Jan. 1842
A building of Prime Coleman at Thorncoat
Reg. by Prime Coleman
BRO, ABN 1/2; ABN 2/367. PRO, RG 31/2, 387

69/9
Archdeaconry   14/14 Sept. 1843
A building of James Foxley at Thorncote
Reg. by James Foxley
BRO, ABN 1/2; ABN 2/371. PRO, RG 31/2, 395

69/10
Archdeaconry   10/12 June 1850
House in occ. of Martha Larkin at Upper Caldecote
Reg. by Christopher Layton of Caldecote in Northill, Samuel Martin, William Wagstaff
BRO, ABN 1/2; ABN 2/418.
Possibly Mormon (see next entry). Certificate addressed to the Bishop of Ely

69/11   Mormon
Archdeaconry   8/12 June 1850
Premises in poss. of William Fisher of Potton at Thorncutt for Latter Day Saints
Reg. by William Fisher, Samuel Martin, William Wagstaff
BRO, ABN 1/2; ABN 2/420. PRO, RG 31/2, 448
Certificate addressed to the Bishop of Ely

69/12
Archdeaconry 24/29 Mar. 1851
House of John Millenier (Millena) of Upper Caldecote
Reg. by John Wesley Wilson
BRO, ABN 1/2; ABN 2/426. PRO, RG 31/2. 452

69/13 Mormon
Worship 8 Feb. 1853
A building in Upper Caldecote
Reg. by John Sears of Upper Caldecote (trustee)
Cancelled on revision, 19 Apr. 1895
OPCS, RG(W) 779

69/14 Wesleyan
Worship 12 July 1855
A building
Reg. by Thomas Wood of Biggleswade, Wesleyan minister
Cancelled on revision, 19 Apr. 1895
OPCS, RG(W) 6528

69/15 Particular Baptist
Worship 23 July 1855
Salem Chapel at Beeston Green
Reg. by Joseph Martin of Beeston in Sandy, shoemaker (proprietor)
Cancelled on revision, 19 Apr. 1895
OPCS, RG(W) 6538

69/16 Wesleyan
Worship 15 Oct. 1856
Wesleyan Methodist Chapel at Upper Caldicote
Reg. by Thomas Wood of Biggleswade, Wesleyan minister
44143 substituted on 3 Oct. 1910
OPCS, RG(W) 7590

69/17 Wesleyan
Marriages 1 Aug. 1901
Wesleyan Methodist Chapel at Upper Caldecote
Cancelled 3 Oct. 1910
OPCS, RG(M) 16212

70. OAKLEY

70/1 Congregational
House of William Finden 16 May 1672
OR, p. 854

70/2
Archdeaconry 2 Oct. 1798
House of William Sperry
BRO, ABN 1/1

70/3   **Baptist**
Archdeaconry   **1/13 Apr. 1805**
Messuage in occ. of Richard Clifton of Oakley
Reg. by Joseph Such, minister, Mary Such, Robert Bowyer, Susannah Hooper, John
Tysoe, Richard Clifton, Catharine Clifton, William Bowyer, Sarah Bowyer, Robert
Tysoe, Thomas Bowyer
BRO, ABN 1/1; ABN 2/118. PRO, RG 31/2, 117
Certificate addressed to the Bishop of Peterborough and amended to Lincoln

70/4
Archdeaconry
House of John Darnel   **13 Nov. 1807**
BRO, ABN 1/1

70/5
Archdeaconry   **13 Nov. 1814**
House of William Hackett
BRO, ABN 1/1

70/6
Archdeaconry   **25 Oct./1 Nov. 1815**
Dwelling house of David Balls
Reg. by John Dean of Bedford
BRO, ABN 1/1; ABN 2/171. PRO, RG 31/2, 170
Certificate addressed to the Bishop of Lincoln

70/7
Archdeaconry   **29 Oct./3 Nov. 1825**
Building of William Chapman (printed form)
Reg. by Samuel Hillyard of Bedford
BRO, ABN 1/2; ABN 2/221; ABN 3/3, 72. PRO, RG 31/2, 243
Probably Wesleyan as the form was printed by T. Cordeux, 14 City Rd., London.
Certificate addressed to the Bishop of Lincoln

70/8   **Primitive Methodist**
Worship   **8 Oct. 1852**
Primitive Methodist Chapel
Reg. by John Symonds Gostling, Gwyn St., Bedford, upholsterer (trustee)
Cancelled 15 Feb. 1898
OPCS, RG(W) 269
Gostling registered a Primitive Methodist chapel at Pavenham on the same day. 70/10
below shows that this licence was not cancelled

70/9   **Congregational**
Worship   **12 Aug. 1860**
Oakley Chapel (connected with Bunyan Meeting, Bedford)
Reg. by John Jukes, Dame Alice St., Bedford, Congregational minister (senior minister)
Cancelled on revision, 8 May 1895
OPCS, RG(W) 9421
Jukes registered Congregational chapels at Cardington, Elstow, Goldington, Kempston &
Stagsden on the same day

70/10
Worship
Primitive Methodist Chapel

Primitive Methodist
15 Feb. 1898

Reg. by William Durrance of Bedford, Primitive Methodist minister
Substituted for 269. 73894 substituted on 25 Jan. 1975
OPCS, RG(W) 36438

70/11
Marriages
Primitive Methodist Chapel

Primitive Methodist
4 Mar. 1898

38041 substituted on 24 Jan. 1875
OPCS, RG(M) 14909

71. ODELL

71/1
House of Thomas Robinson
OR, p. 851

Presbyterian
30 Sept. 1672

71/2
Archdeaconry
A building of Mr Thomas Hinde
BRO, ABN 1/1

26 Oct. 1811

71/3
Archdeaconry
A building of Elizabeth Mason (printed form)

29 Oct./12 Nov. 1814

Reg. by Elizabeth Mason
BRO, ABN 1/1; ABN 2/163. PRO, RG 31/2, 163
Probably Wesleyan as the form was printed by T. Cordeux, 14 City Rd., London.
Certificate addressed to the Bishop of Lincoln

71/4
Archdeaconry
Dwelling house of William Hart, shepherd, late in occ. of John Parrot

17/24 Feb. 1838

Reg. by William Hart (his mark), George Savage (his mark), William Barley
BRO, ABN 1/2; ABN 2/322. PRO, RG 31/2, 345

71/5
Archdeaconry
A Chapel (building) in occ. of Charles Coleman

28 Sept./8 Nov. 1839

Reg. by William Barley, Thomas Cumberland, John Newcombe (householders)
BRO, ABN 1/2; ABN 2/342. PRO, RG 31/2, 366

72. PAVENHAM

72/1
House of Robert Clare
OR, p. 853

Congregational
10 May 1672

72/2
Archdeaconry   17 Nov. 1806
Barn of Ebenezer Cavit
BRO, ABN 1/1

72/3
Archdeaconry   11/17 Mar. 1815
Dwelling house of William Swannell (printed form)
Reg. by John Dean of Bedford, minister
BRO, ABN 1/1; ABN 2/168. PRO, RG 31/2, 166
Probably Wesleyan as the form was printed by T. Cordeux, 14 City Rd., London.
Certificate addressed to the Bishop of Lincoln

72/4   **Wesleyan**
Archdeaconry   4/4 Oct. 1837
Methodist Chapel (printed form)
Reg. by George Riseley of Pavenham, Thomas Staton of Bedford, Wesleyan minister,
George Hulatt of Pavenham
BRO, ABN 1/2; ABN 2/320. PRO, RG 31/2, 343
Certificate addressed to the Bishop of Lincoln

72/5   **Primitive Methodist**
Worship   8 Oct. 1852
Primitive Methodist Chapel
Reg. by John Symonds Gostling, Gwyn St., Bedford, upholsterer (trustee)
Cancelled 31 Dec. 1866
OPCS, RG(W) 270
Gostling registered a Primitive Methodist chapel at Oakley on the same day

72/6   **Wesleyan**
Worship   9 Feb. 1854
Wesleyan Methodist Chapel
Reg. by William Henry Clarkson, Harpur St., Bedford, superintendent minister
Cancelled 3 Mar. 1876
OPCS, RG(W) 1866
Clarkson registered Wesleyan chapels at Bedford, Cardington, Clapham, Kempston,
Milton Ernest, Turvey, Wilshamstead & Wootton on the same day

72/7   **Primitive Methodist**
Worship   25 Mar. 1859
Primitive Methodist Chapel
Reg. by Joseph Hulatt of Pavenham, baker (trustee)
Cancelled on revision, 8 May 1895
OPCS, RG(W) 8743

72/8   **Wesleyan**
Worship   30 Jan. 1861
Wesleyan Methodist Chapel
Reg. by Charles Carter, Harpur St., Bedford, minister
Cancelled 12 July 1968
OPCS, RG(W) 12244
Carter registered a Wesleyan chapel at Kempston on the same day

73. PERTENHALL

73/1
Archdeaconry   **20 Apr. 1798**
House of Francis Abbott
BRO, ABN 1/1

Plate 29: Pertenhall: The Moravian community with houses forming a courtyard round the chapel. The original chapel was licensed in 1823.

(Photograph: Bedfordshire County Council, 1967)

73/2
Archdeaconry   **10/20 Mar. 1823**
Premises of John King Martyn, minister, for Protestants in connection with the Church of England
Reg. by J.K. Martyn, Thomas Marks, carpenter, William Pooles, cordwainer
BRO, ABN 1/2; ABN 2/200; ABN 3/3, 49. PRO, RG 31/2, 221

Plate 30: Pertenhall: The interior of the Moravian church which was built in 1827.
(Photograph: Bedfordshire County Council, 1967)

74. PODINGTON

74/1
Archdeaconry   **26/26 Dec. 1766**
Dwelling house of Anthony King, labourer
Reg. by Anthony King (his mark), William Wilsher of Bedford, victualler
BRO, ABN 1/1; ABN 2/25. PRO, RG 31/2, 24
Certificate addressed to the Commissary & Official of Bedford

74/2
Archdeaconry   **26/26 Dec. 1766**
House of Daniel Abbott
Reg. by Anthony King (his mark), William Wilsher of Bedford, victualler
BRO, ABN 1/1; ABN 2/26. PRO, RG31/2, 25
Certificate addressed to the Commissary & Official of Bedford

74/3
Archdeaconry   **16 Mar./5 Apr. 1794**
House of John Hewet
Reg. by John Hewet (his mark), Benjamin Hotton (his mark), John Davis Vincent,
Nathaniel Haynes, William Lovell
BRO, ABN 1/1; ABN 2/72. PRO, RG 31/2, 73

74/4
Archdeaconry   2 Aug. 1794
House of Richard Carter at Hinwick in Poddington
BRO, ABN 1/1

75. POTSGROVE

75/1
Quarter Sessions   4 July 1792
Dwelling house in occ. of John Farey, farmer
Reg. by John Farey (his mark), John Studds, farmer, Henry Clarke (his mark), labourer,
William Butterfield, dairyman
BRO, QSR 1792, 55; QSM 19, p. 12

75/2
Archdeaconry   5 Oct. 1819
House of George Hitchcock
Reg. by George Hitchcock
BRO, ABN 1/2; ABN 3/3, 16. PRO, RG 31/2, 187

75/3   Wesleyan
Archdeaconry   12/26 Nov. 1824
House of Elizabeth Sayles in Sheep Lane (printed form)
Reg. by John Furness, Elizabeth Sayles, Richard Eland, John Furness, Wesleyan
minister
BRO, ABN 1/2; ABN 2/214; ABN 3/3, 63. PRO, RG 31/2, 234
Form printed by T. Cordeux, London

75/4
Archdeaconry   27/30 Mar. 1830
House of John Creamer in Ship or Sheep Lane
Reg. by W.D. Harris, William Poole
BRO, ABN 1/2; ABN 2/245; ABN 3/3, 95. PRO, RG 31/2, 267

75/5
Archdeaconry   20 Nov. 1849/5 Jan. 1850
**Dwelling house & premises in occ. of Thomas Green in Sheep Lane (printed
form)**
Reg. by William Wigley of Aylesbury (Bucks.)
BRO, ABN 1/2; ABN 2/423. PRO, RG 31/2, 445
Certificate addressed to the Bishop of Bedford

75/6   Wesleyan
Worship   15 July 1863
Wesleyan Chapel in Sheep Lane
Reg. by William Richardson of Leighton Buzzard, bookseller (local preacher)
Cancelled on revision, 22 May 1964
OPCS, RG(W) 15788

76. POTTON

76/1

(Archdeaconry)   11 Jan. 1715/6

Dwelling house and outhouses of Thomas Lake of Potton, glover

Reg. by John Hensman, Samuel Hensman

BRO, P64/7/1

This certificate is with the Potton parish records. It was probably never received by the Registrar of the Archdeaconry

76/2

Archdeaconry   8/8 Apr. 1758

Dwelling house of Jeremiah Negus in Kings Street

Reg. by Jeremiah Negus of Potton, plumber, Thomas Clerk of Everton, servant

BRO, ABN 1/1; ABN 2/10. PRO, RG 31/2, 10

Certificate addressed to the Commissary & Official of Bedford

76/3

Archdeaconry   8/8 Apr. 1758

Dwelling house of Esther Gatward

Reg. by Jeremiah Negus, Thomas Clerk

BRO, ABN 1/1; ABN 2/12. PRO, RG 31/2, 12

Certificate addressed to the Commissary & Official of Bedford

76/4

Archdeaconry   25/5 May 1761 *(sic)*

A Malting in King Street

Reg. by Thomas Thorn (his mark), woolcomber, George Gatward, woolcomber

BRO, ABN 1/1; ABN 2/19. PRO, RG 31/2, 18

Certificate addressed to the Commissary & Official of Bedford

76/5

Archdeaconry   14/15 May 1788

Barn of Mr Ed. Bumbery

Reg. by William Reynolds, George Emery, John Rogers, John Emery, Edmund Bumbery

BRO, ABN 1/1; ABN 2/58. PRO, RG 31/2, 58

The certificate is torn

76/6

Archdeaconry   24/26 Dec. 1789

Barn of Martha Miller, widow - 'being desirous of worshiping God according to the rules of his written word, and the dictates of our own Consciences'

Reg. by John Miller, carpenter, John Rogers, cooper, Elizabeth Rogers, Martha Miller, John Miller, glazier, S. Pedley, Richard Whithead, Martha Norman

BRO, ABN 1/1; ABN 2/63. PRO, RG 31/2, 63

Certificate addressed to Rev. Mr Hornbuckle at Bedford

76/7

Archdeaconry   1/1 May 1802

Newly erected building (Meeting House)

Reg. by John Keeling, Livett Frank, William Bigg, Joseph Miller, Joseph Freshwater, Jeremiah Lee, Thomas Hagger

BRO, ABN 1/1; ABN 2/108. PRO, RG 31/2, 107

116/9. The entry for Potton, 6 Jan. 1838, in ABN 1/2 is a mistake for Wootton

76/8
Archdeaconry   **18 May 1849**
A Chapel
Reg. by Frederick Basden, minister
BRO, ABN 1/2. PRO, RG 31/2, 438

Plate 31: Potton: The Congregational church (opened in 1848) and the old manse.
(Photograph c.1892)

76/9   **Congregational**
Marriages   **12 May 1850**
Congregational Chapel [United Reformed Church]
OPCS, RG(M) 3176

76/10
Archdeaconry   **22/25 Oct. 1851**
A separate building (printed form)
Reg. by John D. Julian of St Neots (Hunts.)
BRO, ABN 1/2; ABN 2/433. PRO, RG 31/2, 457

76/11   **Wesleyan**
Worship   **14 Mar. 1854**
Wesleyan Chapel
Reg. by Adam Fletcher of St Neots (Hunts.), Wesleyan minister
73415 substituted on 16 Nov. 1931
OPCS, RG(W) 3322
Fletcher registered a Wesleyan chapel at Tempsford on the same day

Plate 32: Potton: The interior of the Congregational chapel as it was before the rearrangement of 1899.   (*Photograph: c.1895*)

76/12   **Particular Baptist**
Worship   **2 Apr. 1863**
Wool Warehouse
Reg. by David Noble of Potton, market gardener ('an occupier')
Cancelled 31 Dec. 1866
OPCS, RG(W) 15626

76/13   **Baptist**
Worship   **26 Nov. 1868**
The Baptist Meeting in Horslow Street
Reg. by Henry Hercock of Potton, Baptist minister
OPCS, RG(W) 18801

76/14   **Particular Baptist**
Marriages   **28 Nov. 1868**
Baptist Chapel in Horslow Street
OPCS, RG(M) 6714

76/15   **Wesleyan**
Marriages   **22 Nov. 1875**
Wesleyan Methodist Chapel
25496 substituted on 16 Nov. 1931
OPCS, RG(M) 8702

76/16
Worship

Salvationists
22 May 1890

Salvation Army Barracks
Reg. by Albert Suckley of Biggleswade, Captain, S.A,
OPCS, RG(W) 32160

77. PULLOXHILL

77/1
Archdeaconry   **1/4 Nov. 1802**
Dwelling house of George Rich, labourer
Reg. by J.C. Lepington, John Crouch, Thomas Walker, James Cole, James Deamer, John
Tompson
BRO, ABN 1/1; ABN 2/109. PRO, RG 31/2, 108
Certificate addressed to the Bishop of Lincoln

77/2
Archdeaconry   **27 Mar. 1805**
Dwelling house of John Thompson
BRO, ABN 1/1

77/3
Archdeaconry   **11/11 Mar. 1832**
House of James Spendelow (Spedlow)
Reg. by James Spendelow
BRO, ABN 1/2; ABN 2/267; ABN 3/3, 116. PRO, RG 31/2, 288
Certificate addressed to the Bishop of Lincoln

77/4
Archdeaconry   **25/26 Sept. 1837**
A building recently erected
Reg. by Henry Hyde, John Cain, John Neal (house dwellers)
BRO, ABN 1/2; ABN 2/319. PRO, RG 32/1, 342

78. RAVENSDEN

78/1
Archdeaconry   **8/8 Jan. 1831**
Dwelling house of John Wiles of Ravensden
Reg. by John Wiles
BRO, ABN 1/2; ABN 2/253; ABN 3/3, 102. PRO, RG 31/2, 274
Certificate addressed to the Bishop of Lincoln

78/2
Archdeaconry   **10/10 Jan. 1832**
House of John Allen
Reg. by John Allen
BRO, ABN 1/2; ABN 2/265; ABN 3/3, 114. PRO, RG 31/2, 286
Certificate addressed to the Bishop of Lincoln

78/3
Archdeaconry
Episcopal Church (A Chapel)
Reg. by Timothy Richard Matthews, clerk, of Bedford
BRO, ABN 1/2; ABN 2/290. PRO, RG 31/2, 312
Certificate addressed to the Bishop of Lincoln

Episcopal
27/28 June 1834

78/4
Archdeaconry
A Chapel
Reg. by John Allen
BRO, ABN 1/2. PRO, RG 31/2, 427

8 Apr. 1848

78/5
Worship
Zion Chapel
Reg. by James Shepherd of Bedford, tailor (trustee)
OPCS, RG(W) 1812

Particular Baptist
7 Feb. 1854

79. RENHOLD

79/1
Archdeaconry
House of Thomas Peck of Renhold
BRO, ABN 1/1

21 Apr. 1807

79/2
Archdeaconry
Dwelling house of John Dawson of Renhold
Reg. by John Dawson
BRO, ABN 1/2; ABN 2/264; ABN 3/3, 113. PRO, RG 31/2, 285
Certificate addressed to the Bishop of Lincoln

10/10 Jan. 1832

79/3
Archdeaconry
Dwelling house of Samuel Goodly of Renhold
Reg. by Samuel Goodly
BRO, ABN 1/2; ABN 2/268; ABN 3/3, 117. PRO, RG 31/2, 289
Certificate addressed to the Bishop of Lincoln

14/14 Mar. 1832

80. RIDGMONT

80/1
House of William Jarvis
OR, p. 857

Congregational
1 May 1672

80/2
Archdeaconry
Rebuilt Meeting House for occasional public worship
Reg. by Richard Broughton 'and others'
BRO, ABN 1/1; X347/40
Original licence is with the Ridgmont Baptist Church records

7 Mar. 1812

Plate 33: Ridgmont: The Baptist chapel and manse. The chapel was built in 1811 to replace an earlier meeting house on the site for a church formed in 1701.

(*Photograph: Jack Sharpe, c.1910*)

80/3   **Baptist**
Marriages   **2 Sept. 1837**
Baptist Meeting House
Cancelled 11 May 1993
OPCS, RG(M) 473

80/4   **Wesleyan**
Archdeaconry   **7/7 Oct. 1845**
Wesleyan Chapel
Reg. by John Pickavant, Wesleyan minister, Bedford circuit
BRO, ABN 1/2; ABN 2/380. PRO, RG 31/2, 401

80/5   **Wesleyan**
Marriages   **8 Oct. 1845**
Wesleyan Chapel
Cancelled on revision, 29 June 1954
OPCS, RG(M) 2487

52/6. The entry for Ridgmont, 26 Oct. 1845, in ABN 1/2 is a mistake for Husborne Crawley

Plate 34: Ridgmont: The Wesleyan chapel at the corner of the High Street and Lydds Hill, licensed in 1845.   (*Photograph: Jack Sharpe, c.1910*)

80/6   **Wesleyan**
Worship   **11 Feb. 1854**
Wesleyan Methodist Chapel
Reg. by William Henry Clarkson, 4 Harpur St., Bedford, superintendent minister
Cancelled on revision, 29 June 1954
OPCS, RG (W) 1970
Clarkson registered a Wesleyan chapel at Eversholt on the same day

80/7   **Baptist**
Worship   **12/14 Dec. 1860**
Baptist Chapel
Reg. by Thomas Baker of Ridgmont, minister
Cancelled 11 May 1993
OPCS, RG(W) 10196. BRO, X347/41
Original licence in Ridgmont Baptist Church records

81. RISELEY

81/1
Archdeaconry   **8/8 Apr. 1758**
Dwelling house (Hill Farm) of Nathaniel Harper of Riseley, farmer
Reg. by Nathaniel Harper, John Norman of Little Barford, farmer
BRO, ABN 1/1; ABN 2/11. PRO, RG 31/2, 11
Certificate addressed to the Commissary & Official of Bedford

81/2   **Moravian**
Quarter Sessions   **1/3 Oct. 1759**
Chapel of *Unitas Fratrum* on west side of High Street, adjoining estate bel. to Mr
Allen of Souldrop on south & estate bel. to Mr Woodward of Caldicot on north
Reg. by Robert Dawson, Robert Jackson
BRO, QSP 43/1, QSM 13, 174; MO 44. PRO, RG 31/6, 4
Certificate & draft licence in Quarter Sessions records. Original licence in Bedford
Moravian Church records, and printed in *B.H.R.S.*, vol. 68, p.197

81/3
Quarter Sessions   **6 Oct. 1763**
House of Stephen Dickins
Reg. by Samuel Berry, Joseph Marshall, Robert Day
BRO, QSP 43/6
Draft licence

81/4
Quarter Sessions   **28 Sept. 1773**
House of Stephen Dickins
Reg. by Samuel Berry, Joseph Marshall, Robert Day
BRO, QSP 43/11
Original certificate

81/5
Archdeaconry   **30/30 Dec. 1783**
House of William Curtis
Reg. by William Curtis (his mark), George Dickins, William Dickins
BRO, ABN 1/1; ABN 2/54. PRO, RG 31/2, 54

81/6
Archdeaconry   **30 Mar./5 Apr. 1805**
Room in house of Stephen Dickins
Reg. by Stephen Dickins, William Rootham, William Vallantine, John Goss, [William
Prior *deleted*]
BRO, ABN 1/1; ABN 2/116. PRO, RG 31/2, 116

81/7   **Methodist**
Archdeaconry   **14 Feb. 1807**
Methodist Chapel
BRO, ABN 1/1

81/8
Archdeaconry   **5 Aug./4 Sept. 1830**
Building in occ. of William Fowler, the property of Lord St John
Reg. by Thomas Brown, John Watts, Thomas Woodruff
BRO, ABN 1/2; ABN 2/250; ABN 3/3, 98. PRO, RG 31/2, 270
Certificate addressed to the Bishop of Lincoln

81/9
Archdeaconry   **16/16 June 1838**
A barn in poss. of Mrs Everett
Reg. by Joseph Love, Samuel Beall, Ladds William Lugsdin
BRO, ABN 1/2; ABN 2/329. PRO, RG 31/2, 351

81/10

Archdeaconry   18/18 June 1838

A barn in poss. of Mrs Everett

Reg. by Joseph Love, Samuel Beale, Ladd W. Lugsden
BRO, ABN 1/2; ABN 2/330. PRO, RG 31/2, 353

81/11   Baptist

Archdeaconry   7/17 Nov. 1838

Baptist Chapel

Reg. by James Lugsdin, Joseph Love, Samuel Beall
BRO, ABN 1/2; ABN 2/331. PRO, RG 31/2, 354

81/12

Archdeaconry   19/27 Apr. 1839

Dwelling house of Isaac Flavel

Reg. by Isaac Flavel
BRO, ABN 1/2; ABN 2/339. PRO, RG 31/2, 362
Certificate addressed to the Bishop of Ely

81/13   Wesleyan

Worship   29 May 1854

Wesleyan Methodist Chapel

Reg. by Thomas Jeffery of Higham Ferrers (Northants.), Wesleyan minister
72109 substituted on 17 Apr. 1970
OPCS, RG(W) 5144
Jeffery registered a Wesleyan chapel at Yelden on the same day

81/14   Moravian

Worship   12 Aug. 1858

Moravian Chapel

Reg. by John Hull of Riseley, minister
Cancelled on revision, 18 Mar. 1971
OPCS, RG(W) 8451

81/15   Moravian

Marriages   14 Aug. 1858

Moravian Chapel

Cancelled 18 Mar. 1971
OPCS, RG(M) 4288

82. ROXTON

82/1

Archdeaconry   17/17 Nov. 1753

Dwelling house of Paul Freshwater

Reg. by Thomas Craner of Blunham, gent., Samuel Butler of Bedford, wheelwright
BRO, ABN 1/1; ABN 2/3. PRO, RG 31/2, 2
Certificate addressed to the Commissary & Official of Bedford. Attributed to Blunham in
RG 31/2

Plate 35: Roxton: The Congregational chapel established in 1808 by the squire, Charles James Metcalfe of Roxton House. The thatched chapel was given its rustic appearance when the building was enlarged in about 1825.   (*Photograph: A.Reynolds, c.1914*)

82/2

Archdeaconry   **8 Aug. 1808**

Building & premises of Charles James Metcalfe of Roxton House, esq., now in occ. of William Brown, between premises of Mary Garratt on N, premises of Ann Rouston on W, close of C.J. Metcalfe on S & road on E

Reg. by C.J. Metcalfe, William Brown, John Savile

BRO, ABN 1/1; ABN 2/132. PRO, RG 31/2, 130

Probably Congregational (H.G. Tibbutt, *Roxton Congregational Church*, Bedford, 1958). Certificate undated

82/3

Archdeaconry   **6/11 Dec. 1811**

Chapel bel. to Ann Rowlson

Reg. by John Sydserff, William Hall, Peaceson George, William Saunderson

BRO, ABN 2/143. PRO, RG 31/2, 142

82/4   **Independent**

Marriages   **11 Aug. 1837**

Roxton Chapel

OPCS, RG(M) 375

83. SALFORD

83/1
Archdeaconry   **5 Apr. 1816**
House of John Barber
BRO, ABN 1/1

Plate 36: Salford: The Wesleyan chapel was "erected 1814" but not registered until 1854.
(*Photograph: c.1900*)

83/2
Archdeaconry   **9/12 May 1827**
A chapel lately erected (printed form)
Reg. by John Stevens of Newport Pagnell (Bucks.), minister
BRO, ABN 1/2; ABN 2/229; ABN 3/3, 80. PRO, RG 31/2, 252

83/3   **Wesleyan**
Worship   **20 June 1854**
Wesleyan Chapel
Reg. by William Britten of Bow Brickhill (Bucks.), baker (trustee)
Cancelled 14 Mar. 1876
OPCS, RG(W) 5393
Britten registered a Wesleyan chapel at Aspley Guise on the same day

WESLEYAN CHAPEL, SALFORD

Plate 37: Salford: The interior of the Wesleyan chapel.   (*Photograph: c.1900*)

84. SANDY

84/1
Archdeaconry   **15 June 1791**
House of Jeremy Skilliter
BRO, ABN 1/1

84/2
Archdeaconry   **15/15 June 1791**
House of John Purser
Reg. by Turners Squire, John Skilleter, Robert Skilleter, Joseph Skilleter, Samuel
Freeman
BRO, ABN 1/1; ABN 2/68. PRO, RG 31/2, 68

84/3
Archdeaconry   **18/18 Apr. 1797**
Dwelling house of John Cooper of Beeston in Sandy
Reg. by John Cooper, James Schofield
BRO, ABN 1/1; ABN 2/79. PRO, RG 31/2, 79

84/4
Archdeaconry   **1/1 May 1797**
House in poss. of Henry Huckle at Girtford in Sandy
Reg. by Henry Huckle (his mark), Stephen Wilson, John Freeman, James Watson, James
Ellis, Thomas Eagle
BRO, ABN 1/1; ABN 2/81. PRO, RG 31/2, 80

84/5
Archdeaconry   **25 July 1801**
House of John Harwood
BRO, ABN 1/1

84/6
Archdeaconry   **25 June 1813**
House of William Christmas, cordwainer
Reg. by William Christmas, John Skilleter, Jeremy Skilleter, Joseph Keep, William
Whittlemore, John Harwood
BRO, ABN 1/1; ABN 2/153. PRO, RG 31/2, 153

84/7
Archdeaconry   **29 Apr. 1816**
House of Jeremy Skilleter
BRO, ABN 1/1

84/8
Archdeaconry   **2/2 Feb. 1821**
House of Thomas Blewitt in Girtford
Reg. by James Sirket, William Baldrey, William Braybrooks
BRO, ABN 1/2; ABN 2/177; ABN 3/3, 23. PRO, RG 31/2, 194

84/9   **Baptist**
Archdeaconry   **25/26 Feb. 1831**
Building in poss. of John Foster to be used as a Baptist chapel
Reg. by Thomas Middleditch, John Foster, Blyth Foster
BRO, ABN 1/2; ABN 2/254; ABN 3/3, 103. PRO, RG 31/2, 275

84/10
Archdeaconry   **13 May/21 June 1834**
A Chapel (printed form)
Reg. by William Davies of Biggleswade
BRO, ABN 1/2; ABN 2/285. PRO, RG 31/2, 310
Certificate addressed to the Bishop of Lincoln

84/11
Archdeaconry   **5/15 July 1834**
Building in occ. of Elizabeth Page in Beeston
Reg. by Joseph Hindes of Blunham
BRO, ABN 1/2; ABN 2/292. PRO, RG 31/2, 314

84/12
Archdeaconry   **19/19 Mar. 1849**
Dwelling house of William Barnes jun.
Reg. by Thomas Smith of Bedford
BRO, ABN 1/2; ABN 2/408. PRO, RG 31/2, 435

84/13
Archdeaconry   **8/8 Mar. 1852**
House of John Ball at Girtford
Reg. by William Knight, William Bywaters, Joseph Harris
BRO, ABN 1/2; ABN 2/435. PRO, RG 31/2, 460
Certificate addressed to the Bishop of Lincoln

84/14   **Wesleyan**
Worship   **9 Feb. 1854**
Wesleyan Chapel at Beeston
Reg. by Robert Maxwell of Biggleswade, Wesleyan minister
Cancelled 6 Mar. 1876
OPCS, RG(W) 1876
Maxwell registered Wesleyan chapels at Biggleswade, Langford, Shefford & Stotfold on
the same day

84/15   **Baptist**
Worship   **11 Sept. 1854**
Baptist Chapel
Reg. by William Skilleter of Sandy, gardener (trustee)
46995 substituted on 12 Mar. 1917
OPCS, RG(W) 5799

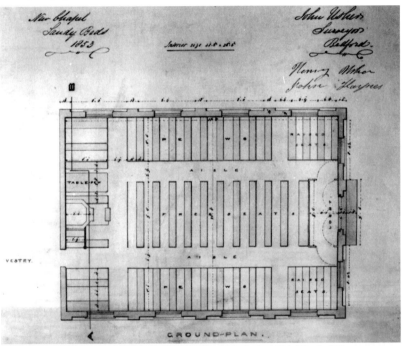

Plate 38: Sandy: A plan of the new Baptist chapel built in 1854. The building gave way
to a new chapel in 1887-8.   (*Architectural drawing: John Usher, 1854*)

84/16   **Baptist**
Worship   **14 Mar. 1861**
Baptist Meeting
Reg. by Thomas Voysey of Sandy, Baptist minister
30946 substituted on 20 June 1888
OPCS, RG(W) 13493

84/17   **Baptist**
Marriages   **2 July 1863**
Baptist Meeting
Cancelled 31 Aug. 1888
OPCS, RG(M) 5279
This number is duplicated in the register

84/18   **Mormon**
Worship   **6 June 1867**
Building in occ. of William Maylin in Back Street, Girtford for Latter Day Saints
Reg. by William Maylin of Girtford, rag & bone dealer (occupier)
Cancelled 6 Mar. 1876
OPCS, RG(W) 17956

84/19   **Wesleyan**
Worship   **21 July 1868**
Wesleyan Chapel at Beeston
Reg. by John Carey Pengelly of Biggleswade, Wesleyan minister
OPCS, RG(W) 18620

84/20   **Primitive Methodist**
Worship   **15 May 1869**
Primitive Methodist Chapel at Girtford
Reg. by William Birks, Commercial Rd., Bedford, minister
44705 substituted on 14 Mar. 1911
OPCS, RG(W) 19093

84/21   **Wesleyan**
Marriages   **29 June 1870**
Wesleyan Chapel at Beeston
OPCS, RG(M) 7185

84/22   **Baptist**
Worship   **20 June 1888**
Baptist Chapel
Reg. by George Andrew Gregg of Sandy, deacon
Substituted for 13493
OPCS, RG(W) 30946

84/23   **Baptist**
Marriages   **31 Aug. 1888**
Baptist Chapel
OPCS, RG(M) 12038

84/24   **Salvationists**
Worship   **19 Nov. 1888**
Salvation Army Barracks
Reg. by Mary Bird of Sandy, Captain, S.A.
Cancelled 19 Apr. 1895
OPCS, RG(W) 31235

85. SHARNBROOK

85/1
Archdeaconry 30 Sept./2 Oct. 1790
Rebuilt Meeting House
Reg. by R. Grindon, S. Dickins, Jesse Woodham, William Curtis (his mark), Charles Archer (trustees)
BRO, ABN 1/1; ABN 2/66. PRO, RG 31/2, 65

85/2
Archdeaconry 27 Sept. 1816
House of Marshall Tebbutt
BRO, ABN 1/1

85/3
Archdeaconry 20/27 May 1826
House of William Archer of Sharnbrook, carrier
Reg. by William Archer, Thomas Grindon, Philip Wodham, William Peck
BRO, ABN 1/2; ABN 2/225; ABN 3/3, 74. pRO, RG 31/2, 246

85/4
Archdeaconry 17/21 Nov. 1827
Schoolroom of Thomas Grindon of Sharnbrook, shopkeeper
Reg. by Thomas Grindon, Philip Woodham, William Peck, William Archer
BRO, ABN 1/2; ABN 2/232; ABN 3/3, 82. PRO, RG 31/2, 254

85/5
Archdeaconry 30 Aug./7 Sept. 1833
Barn & tenement of Thomas Grindon, shopkeeper, to be used as a chapel
Reg. by Thomas Grindon, William Peck, Thomas Spencer, John Payne
BRO, ABN 1/2; ABN 2/279A. PRO, RG 31/2, 301

85/6 **Baptist**
Marriages 18 Oct. 1843
Old Baptist Meeting House
OPCS, RG(M) 2154

85/7
Archdeaconry 13/13 May 1848
A Barn (printed form)
Reg. by William Henry Stewart of Wellingborough (Northants.)
BRO, ABN 1/2; ABN 2. PRO, RG 31/2, 417
Form printed at Northampton. Certificate addressed to the Bishop of Peterborough and amended to Ely

85/8 **Particular Baptist**
Worship 20 Jan. 1862
Bethlehem Chapel at top of Bodycroft Lane
Reg. by Thomas Corby of Radwell in Felmersham, Baptist minister
Cancelled 21 Jan. 1939
OPCS, RG(W) 14805

85/9   **Particular Baptist**
Worship   **8 Apr. 1862**
The Old Meeting House in High Street
Reg. by James Pacey, Kennel Hill, Sharnbrook, labourer (deacon)
OPCS, RG(W) 15064

86. SHEFFORD

86/1
Archdeaconry   **14/14 Dec. 1777**
House of William Tansley for occasional public worship
Reg. by William Tansley, Thomas Barnes
BRO, ABN 1/1; ABN 2/44. PRO, RG 31/2, 44
ABN 2/44 dates the registration 27 Dec.

86/2
Quarter Sessions   **7 Aug. 1791**
House of Thomas Churchman Dumvile
Reg. by William Tansley, Thomas Dumvile
BRO, QSR 1791, 92; QSM 18, p. 254. PRO, RG 31/6, 13

Plate 39: Shefford: The Roman Catholic mission at Shefford was established in 1728 and the first chapel built in 1791.   (*Watercolour: Thomas Fisher, c.1820*)

86/3
Archdeaconry   **15 Nov. 1808**
House of Samuel Sheffield
BRO, ABN 1/1

86/4
Archdeaconry   **23/23 Feb. 1814**
Barn in occ. of Benjamin Briggs of Shefford, tailor
Reg. by Benjamin Briggs, Edward Chew, George Nash
BRO, ABN 1/1; ABN 2/161. PRO, RG 31/2, 160

86/5
Archdeaconry   **26 Nov. 1825**
Newly erected building at North End of Shefford Hardwick
Reg. by Thomas Inskip, John Impey
BRO, ABN 2/223. PRO, RG 31/2, 244

Plate 40: Shefford: The original Wesleyan Methodist chapel. It was built in 1835 and
replaced by the present chapel in 1912. No licence is recorded.   (*Photograph: c.1910*)

86/6   **Roman Catholic**
Marriages   **8 Mar. 1838**
Catholic Chapel
Cancelled for informality, lack of information, 9 Mar. 1838. See next entry
OPCS, RG(M) 1058

86/7   **Roman Catholic**
Marriages   **9 Mar. 1838**
Catholic Chapel [St Francis' Church in High Street]
OPCS, RG(M) 1095

86/8   **Union**
Marriages   **23 Apr. 1838**
Union Meeting House in Little Hardwick [Baptist Church]
OPCS, RG(M) 1121

86/9   **Wesleyan**
Worship   **9 Feb. 1854**
Wesleyan Chapel in Ampthill Road
Reg. by Robert Maxwell of Biggleswade, Wesleyan minister
45492 substituted on 5 Dec. 1912
OPCS, RG(W) 1875
Maxwell registered Wesleyan chapels at Biggleswade, Langford, Sandy & Stotfold on
the same day

86/10   **Salvationists**
Worship   **29 Dec. 1887**
Salvation Army Barracks
Reg. by Edward Batten of Meppershall, Captain, S.A.
Cancelled on revision, 19 Apr. 1895
OPCS, RG(W) 30571
Batten registered a barracks at Meppershall on the same day

86/11   **Salvationists**
Worship   **13 Oct. 1888**
Salvation Army Barracks
Reg. by Alfred Wood of Shefford, Captain, S.A.
38352 substituted on 27 Apr. 1901
OPCS, RG(W) 31162

86/12   **Wesleyan**
Marriages   **18 Jan. 1897**
Wesleyan Chapel in Ampthill Road
20361 substituted on 5 Dec. 1912
OPCS, RG(M) 14517

86/13   **Salvation Army**
Worship   **27 Apr. 1901**
Salvation Army Barracks in Bridge Street
Reg. by John Williams, Meppershall Rd., Shefford, Captain, S.A.
Substituted for 31162. 45788 substituted on 25 June 1913
OPCS, RG(W) 38352

87. SHELTON

87/1
Quarter Sessions   **17 July 1715**
The now dwelling house of Samuel Knighton
BRO, QSM 2, p. 134. PRO, RG 31/6, 1

87/2
Archdeaconry   **1/8 Feb. 1777**
House of Thomas Peck
Reg. by Thomas Peck, John Emery
BRO, ABN 1/1; ABN 2/43. PRO, RG 31/2, 43

87/3
Archdeaconry   **16 Jan. 1808**
House of John Button
BRO, ABN 1/1

87/4
Archdeaconry   **26 July/9 Aug. 1813**
House of Henry Harris (printed form)
Reg. by Henry Harris
BRO, ABN 1/1; ABN 2/154. PRO, RG 31/2, 152
Probably Wesleyan as the form was printed by T. Cordeux, 14 City Rd., London.
Certificate addressed to the Bishop of Lincoln

88. SHILLINGTON

88/1
Archdeaconry   **28 Nov./1 Dec. 1788**
Dwelling house in occ. of Thomas Hare
Reg. by James Bowers, John Savile, John Foster
BRO, ABN 1/1; ABN 2/60. PRO, RG 31/2, 60

88/2
Quarter Sessions   **17 July 1793**
Dwelling house of William Hill at Upper Stondon
Reg. by William Stevens, John Groom (his mark), James Smith, landlord, Thomas
Hopkins
PRO, RG 31/6, 19

88/3
Archdeaconry   **14//20 June 1798**
Dwelling house in occ. of Ann Haire
Reg. by John Foster, Edward Foster
BRO, ABN 1/1; ABN 2/96. PRO, RG 31/2, 95

88/4
Archdeaconry   **18/22 Oct. 1798**
Dwelling house in occ. of John Foster
Reg. by John Foster, David Tompson, Edward Foster
BRO, ABN 1/1; ABN 2/99. PRO, RG 31/2, 98

88/5
Archdeaconry   **12 Sept. 1814**
A building
BRO, ABN 1/1

88/7
Archdeaconry   12 June 1815
A Chapel
BRO, ABN 1/1

88/8
Archdeaconry   6 Aug. 1822
Premises of John Flint in own occ.
Reg. by John Flint
BRO, ABN 1/2; ABN 2/193; ABN 3/3, 40. PRO, RG 31/2, 211

88/9
Archdeaconry   6/7 Apr. 1830
Building at Lower Stondon in poss. of John Brown
Reg. by Samuel Hillyard of Bedford, Thomas Green, John Brashier
BRO, ABN 1/2; ABN 2/247; ABN 3/3, 96. PRO, RG 31/2, 268

88/10
Archdeaconry   19/19 Nov. 1841
A building intended to be a chapel (12 trustees)
Reg. by Charles James Metcalf jun., Thomas Newling (trustees)
BRO, ABN 1/2; ABN 2/358. PRO, RG 31/2, 381

Plate 41: Shillington: The Congregational church which was built as the Union Chapel and opened in 1840.   (*Photograph: c.1950*)

88/11   **Wesleyan**
Archdeaconry   **18/23 Sept. 1846**
Wesleyan Methodist Chapel in Pegsden (printed form)
Reg. by John Crofts
BRO, ABN 1/2; ABN 2/389. PRO, RG 31/2, 413
Certificate addressed to the Bishop of Lincoln and amended to Ely. Crofts registered
Wesleyan chapels at Luton & Upper Gravenhurst on the same day

88/12   **Wesleyan**
Archdeaconry   **18/23 Sept. 1846**
Wesleyan Methodist Chapel (printed form)
Reg. by John Crofts
BRO, ABN 1/2; ABN 2/390. PRO, RG 31/2, 412
Certificate addressed to the Bishop of Lincoln and amended to Ely

88/13   **Wesleyan**
Worship   **9 Feb. 1854**
Wesleyan Methodist Chapel in Pegsdon
Reg. by Wright Shovelton, Chapel St., Luton, superintendent minister
Cancelled 21 June 1977 (advertised 21 June)
OPCS, RG(W) 1902

88/14   **Wesleyan**
Worship   **9 Feb. 1854**
Wesleyan Methodist Chapel
Reg. by Wright Shovelton, Chapel St., Luton, superintendent minister
Cancelled on revision, 8 May 1897
OPCS, RG(W) 1903

88/15   **Independent**
Marriages   **25 Oct. 1860**
Union Chapel [Congregational Church in Church Street]
OPCS, RG(M) 4691

88/16   **Wesleyan**
Worship   **17 Sept. 1872**
A building belonging to the Wesleyan Methodists [Wesleyan Methodist Chapel]
Reg. by Robert Eland, Church St., Luton, minister
OPCS, RG(W) 20920

88/17   **Primitive Methodist**
Worship   **20 Dec. 1887**
Primitive Methodist Chapel
Reg. by William Brass, Pembroke Rd., Baldock (Herts.), Primitive Methodist minister
Substituted 42872 on 27 Jan. 1908
OPCS, RG(W) 30556

88/18   **Wesleyan**
Marriages   **22 Nov. 1897**
Wesleyan Methodist Chapel
OPCS, RG(M) 14820

89. SILSOE

89/1
Archdeaconry   **1/7 Apr. 1794**
Dwelling house of Catherine Studman, widow
Reg. by Catherine Studman (her mark), John Hickling, Jonathan Clark, James Schofield
BRO, ABN 1/1; ABN 2/73. PRO, RG 31/2, 72
Certificate addressed to the Bishop of Lincoln

89/2
Archdeaconry   **5 June 1802**
Dwelling house of James Chapman of Silsoe
BRO, ABN 1/1

89/3
Archdeaconry   **9/10 Sept. 1806**
Dwelling house of William Austin
Reg. by John Aikenhead, William Austin, John Bedford, James Chapman, [William
Waldock, Peter Stonebanks *deleted*]
BRO, ABN 1/1; ABN 2/122. PRO, RG 31/2, 125

89/4
Archdeaconry   **19 Nov. 1808**
House of James Chapman
BRO, ABN 1/1

89/5
Archdeaconry   **24/24 Mar. 1824**
House in occ. of Mrs Whitbread
Reg. by Samuel Hobson of Maulden
BRO, ABN 1/2; ABN 2/208; ABN 3/3, 57. PRO, RG 31/2, 228

89/6   **Primitive Methodist**
Worship   **27 Feb. 1861**
Dwelling house in occ. of Jacob Swannell
Reg. by Edward Bishop, 6 Adelaide Sq., Bedford, minister
Cancelled 29 Aug. 1894
OPCS, RG(W) 13134
Bishop registered Primitive Methodist chapels at Flitton, Marston Morteyne & Maulden
on the same day

90. SOULDROP

90/1
Archdeaconry   **19/20 Nov. 1822**
House in occ. of Richard Gadsby
Reg. by Joseph Hindes of Sharnbrook
BRO, ABN 1/2; ABN 2/198; ABN 3/3, 46. PRO, RG 31/2, 219

91. SOUTHILL

91/1
Archdeaconry   **26/26 Mar. 1762**
Dwelling house of Francis Piggot of Broom, labourer
Reg. by Francis Piggot (his mark), William Chew (his mark)
BRO, ABN 1/1; ABN 2/20. PRO, RG 31/2, 19
Certificate addressed to the Commissary & Official of Bedford

91/2
Archdeaconry   **2 Sept./4 Oct. 1805**
New Meeting House being erected
Reg. by Joseph Patrick, Thomas Preston, Griffith Dunton, Edward Chew, John
Peppercorn, Anthony Thody
BRO, ABN 1/1; ABN 2/120. PRO, RG 31/2, 118

91/3
Archdeaconry   **15 Mar. 1811**
House of Edward Hawkins
BRO, ABN 1/1

91/4
Archdeaconry   **8 Jan. 1819**
House of Edward Wright at Stanford
Reg. by John Mason, John Lockey
ABN 1/2. PRO, RG 31/2, 182

91/5
Archdeaconry   **16 Nov. 1820**
House of John Cowland at Ireland in Southill
Reg. by Thomas Fay
BRO, ABN 1/2; ABN 2; ABN 3/3, 20. PRO, RG 31/2, 191
Fay requests a licence 'As some of our friends have been desirous for a long time to
oppen a house for prayer at Ireland and as we consider it would not be safe unless the
house was licenced ...'

91/6
Archdeaconry   **15 Sept. 1832**
Dwelling house in occ. of William Hale in Broom in Southill
Reg. by Thomas Middleditch of Biggleswade, Samuel Hale of Broom
BRO, ABN 1/2; ABN 2/272. PRO, RG 31/2, 294

91/7   **Baptist**
Marriages   **17 Feb. 1852**
Southill Meeting [Strict Baptist Chapel]
OPCS, RG(M) 3391

92. STAGSDEN

92/1   **Congregational**
House of William Man   **10 May 1672**
OR, p. 854

92/2
Quarter Sessions   5 Oct. 1768
House of Samuel Ward
Reg. by Joshua Symonds, Thomas Woodward, Thomas Kilpin, Thomas Rush, Samuel
Ward (his mark)
BRO, QSP43/7
Probably Congregational as Joshua Symonds was the minister of Bunyan Meeting.
Original certificate

92/3
Quarter Sessions   29 Dec. 1769/25 Apr. 1770
House of John Goodman
Reg. by Amos Bass, Thomas Syckes, Thomas Bass, John Goodman
BRO, QSM 15, 61; QSP 43/9. PRO, RG 31/6, 7
Original certificate

92/4
Archdeaconry   10/10 May 1832
Dwelling house of Richard Barcock
Reg. by Richard Barcock
BRO, ABN 1/2; ABN 2/269; ABN 3/3, 118. PRO, RG 31/2, 290

92/5
Archdeaconry   13 July 1844
House of James Henman
Reg. by James Henman
BRO, ABN 1/2

92/6   **Congregational**
Worship   **12 July 1860**
Stagsden Chapel (in connection with Bunyan Meeting, Bedford)
Reg. by John Jukes, Dame Alice St., Bedford, Congregational minister (senior minister)
54417 substituted on 27 Apr. 1933
OPCS, RG(W) 9420
Jukes registered Congregational chapels at Cardington, Elstow, Goldington, Kempston &
Oakley on the same day

93. STANBRIDGE

93/1
Archdeaconry   21/24 Sept. 1795
House in poss. of Nicholas Lucas in Stanbridge (Leighton Buzzard)
Reg. by Nicholas Lucas, John Olney, Joseph Emearton
BRO, ABN 2/76. PRO, RG31/2, 76

93/2
Quarter Sessions   11/16 Apr. 1817
Dwelling house of John Tearle of Stanbridge
Reg. by John Hodgson of Leighton Buzzard, preacher
BRO, QSR 1817, 285
This licence is probably duplicated by the next entry

93/3
Peculiar Jurisdiction 7 July 1817
Dwelling house of John Tearle of Stanbridge
Reg. by John Hodgson of Leighton Buzzard
BRO, RI 3/6824b
Certificate addressed to the County Quarter Sessions. See previous entry

93/4
Archdeaconry 4/18 Nov. 1833
A Chapel
Reg. by William Piggott of Leighton Buzzard
BRO, ABN 1/2; ABN 2/281. PRO, RG 31/2, 303

93/5
Archdeaconry 13 Mar./3 Apr. 1850
House of Mr David Squires
Reg. by Benjamin Johnson of Northall in Eddlesborough (Bucks.), Jeremiah Borham, John Mead
BRO, ABN 1/2; ABN 2/421. PRO, RG 31/2, 447
Certificate addressed to the Bishop of Ely

93/6 Primitive Methodist
Worship 9 Jan. 1861
Primitive Methodist Chapel
Reg. by Matthew Plummer of Luton, bonnet manufacturer (trustee)
Cancelled on revision, 5 Aug. 1954
OPCS, RG(W) 11814

93/7 Wesleyan
Worship 15 Mar. 1861
Wesleyan Methodist Chapel
Reg. by James S. Haigh of Leighton Buzzard, Wesleyan minister
Cancelled 18 Mar. 1876
OPCS, RG(W) 13532
Haigh registered Wesleyan chapels at Eaton Bray & Heath, Ivinghoe & Wing (Bucks.) on the same day

93/8 Wesleyan
Worship 30 Aug. 1870
A building belonging to Wesleyan Methodists in Mill Lane
Reg. by John Cooper of Leighton Buzzard, superintendent minister
Cancelled 21 Jan. 1972
OPCS, RG(W) 19785

94. LITTLE STAUGHTON

94/1
Archdeaconry 21/25 Apr. 1766
Dwelling house of William Pearson, husbandman
Reg. by William Pearson, John Hawkins of Wilden, husbandman (his mark)
BRO, ABN1/1; ABN 2/22B. PRO, RG 31/2, 21
Certificate addressed to the Commissary & Official of Bedford

94/2
Quarter Sessions 26 Apr. 1786
Newly erected building
BRO, QSM 18, p. 56. PRO, RG 31/6, 10

Plate 42: Staughton, Little: The Baptist meeting here was licensed in 1786, enlarged in 1793, and demolished for defence purposes in 1944. (*Postcard: c.1910*)

94/3
Archdeaconry **22/27 Apr. 1799**
Meeting House
Reg. by William Lugsdin, James Lugsdin, James Peppercorn
BRO, ABN 1/1; ABN 2/102. PRO, RG 31/2, 102

94/4
Archdeaconry **7/8 Dec. 1838**
A building in poss. of Thomas Slaney
Reg. by M.W. Flanders, Robert Lusdin, Joseph Parish
BRO, ABN 1/1; ABN 2/332. PRO, RG 31/2, 356

94/5 **Baptist**
Marriages **19 July 1843**
Baptist Meeting
28932 substituted on 11 Oct. 1944
OPCS, RG(M) 2118

95. STEPPINGLEY

95/1
Archdeaconry   **19/19 June 1756**
Dwelling house of James Lyne, husbandman
Reg. by James Lyne, Samuel Everitt of Ampthill, miller
BRO, ABN 1/1; ABN 2/6. PRO, RG 31/2, 7
Certificate addressed to the Vicar-general of Lincoln. RG 31/2 dates this 1755

95/2
Quarter Sessions   **15 Jan. 1794**
Dwelling house of Mrs Judith Cook
BRO, QSM 19, 71. PRO, RG 31/6, 20

95/3
Archdeaconry   **24 Mar./20 Apr. 1798**
Building in occ. of Ann Burridge, with house in occ. of Thomas Phillips on one side
& house in occ. of William Bunker on other
Reg. by Ann Burridge (her mark), Thomas Cooke, Robert Makeham, James Oliver
BRO, ABN 1/1; ABN 2/88. PRO, RG 31/2, 88

95/4
Archdeaconry   **15 Jan. 1823**
House of John Squires
Reg. by John Squires
BRO, ABN 1/2

95/5
Archdeaconry   **16/23 Apr. 1827**
Meeting House (printed form)
Reg. by Richard Cook
BRO, ABN 1/2; ABN 2/230; ABN 3/3, 79. PRO, RG 31/2, 251
Probably Wesleyan as the form was printed by T. Cordeux, London

95/6   **Wesleyan**
Worship   **5 Feb. 1861**
Wesleyan Methodist Chapel
Reg. by Charles Carter, Harpur St., Bedford, minister
Cancelled 9 Feb. 1904
OPCS, RG(W) 12468
Carter registered Wesleyan chapels at Marston Morteyne & Millbrook on the same day

96. STEVINGTON

96/1   **Congregational**
House of Widow Reade   **16 May 1672**
OR, p. 853

Plate 43: Stevington: The interior of the Baptist church. An Independent church at Stevington was formed in 1655 and the present meeting house dates from 1720.

(*Photograph: Bedfordshire County Council, 1969*)

96/2
Archdeaconry   **2/2 Oct. 1798**
Meeting House
Reg. by John Millard, minister, William Bowyer, Robert Bowyer, John Tyso, Samuel Rose
BRO, ABN 1/1; ABN 2/98. PRO, RG 31/2, 97
John Millard was a Congregational minister trained at Newport Pagnell Academy

96/3
Archdeaconry   **2 Oct. 1798**
House of John Tyso
BRO, ABN 1/1

96/4   **Baptist**
Archdeaconry   **7/17 Oct. 1807**
Messuage or tenement in occ. of Sarah Bowyer
Reg. by Joseph Such, minister, William Bowyer, William Prall, Lawrence Cumberland,
Robert Bowyer, John Wheaton, Thomas Cox, Richard Barcock, Sarah Bowyer
BRO, ABN 1/1; ABN 2/133. PRO, RG 31/2, 127

96/5
Archdeaconry   **13 Sept. 1808**
House of James Prasslow
BRO, ABN 1/1

96/6
Archdeaconry   **22 Oct./24 Nov. 1813**
Building the property of Mrs Margaret Poole
Reg. by Joseph Such of Stevington, minister, Margaret Poole, William Pratt
BRO, ABN 1/1; ABN 2/158. PRO, RG 31/2, 157

96/7
Archdeaconry   **17/19 Oct. 1822**
Messuage of Thomas Bowyer (Bower)
Reg. by Robert Bowyer of Stevington, matmaker, Joseph Such, minister, Thomas Bowyer, William Bowyer, John Fobee
BRO, ABN 1/2; ABN 2/196; ABN 3/3, 44. PRO, RG 31/2, 215

96/8
Archdeaconry   **5/10 Nov. 1824**
Messuage of Jeremiah Sansome of Turvey, in occ. of Robert Tyso of Stevington
Reg. by Robert Tyso (his mark), Dinah Such
BRO, ABN 1/2; ABN 2/211; ABN 3/3, 62. PRO, RG 31/2, 233

96/9   **Baptist**
Marriages   **29 May 1840**
Baptist Meeting House at West End
OPCS, RG(M) 1668

96/10
Archdeaconry   **15/15 Jan. 1842**
A building in occ. of Mr Richard Lilley for occasional public worship
Reg. by Jeremiah Dodsworth of Bedford
BRO, ABN 1/2; ABN 2/369. PRO, RG 31/2, 386

96/11   **Primitive Methodist**
Worship   **28 Dec. 1860**
Dwelling house belonging to Thomas White
Reg. by Edward Bishop, 6 Adelaide Sq., Bedford, minister
Cancelled 31 Dec. 1866
OPCS, RG(W) 10907
Bishop registered a Primitive Methodist chapel at Clapham on the same day

96/12   **Primitive Methodist**
Worship   **19 Nov. 1863**
Primitive Methodist Chapel
Reg. by Edward Bishop, 6 Adelaide Sq, Bedford, minister
Cancelled 9 Aug. 1957
OPCS, RG(W) 15920

97. STOTFOLD

97/1
Archdeaconry   **12/12 July 1780**
House of Roger Irons
BRO, ABN 1/1; ABN 2/50. PRO, RG 31/2, 51
No names given on certificate

97/2
Archdeaconry   16 Sept. 1786
Building the property of Mr Bristow, in occ. of William Bennet
Reg. by James Leevitt, William Leevitt, Edward Saunders, Henry Pottrell, William Sarll
BRO, ABN 1/1; ABN 2/57. PRO, RG 31/2, 56

97/3
Quarter Sessions   18 Apr. 1787
Formerly a barn the property of Timothy Bristow of Hitchin (Herts.), now the property of John Payne of Stotfold. Richard Charles has permission to preach there
Reg. by John Payne, Roger Irons, Edward Saunders, William Ganes (his mark)
BRO, QSR 1787, 5; QSM 18, p. 98

97/4
Archdeaconry   30 Dec. 1819
House of Joseph Ansell
Reg. by Joseph Ansell & other
BRO, ABN 1/2; ABN 3/3, 18. PRO, RG 31/2, 189

97/5
Archdeaconry   21/21 Dec. 1824
A Chapel
Reg. by Samuel Gentle, Edward Gentle, Samuel Castle (his mark)
BRO, ABN 1/2; ABN 2/215; ABN 3/3, 65. PRO, RG 31/2, 235

97/6
Archdeaconry   28/ 30 Nov. 1833
A Chapel lately built
Reg. by John Hide, Thomas Howard, John Randal, George Harris, John Harris, James Harris
BRO, ABN 1/2; ABN 2/282. PRO, RG 31/2, 304
Certificate addressed to the Bishop of Lincoln

97/7
Archdeaconry   19/19 Apr. 1845
Building in occ. of Edward Gentle (printed form)
Reg. by Edward Gentle of Stotfold
BRO, ABN 1/2; ABN 2/378. PRO, RG 31/2, 400
Certificate addressed to the Bishop of Ely and amended to the Archdeacon of Bedford

97/8   **Primitive Methodist**
Archdeaconry   **12 Sept./7 Oct. 1848**
Chapel & premises of Thomas Marriot & George Howard, trustees (printed form)
Reg. by John Guy of Baldock (Herts.), Edward Powell
BRO, ABN 1/2; ABN 2/398. PRO, RG 31/2, 422
Certificate addressed to the Bishop of Ely

97/9   **Wesleyan**
Worship   **9 Feb. 1854**
Wesleyan Chapel
Reg. by Robert Maxwell of Biggleswade, Wesleyan minister
Cancelled 6 Mar. 1876
OPCS, RG(W) 1874
Maxwell registered Wesleyan chapels at Biggleswade, Langford, Sandy & Shefford on the same day

97 / 10   **Primitive Methodist**
Worship   29 Nov. 1860
Primitive Methodist Chapel
Reg. by James Young, Sun St., Biggleswade, Primitive Methodist minister
47220 substituted on 12 Feb. 1918
OPCS, RG(W) 9836
Young registered Primitive Methodist chapels at Arlesey, Biggleswade & Wrestlingworth
on the same day

97 / 11   **Baptist**
Worship   30 Mar. 1865
The Old Baptist Meeting (in Rook Tree Lane)
Reg. by Charles Galer of Stotfold, baker (attendant)
71126 substituted on 17 Oct. 1967
OPCS, RG(W) 16642

97 / 12   **Baptist**
Marriages   11 Nov. 1865
Old Baptist Chapel in Rock Tree Lane
35879 substituted on 17 Oct. 1967
OPCS, RG(M) 5856

97 / 13   **Wesleyan**
Worship   8 Nov. 1869
Wesleyan Chapel in High Street
Reg. by Jonathan Dent of Biggleswade, Wesleyan minister
OPCS, RG(W) 19339

Plate 44: Stotfold: The Wesleyan chapel built and licensed in 1869.   (*Postcard c.1910*)

97/14   Wesleyan
Marriages   26 Apr. 1871
Wesleyan Chapel in High Street
OPCS, RG(M) 7386

97/15   Strict Baptist
Worship   8 Feb. 1886
Hope Baptist Chapel in Mill Lane
Reg. by Henry Bull Mehew of Stotfold, smith (proprietor)
OPCS, RG(W) 29167

97/16   Salvation Army
Worship   31 Aug. 1887
Salvation Army Barracks
Reg. by Stephen File of Stotfold, Captain, S.A.
Cancelled 30 Jan. 1890
OPCS, RG(W) 30309

97/17   Salvationists
Worship   30 Jan. 1890
Salvation Army Barracks
Reg. by Albert Suckley of Stotfold, Captain, S.A.
67045 substituted on 9 Dec. 1958
OPCS, RG(W) 31983

98. STREATLEY

98/1
Quarter Sessions   6 Mar. 1765
Dwelling house of Joseph Mead of Streatley
Reg. by Joseph Mead, Christopher Hall
BRO, QSR 1765, 48

98/2
Quarter Sessions   26 Sept./4 Oct. 1809
Dwelling house of Thomas Blindell
Reg. by William Holdstock, James Newberry, William Cain, Thomas Spiggins
(householders)
BRO, QSR 1809, 89. PRO, RG 31/6, 32

98/3
Archdeaconry   16/21 Mar. 1812
House of William Cain of Streatley
Reg. by E. Daniel, William Cain (his mark), John Holdstock, William Holdstock
BRO, ABN 1/1; ABN 2/144. PRO, RG 31/2, 143

98/4   Baptist
Archdeaconry   25/27 Jan. 1849
Baptist Chapel
Reg. by Francis Davis, George Woodham, James Peck, George Adams
BRO, ABN 1/2; ABN 2/405. PRO, RG 31/2, 432

98/5   **Primitive Methodist**
Worship   **3 Jan. 1861**
Primitive Methodist Chapel at Sharpenhoe
Reg. by Thomas Huckle of Luton, bonnet manufacturer (trustee)
Cancelled 8 Sept. 1964 (advertised 8 Sept.)
OPCS, RG(W) 11638

99. STUDHAM

99/1   **Independents**
Archdeaconry   **21 Jan./3 Feb. 1800**
Cottage & premises in occ. of Mr Jonathan Munn for use of Independents
Reg. by John Coupees, Edward Briden, Samuel Ames, Joseph Hawkes, Joseph Wright,
James Leete
BRO, ABN 1/1; ABN 2/104. PRO, RG 31/2, 104
Certificate addressed to the Bishop of Lincoln

99/2
Archdeaconry   **7/15 July 1848**
**House & premises in occ. of Cornelius Goodyear in Market (Maryate) Street,
Humbertone (Humbershoe)**
Reg. by Robert Hodgert of Billington (Leighton Buzzard)
BRO, ABN 1/2; ABN 2/397. PRO, RG 31/2, 421
Certificate addressed to the Bishop of Ely

99/3
Archdeaconry   **25/26 Sept. 1848**
House & premises of John Grace
Reg. by Robert Hodgert of Leighton Buzzard
BRO, ABN 1/2; ABN 2/399. PRO, RG 31/2, 420
Certificate addressed to the Bishop of Ely

99/4
Archdeaconry   **13/17 Oct. 1850**
House & premises belonging to Thomas Birdsey
Reg. by William Webb of Studham, John Austin (his mark), John Pratt
BRO, ABN 1/2; ABN 2/417
Certificate addressed to the Bishop of Ely

99/5   **Wesleyan**
Worship   **14 Oct. 1853**
Building lately used by George Barnard as a timber storehouse
Reg. by George Barnard of Studham, wheelwright (proprietor)
Cancelled 31 Dec. 1866
OPCS, RG(W) 1268

99/6   **Wesleyan**
Worship   **23 Aug. 1861**
Wesleyan Methodist Chapel
Reg. by Joseph Midgley, London Rd., Luton, minister
Cancelled 22 Feb. 1966
OPCS, RG(W) 14538
The chapel is mistakenly described as being in Herts.

99/7	**Wesleyan**
Marriages	**16 Oct. 1869**
Wesleyan Chapel	
OPCS, RG(M) 6958	

100. SUNDON

100/1

Quarter Sessions	**6 Mar. 1748/9**

House in poss. of William Brown
Reg. by Henry Finch, John Fowler, Kingston Fowler
BRO, QSR 1748, 41
BRO, QSM 7, p. 145 records the registration of Quaker ministers at Sundon

100/2

Quarter Sessions	**17 July 1793**

Dwelling house of William Hill of Upper Sandon
Reg. by William Stevens, John Groom (his mark), James Smith, landlord, Thomas Hopkins
BRO, QSR 1793, 56; QSM 19, 50

100/3

Archdeaconry	**9 June 1798**

House near centre of Sundon in occ. of Samuel Mayles
Reg. by John Groom, Samuel Mayles
BRO, ABN 1/1; ABN 2/94. PRO, RG 31/2, 90

100/4

Archdeaconry	**22 Nov. 1806**

Dwelling house of Thomas Pointer
Reg. by Thomas Pointer, John Heady, Joseph Smith, Joseph Martin, [Elizabeth Clark, Charles Pointer *deleted*]
BRO, ABN 1/1; ABN 2/125. PRO, RG 31/2, 124

100/5

Archdeaconry	**21 Mar. 1808**

House of Philip Worker
BRO, ABN 1/1

100/6

Archdeaconry	**Baptist** **4/7 May 1851**

Baptist Chapel for occasional public worship
Reg. by William Randall, dyer, Joseph Cooper, farmer, Samuel Hopkins, farmer, William Deacon, farmer
BRO, ABN 1/2; ABN 2/427. PRO, RG 31/2, 453

100/7

Worship	**Wesleyan** **9 Feb. 1854**

Wesleyan Methodist Chapel
Reg. by Matthew Trevan Male of Dunstable, superintendent minister
45802 substituted on 10 July 1913
OPCS, RG(W) 1898
Male registered Wesleyan chapels at Dunstable, Houghton Regis, Kensworth & Leagrave on the same day

101. SWINESHEAD

Swineshead was transferred from Hunts. to Beds. in 1888

101/1
Archdeaconry   **10 June 1798**
House & premises on south-west side of street leading to Dean, belonging to Isaac Dickins & in occ. of Simon Bass and others
Reg. by Isaac Dickins, Simon Bass, William Wagstaff, John Sparrow, Richard Islip
CRO, A 277/24

101/2
Archdeaconry   **10/20 Nov. 1813**
House in occ. of John Robins
Reg. by John Robbins of Yelden
CRO, A 277/98

101/3   **Wesleyan**
Worship   **3 Mar. 1861**
Wesleyan Chapel
Reg. by Charles Edward Woolmer of Higham Ferrers (Northants.), minister
Cancelled 31 Dec. 1866
OPCS, RG(W) 13432

101/4   **Wesleyan**
Worship   **27 Sept. 1865**
Wesleyan Methodist Chapel
Reg. by Josiah Jutsum of Higham Ferrers (Northants.), Wesleyan minister
Cancelled 6 Aug. 1970
OPCS, RG(W) 16892

102. TEMPSFORD

102/1
Archdeaconry   **13/13 Nov. 1756**
Newly erected building, late a granary, in poss. of Joseph Field of Tempsford, coal merchant
Reg. by John Moors of Tempsford, farmer, John Arch of Thurleigh, farmer
BRO, ABN 1/1; ABN 2/9. PRO, RG 31/2, 8
Certificate addressed to the Commissary & Official of Bedford

102/2
Archdeaconry   **15 Jan./20 Feb. 1794**
Brewhouse of (converted by) Samuel Bennett of Tempsford, farmer
Reg. by Samuel Bennett, James Scholefield, John Hickling
BRO, ABN 1/1; ABN 2/71. PRO, RG 31/2, 71

102/3   **Methodist**
Archdeaconry   **16 Jan. 1805**
Methodist Chapel
BRO, ABN 1/1

102/4
Archdeaconry   **17 Dec. 1813/9 Feb. 1814**
Dwelling house of George Smart, cordwainer
Reg. by George Smart, Robert Ardines
BRO, ABN 1/1; ABN 2/160. PRO, RG 31/2, 159
Certificate addressed to the 'Registrar of Places of Religious Worship at Bedford'

102/5   **Wesleyan**
Marriages   **3 Apr. 1838**
Wesleyan Chapel
OPCS, RG(M) 1135

102/6
Archdeaconry   **15/15 Nov. 1839**
A building in poss. of William Wells
Reg. by Joseph Hindes
BRO, ABN 1/2; ABN 2/344. PRO, RG 31/2, 368
Certificate addressed to 'Sam. Bailey Registerer'

102/7   **Wesleyan**
Worship   **14 Mar. 1854**
Wesleyan Chapel
Reg. by Adam Fletcher of St Neots (Hunts.), Wesleyan minister
OPCS, RG(W) 3323
Fletcher registered a Wesleyan chapel at Potton on the same day

103. THURLEIGH

103/1
Quarter Sessions   **13/13 July 1763**
House of Samuel Tyso
Reg. by Samuel Tyso, Richard Ward, John Pettit, Edmund Ward
BRO, QSP43/5
Original certificate & licence (seal defaced). The name of Samuel Tyso as owner added
to certificate later. Dorse of licence used to calculate wages

103/2
Archdeaconry   **18 July 1818**
House of Mark Smith
Reg. by Mark Smith & others
BRO, ABN 1/2; ABN 3/3, 3. PRO, RG 31/2, 174

103/3
Archdeaconry   **15 Nov. 1821**
House of William Swale
Reg. by Anthony Byrd Seckerson
BRO, ABN 1/2; ABN 3/3, 33. PRO, RG 31/2, 204

103/4
Archdeaconry   **23/25 July 1827**
**Newly erected Chapel (building) on premises of Mr John Williams & in occ. of John
Cowley**

Reg. by Thomas Pestell, James Parkwood, Peter Brown, William Desborough, William Howkins
BRO, ABN 1/2; ABN 2/231; ABN 3/3, 81. PRO, RG 31/2, 253

103/5
Archdeaconry   **15/15 May 1838**
Dwelling house of John Allen
Reg. by John Allen
BRO, ABN 1/2; ABN 2/326. PRO, RG 31/2, 350
Certificate addressed to the Bishop of Ely

103/6   **Baptist**
Worship   **17 May 1861**
Baptist Chapel
Reg. by Thomas Wagstaff of Thurleigh, shoemaker (deacon)
Cancelled 17 July 1897
OPCS, RG(W) 14321

Plate 45: Thurleigh: The Baptist chapel as rebuilt in 1888.   (*Postcard, c.1920*)

103/7   **Baptist**
Worship   **22 Apr. 1901**
Baptist Chapel
Reg. by George Chandler of Thurleigh, Baptist minister
OPCS, RG(W) 38335

103/8   **Baptist**
Marriages   **7 May 1901**
Baptist Chapel
OPCS, RG(M) 16104

104. TILBROOK

Tilbrook was transferred from Beds. to Hunts. in 1888

104/1
Archdeaconry   **22 Jan./15 Feb. 1798**
House of John Measures
Reg. by John Measures, Chris. Sibley, Matthias Baker
BRO, ABN 1/1; ABN 2/84. PRO, RG 31/2, 82
Licence 'required by bearer'

104/2
Archdeaconry   **23/23 May 1838**
House in occ. of William Porter
Reg. by William Piggott of Higham Ferrers (Northants.)
BRO, ABN 1/2; ABN 2/327. PRO, RG 31/2, 349
Certificate addressed to the Bishop of Ely

104/3   **Moravian**
Archdeaconry   **7/10 Jan. 1839**
A building on premises of Rev. John King Martyn for the Episcopal Church of the United Brethren
Reg. by Benjamin Sufferth, Thomas Flanders, Thomas William West, Thomas Marks, Joseph Bell
BRO, ABN 1/2; ABN 2/336. PRO, RG 31/2, 359

104/4   **Moravian**
Worship   **29 Oct. 1853**
Moravian Church
Reg. by Thomas Flanders of Kimbolton (Hunts.), baker (trustee)
Cancelled on revision, 1 Sept. 1954
OPCS, RG(W) 1294

104/5   **Wesleyan**
Worship   **28 Jan. 1858**
Wesleyan Methodist Chapel
Reg. by Joseph Payne of Higham Ferrers (Northants.), Wesleyan minister
Cancelled on revision, 31 Jan. 1980
OPCS, RG(W) 8254

105. TILSWORTH

105/1
Archdeaconry   **12/14 June 1798**
House in occ. of Mr Richard Partridge
Reg. by Richard Partridge, William Edwards, William Foard (his mark), John Stirman (his mark), Joseph Souster (his mark), William Emerton
BRO, ABN 1/1; ABN 2/95. PRO, RG 31/2, 93
Certificate addressed to the Bishop of Lincoln

105/2
Archdeaconry   **28 Feb./15 Mar. 1821**
House in occ. of Joseph Tompson
Reg. by William Goodson, shopkeeper, Joseph Tompson (his mark), William S. Partridge, farmer
BRO, ABN 1/2; ABN 2/180; ABN 3/3, 25. PRO, RG 31/2, 196

105/3
Archdeaconry   **4/14 Mar. 1831**
Building or chapel in occ. of William Goodson
Reg. by William Goodson
BRO, ABN 1/2; ABN 2/255; ABN 3/3, 104. PRO, RG 31/2, 276

105/4   **Wesleyan**
Worship   **4 Oct. 1862**
Wesleyan Chapel
Reg. by William Richardson of Leighton Buzzard, stationer (trustee)
Cancelled 8 Feb. 1991
OPCS, RG(W) 15326

106. TODDINGTON

106/1
Quarter Sessions   **7 Oct. 1724**
Dwelling house of Thomas Brittain of Chalton in Toddington, cordwainer
Reg. by Thomas Brittain
BRO, QSR 1724, 65

106/2
Quarter Sessions   **28 Apr. 1802**
Dwelling house of John Holdstock, the property of James Fowler
Reg. by F. Hews, minister, James Fowler, Elizabeth Fowler, John Holdstock, Mary Holdstock, John Spring, Richard Marting (his mark), Henry Dale (his mark), Sarah Dale (her mark), Hannah Kingham (her mark), Ann Hallworth, William Fowler, Hannah Fowler
BRO, QSR 1802, 81; QSM 21, p. 108, RG 31/6, 27
Hews also registered 61/4 & 5

106/3
Archdeaconry   **12 Jan. 1803**
Dwelling house of Thomas Pointer
BRO, ABN 1/1

106/4
Archdeaconry   **9/9 Apr. 1804**
Dwelling house & premises in occ. of Henry Saunders, next to the house of Mrs Alice Wheeler
Reg. by Henry Saunders, T. Willis, Alice Willis, James Bailey, Mary Saunders, Thomas Saunders, John Lee
BRO, ABN 1/1; ABN 2/114. PRO, RG 31/2, 115

106/5
Archdeaconry   **5 Dec. 1810**
House of G. Waller at Chalton
BRO, ABN 1/1

106/6
Archdeaconry   **17 Oct. 1811**
House of Joseph Butt
BRO, ABN 1/1

106/7
Archdeaconry   **2 June 1812**
House of Reuben Randall
BRO, ABN 1/1

106/8
Archdeaconry   **13 June 1812**
Meeting House
BRO, ABN 1/1

106/9   **Wesleyan**
Archdeaconry   **4/4 Oct. 1823**
Wesleyan Methodist Chapel (printed form)
Reg. by Richard Elland of Toddington
BRO, ABN 1/2; ABN 2/206; ABN 3/3, 53. PRO, RG 31/2, 225
Form printed by T. Cordeux, London

106/10   **Wesleyan**
Archdeaconry   **19/19 May 1835**
Wesleyan Chapel (printed form)
Reg. by Thomas Rogerson of Luton
BRO, ABN 1/2; ABN 2/305. PRO, RG 31/2, 323
Rogerson registered Wesleyan chapels at Barton, Houghton Regis, Leagrave, Luton, Tebworth & Whipsnade on the same day

35/8. The entry for a room in Toddington, 17 Nov. 1835, in ABN 1/2 is a mistake for Eversholt

106/11   **Wesleyan**
Archdeaconry   **11/12 Sept. 1846**
Wesleyan Chapel (printed form)
Reg. by Wright Shovelton of Dunstable
BRO, ABN 1/2; ABN 2/387. PRO, RG 31/2, 410
Certificate addressed to the Bishop of Ely

106/12
Quarter Sessions   **19/19 Oct. 1847**
A building (printed form)
Reg. by Thomas Hobson, minister
BRO, QSR 47/4. PRO, RG 31/6, 39
Hobson registered a building at Houghton Regis on the same day

Plate 46: Toddington: The Wesleyan chapel erected in 1846.

(Engraving: Rock & Co., c.1850)

106/13   **Baptist**
Marriages   **15 Oct. 1851**
Baptist Chapel
11904 substituted on 8 Feb. 1888
OPCS, RG(M) 3344

106/14   **Wesleyan**
Worship   **9 Feb. 1854**
Wesleyan Methodist Chapel in High Street
Reg. by Matthew Trevan Male of Dunstable, superintendent minister
OPCS, RG(W) 1854
Male registered Wesleyan chapels at Chalgrave, Harlington & Hockliffe on the same day

106/15   **Wesleyan**
Worship   **9 Feb. 1854**
Wesleyan Methodist Chapel at Chalton
Reg. by Matthew Trevan Male of Dunstable, superintendent minister
Cancelled 20 July 1922 (advertised 20 July)
OPCS, RG(W) 1858

106/16   **Primitive Methodist**
Worship   **1 Apr. 1854**
Primitive Methodist Chapel
Reg. by Samuel Wells of Toddington (trustee)
Cancelled on revision, 5 Feb. 1897
OPCS, RG(W) 4632

106/17   Wesleyan
Marriages   21 Feb. 1863
Wesleyan Methodist Chapel [in High Street]
OPCS, RG(M) 5190

106/18   Salvationists
Worship   2 Apr. 1887
Salvation Army Barracks in High Street
Reg. by Edward Henry Marson, High St., Houghton Regis, Captain, S.A.
Cancelled on revision, 5 Feb. 1897
OPCS, RG(W) 30048

106/19   Baptist
Worship   2 Feb. 1888
Baptist Chapel in Ampthill Street [Station Road]
Reg. by Edward Sear jun. of Toddington (trustee)
OPCS, RG(W) 30644

106/20   Baptist
Marriages   8 Feb. 1888
Baptist Chapel in Ampthill Street [Station Road]
Substituted for 3344
OPCS, RG(M) 11904

107. TOTTERNHOE

107/1   Baptist
Quarter Sessions   17 July 1793
Dwelling house of Mrs Mary Hudnall
Reg. by Francis Hews, minister, William Cheshire, Mary Hudnall, Daniel Ellingham,
John Herbert
BRO, QSR 1793, 56; QSM 19, p.50. PRO, RG 31/6, 18

107/2
Archdeaconry   23 Mar. 1808
Dwelling house of Fisher Scroggs
BRO, ABN 1/1

107/3
Archdeaconry   18/18 June 1825
School room (Brick building)
Reg. by John Cook of Houghton Regis
BRO, ABN 1/2; ABN 2/220; ABN 3/3, 69. PRO, RG 31/2, 240
Certificate addressed to the Bishop of Lincoln

107/4
Archdeaconry   13/15 Oct. 1834
Farmhouse, open field & little meadow of James Purton, in occ. of Henry Purton
Reg. by Henry Purton, Joseph Holland, John East, William Jefts, William Tompkins
BRO, ABN 1/2; ABN 2/296. PRO, RG 31/2, 318

107/5   **Wesleyan**
Archdeaconry   **23/28 Dec. 1841**
A Chapel (printed form)
Reg. by Joseph Wilson of Leighton Buzzard, Wesleyan minister
BRO, ABN 1/2; ABN 2/359. PRO, RG 31/2, 384
Certificate addressed to the Bishop of Lincoln

107/6
Archdeaconry   **17/24 Sept. 1842**
House in occ. of Thomas Pratt (printed form)
Reg. by James Warner of Luton
BRO, ABN 1/2; ABN 2/362. PRO, RG 31/2, 392
Certificate addressed to the Bishop of Ely

107/7
Archdeaconry   **19/19 Oct. 1848**
A Chapel (printed form)
Reg. by Joseph Eustace of Eaton Bray
BRO, ABN 1/2; ABN 2/400. PRO, RG 31/2, 423
Certificate addressed to the Bishop of Ely

107/8
Archdeaconry   **14/17 Aug. 1849**
House in occ. of Jeffry Janes
Reg. by John Mead of Eaton Bray, Jeffery [*sic*] Janes (his mark), William Folkes (his mark)
BRO, ABN 1/2; ABN 2/413. PRO, RG 31/2, 441
Certificate addressed to the Bishop of Ely

107/9   **Wesleyan**
Worship   **19 June 1861**
Wesleyan Methodist Chapel [in Castle Hill Road]
Reg. by Joshua Mottram of Leighton Buzzard, minister
Cancelled 28 Aug. 1990
OPCS, RG(W) 14391

107/10   **Primitive Methodist**
Worship   **22 Feb. 1864**
Primitive Methodist Chapel
Reg. by James Langham, Hightown, Luton, minister
Cancelled 11 July 1932 (advertised 11 July)
OPCS, RG(W) 16046

108. TURVEY

108/1   **Congregational**
House of Stephen Hawthorne   **16 May 1672**
OR, p. 853

108/2
Archdeaconry   **10/10 Apr. 1740**
Dwelling house of John Stratton, labourer
Reg. by William Spencer of Turvey, labourer, James Pain of Oakley, blacksmith
BRO, ABN 1/1; ABN 2/1. PRO, RG 31/2, 1

108/3
Archdeaconry   20/20 May 1758
Dwelling house of Sarah Tysoe, spinster, at Stockers End
Reg. by William Spencer of Turvey, labourer (his mark), William Davison of Turvey, farmer
BRO, ABN 1/1; ABN 2/13. PRO, RG 31/2, 13
Certificate addressed to the Commissary & Official of Bedford

108/4
Archdeaconry   11 Mar. 1771
Dwelling house of William Adams, labourer
Reg. by Joseph Clayton, Samuel Bigrave
BRO, ABN 1/1; ABN 2/30. PRO, RG 31/2, 31
Certificate addressed to the Commissary & Official of Bedford. Describes Adams as 'a sober Honest well meaning Man and a protistant Disenter'

108/5
Archdeaconry   9/9 Aug. 1822
Dwelling house of Mary Tyso, widow, & property of John Higgins, esq., of Turvey
Reg. by Thomas Abraham of Turvey
BRO, ABN 1/2; ABN 2/194; ABN 3/3, 41. PRO, RG 31/2, 212

108/6
Archdeaconry   21/21 Mar. 1828
Building in poss. of John Whitworth
Reg. by Joseph Vincent, Joseph Parris, Joel Gaskin, William Buttler, John Whitworth (G. Finch)
BRO, ABN 1/2; ABN 2/236; ABN 3/3, 87. PRO, RG 31/2, 259

108/7   Independent
Archdeaconry   13 Nov./13 Sept. 1828 [*sic*]
House of George Finch (Fynch) of Turvey
Reg. by George Finch (Vincent)
BRO, ABN 1/2; ABN 2/241; ABN 3/3, 89. PRO, RG 31/2, 262
Finch *required* the registrar to register his house. See also previous entry

108/8   Independent
Archdeaconry   16/25 Mar. 1829
A chapel
Reg. by John Morris, Thomas Palmer Bull, H.B. Bull
BRO, ABN 1/2; ABN 2, 242; ABN 3/3, 91. PRO, RG 31/2, 263
Letter of W[illiam] Bull, [Congregational minister of Newport Pagnell (Bucks.)], to his 'Dear Brother' asking him 'to apply to the proper person to register the Turvey Church' attached to certificate

108/9   Independent
Marriages   4 Jan. 1839
Independent Chapel [United Reformed Church]
Cancelled 24 Oct. 1985
OPCS, RG(M) 1361

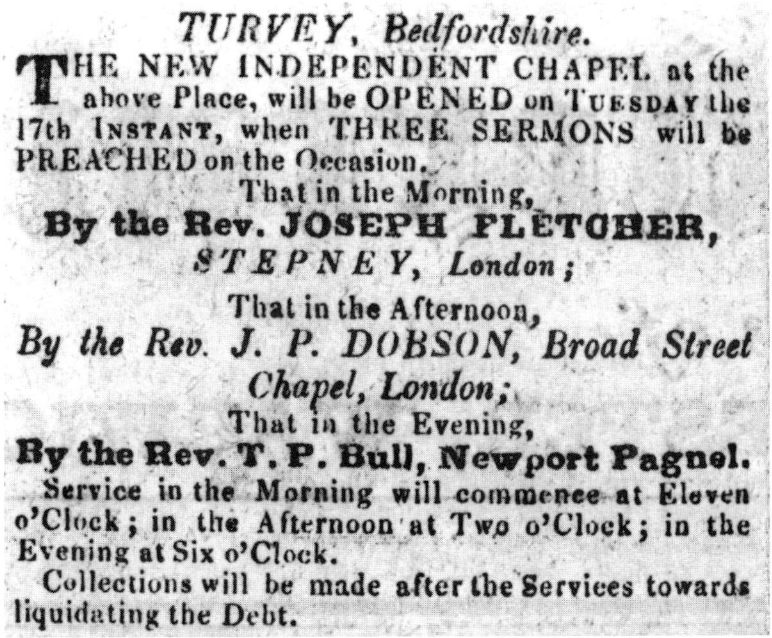

TURVEY, Bedfordshire.

THE NEW INDEPENDENT CHAPEL at the
above Place, will be OPENED on Tuesday the
17th Instant, when THREE SERMONS will be
PREACHED on the Occasion.

That in the Morning,

By the Rev. JOSEPH FLETCHER,

STEPNEY, London;

That in the Afternoon,

*By the Rev. J. P. DOBSON, Broad Street
Chapel, London;*

That in the Evening,

By the Rev. T. P. Bull, Newport Pagnel.

Service in the Morning will commence at Eleven
o'Clock; in the Afternoon at Two o'Clock; in the
Evening at Six o'Clock.

Collections will be made after the Services towards
liquidating the Debt.

Plate 47: Turvey: Advertisement for the opening of the Independent chapel on 17th March 1829 from the *Northampton Mercury*.

108/10   **Wesleyan**
Worship   **9 Feb. 1854**
Wesleyan Methodist Chapel
Reg. by William Henry Clarkson, Harpur St., Bedford, superintendent minister
Cancelled on revision 18 Aug. 1971 (advertised 19 Feb.)
OPCS, RG(W) 1870
CLarkson registered Wesleyan chapels at Bedford, Cardington, Clapham, Kempston, Milton Ernest, Pavenham, Wilshamstead & Wootton on the same day

108/11   **Independent**
Worship   **4 Oct. 1861**
Independent Chapel [United Reformed Church]
Reg. by Richard Cecil of Turvey, Independent minister
Cancelled 24 Oct. 1985
OPCS, RG(W) 14614

109. OLD WARDEN

109/1
Archdeaconry   **13/13 June 1778**
House of Thomas Preston
Reg. by William Tansley, Thomas Preston
BRO, ABN 1/1; ABN 2/46. PRO, 31/2, 46

110. WESTONING

110/1

Quarter Sessions   **7 Jan. 1799**

Dwelling house of Joseph Rawley of Westoning

Reg. by Francis Hews, minister, Richard Guttridge, William Cheshire, Thomas Hill, William Tossey, Joseph Rawley, William Mayles

BRO, QSR 1799, 57; QSM 20, p. 103. PRO, RG 31/6, 23

110/2

Archdeaconry   **12 Jan. 1813**

A building

BRO, ABN 1/1

110/3

Archdeaconry   **23/23 Sept. 1813**

A building

Reg. by John Smith, H. Martindale, Henry Martin, Thomas Oliver

BRO, ABN 1/1; ABN 2/156. PRO, RG 31/2, 155

110/4

Archdeaconry   **27/31 Oct. 1828**

House in occ. of William Stanley (printed form)

Reg. by William Stanley

BRO, ABN 1/2; ABN 2/240; ABN 3/3, 90. PRO, RG 31/2, 261

Plate 48: Westoning: The Baptist church erected in 1835 for a meeting established in the late eighteenth century.   (*Photograph: c.1890*)

110/5
Archdeaconry   **24/25 July 1846**
Building in occ. of William Aldrich (Aldridge), farmer
Reg. by Thomas Flower of Dunstable
BRO, ABN 1/2; ABN 2/385. PRO, RG 31/2, 408
Certificate addressed to the Bishop of Ely

110/6   **Wesleyan**
Worship   **27 Aug. 1863**
Wesleyan Chapel
Reg. by Thomas Chope of Dunstable, Wesleyan minister
OPCS, RG(W) 15829

110/7   **Baptist**
Worship   **2 June 1894**
Particular Calvinistic Baptist Chapel [Hope Strict Baptist Chapel in Greenfield Road]
Reg. by John Neal of Toddington, deacon
78065 substituted on 9 Jan. 1990
OPCS, RG(W) 34375

110/8   **Baptist**
Marriages   **2 June 1894**
Particular Calvinistic Baptist Chapel [Hope Street Strict Baptist Chapel in Greenfield Road]
41215 substituted on 9 Jan. 1990
OPCS, RG(M) 13669

111. WHIPSNADE

111/1
Archdeaconry   **19/19 May 1835**
Dwelling house of John Searle (printed form)
Reg. by Thomas Rogerson of Luton
BRO, ABN 1/2; ABN 2/299. PRO, RG 31/2,329
Rogerson registered Wesleyan chapels at Barton, Houghton Regis, Leagrave, Luton, Tebworth & Toddington on the same day, so this was probably Wesleyan too

112. WILDEN

112/1   **Congregational**
House of John Conquest   **10 May 1672**
OR, p. 856

112/2
Archdeaconry   **10/10 Aug. 1771**
House in poss. of Thomas Beard
Reg. by Thomas Lee of Wilden, farmer, Daniel Marshall of Wilden, tailor
BRO, ABN 1/1; ABN 2/31. PRO, RG 31/2, 30
Certificate addressed to the Commissary & Official of Bedford

112/3
Archdeaconry   31 Mar. 1798
House of Samuel Woods
BRO, ABN 1/1

112/4
Archdeaconry   3 Aug. 1805
Building, the property of Thomas Willmore
BRO, ABN 1/1

112/5
Archdeaconry   6 Sept. 1819
House of Henry Clapham
Reg. by Henry Clapham
BRO, ABN 1/2; ABN 3/3, 14. PRO, RG 31/2, 185

112/6
Archdeaconry   11/11 Dec. 1830
House of William Medlow of Wilden
Reg. by William Medlow (his mark). Witness - Samuel Bailey
BRO, ABN 1/2; ABN 2/252; ABN 3/3, 101. PRO, RG 31/2, 273
Certificate addressed to the Bishop of Lincoln

112/7
Archdeaconry   22/23 Apr. 1831
Dwelling house of Susan Bull of Wilden
Reg. by Susan Bull
BRO, ABN 1/2; ABN 2/257; ABN 3/3, 106
Certificate addressed to the Bishop of Lincoln

112/8   **Baptist**
Worship   **5 Feb. 1870**
Baptist Chapel
Reg. by Henry Burt, Mill St., Bedford, minister
OPCS, RG(W) 19484

113. WILLINGTON

113/1
Archdeaconry   3/3 Apr. 1779
House of Mercy Wells for occasional public worship
Reg. by Thomas Wootton, James Lambe
BRO, ABN 1/1; ABN 2/48. PRO, RG 31/2, 48

113/2   **Moravian**
Quarter Sessions   **9 Oct. 1811**
House in occ. of Richard Sharp in Willington for Episcopal Protestant Church of
the United Brethren
Reg. by Christian Frederick Ramler (Ramsher), Benjamin Trapp
BRO, QSR 1811, 176; QSM 24, p.18. PRO, RG 31/6, 33

113/3 **Moravian**
Quarter Sessions **19//19 Oct. 1814**
Dwelling house of Mary Gurney, for Church of the United Brethren
Reg. by Benjamin Trapp
BRO, QSR 1814, 176; QSM 25, p. 52. PRO, RG 31/6, 34

113/4 **Methodist**
Archdeaconry **26/31 May 1823**
House of John Robinson (printed form)
Reg. by Aquila Barber, Methodist minister
BRO, ABN 1/2; ABN 2/202; ABN 3/3, 51. PRO, RG 31/2, 223
Form printed by T, Cordeux, 14 City Rd, London

113/5
Archdeaconry **5/6 May 1829**
House of Mr John Day
Reg. by John Holloway, minister at Cotton End in Cardington
BRO, ABN 1/2; ABN 2/243; ABN 3/3, 92. PRO, RG 31/2, 264
John Holloway was a Congregational minister

113/6 **Wesleyan**
Worship **29 Aug. 1868**
Wesleyan Chapel
Reg. by John Relph, Westbourne Villas, Bedford, Wesleyan minister
OPCS, RG(W) 18670

113/7 **Wesleyan**
Marriages **12 Oct. 1869**
Wesleyan Chapel
OPCS, RG(M) 6952

114. WILSHAMSTEAD

114/1
Archdeaconry **26 Mar./20 Apr. 1798**
House of Jabez Paine
Reg. by Jabez Paine, Thomas Liles
BRO, ABN 1/1; ABN 2/89. PRO, RG 31/2, 85

114/2
Archdeaconry **4 Nov. 1807**
House of Henry Peacock
BRO, ABN 1/1

114/3
Archdeaconry **25 Nov. 1807**
House of William Armstrong
BRO, ABN 1/1

114/4
Archdeaconry **4 Aug. 1810**
Meeting House
BRO, ABN 1/1

Plate 49: Wilshamstead: The Wesleyan chapel erected in 1841. (*Photograph: c.1875*)

114/5
Archdeaconry **14/16 June 1849**
House in occ. of Thomas Bridges jun.
Reg. by Thomas Bridges, Henry Goss
BRO, ABN 1/2; ABN 2/412. PRO, RG 31/2, 440

114/6 **Wesleyan**
Worship **9 Feb. 1854**
Wesleyan Methodist Chapel
Reg. by William Henry Clarkson, Harpur St., Bedford, superintendent minister
71172 substituted on 28 Nov. 1967
OPCS, RG(W) 1867
Clarkson registered Wesleyan chapels at Bedford, Cardington, Clapham, Kempston,
Milton Ernest, Pavenham & Wootton on the same day

114/7 **Wesleyan**
Marriages **25 Jan. 1870**
Wesleyan Chapel
35912 substituted on 28 Nov. 1962
OPCS, RG(M) 7042

114/8 **Free Methodist**
Worship **17 Apr. 1895**
Wilshamstead Mission Hall
Reg. by Charles Smith of Wilstead [*sic*], grocer (trustee)
66151 substituted on 20 May 1957
OPCS, RG(W) 34805

115. WOBURN

115/1
Quarter Sessions   **20 Apr. 1789**
House & outhouse belonging & in occ. of Mrs Sarah Edmunds in West Street
Reg. by Joseph Harris, plumber, Robert Carey, surgeon, Joseph Barnes, ropemaker,
Samuel Handscomb, watchmaker
BRO, QSR 1789, 200

115/2
Archdeaconry   **30 June 1797/15 Jan. 1798**
Formerly a plumber's casting house in occ. of Mr Carey, surgeon, with premises of
Mr Joseph Perrin of Hitchin (Herts.), gent. on the one side, near the garden of Rev.
John Scroxton on the other & next the garden of Mr Cook Wheeler
Reg. by R. Carey, John Cobb, John Stevens
BRO, ABN 1/1, ABN 2, 80. PRO, RG 31/2, 84

115/3
Archdeaconry   **7 Mar./21 Apr. 1804**
Building & ground, bounded by close in occ. of Mr Fane on N, tenement in occ. of
John Keen on E, garden of - Goodman on S, close in occ. of Mr Parrot on W
Reg. by Michael Castleden, R. Carey, John Buttfield
BRO, ABN 1/1; ABN 2/112. PRO, RG 31/2, 113

115/4   **Baptist**
Archdeaconry   **30/30 June 1835**
Baptist Chapel
Reg. by James Fowler
BRO, ABN 1/2; ABN 2/307. PRO, RG 31/2, 330
Certificate addressed to the Bishop of Lincoln

115/5
Archdeaconry   **6/8 June 1840**
Room in Malthouse in occ. of James Fowler
Reg. by James Fowler
BRO, ABN 1/2; ABN 2/349. PRO, RG 31/2, 372
Certificate addressed to the Bishop of Lincoln

115/6
Archdeaconry   **26/26 May 1841**
Building in occ. of James Fowler
Reg. by James Fowler
BRO, ABN 1/2; ABN 2/352. PRO, RG 31/2, 378
Certificate addressed to the Bishop of Lincoln

115/7   **Independent**
Marriages   **26 Aug. 1843**
Independent Chapel
Cancelled on revision, 1964
OPCS, RG(M) 2123

115/8
Archdeaconry   **12/12 Mar. 1852**
House in occ. of James Fowler in George Street
Reg. by James Fowler, Ebenezer Careless
BRO, ABN 1/2; ABN 2/436. PRO, RG 31/2, 461
Certificate addressed to the Bishop of Ely

115/9   **Baptist**
Worship   **6 Apr. 1853**
A building in occ. of James Fowler, common brewer, in Leighton Street
Reg. by James Fowler of Woburn, common brewer (occupier)
43439 substituted on 16 Dec. 1908
OPCS, RG(W) 899

115/10   **Wesleyan**
Worship   **15 Feb. 1861**
Wesleyan Chapel
Reg. by Thomas White Smith of Newport Pagnell (Bucks.), Wesleyan minister
Cancelled 22 May 1964
OPCS, RG(W) 12752

115/11   **Baptist**
Worship   **7 June 1867**
Baptist Chapel in Leighton Street
Reg. by Eliza House, High St., Woburn (member)
Cancelled on revision, 5 Feb. 1897
OPCS, RG(W) 17959

116. WOOTTON

116/1
Archdeaconry   **13 Mar. 1806**
House of Daniel Cook
BRO, ABN 1/1

116/2
Archdeaconry   **17 Mar. 1807**
House of James Negus
BRO, ABN 1/1

116/3
Archdeaconry   **21 Apr. 1807**
House of Samuel Sheffield
BRO, ABN 1/1

116/4
Archdeaconry   **6 Apr. 1810**
House of John Vaux, labourer
Reg. by John Curtis jun., Thomas Warren, John Thompson, Daniel Cook
BRO, ABN 1/1; ABN 2/138. PRO, RG 31/2, 137
ABN 1/1 dates this 1811

116/5
Archdeaconry
Methodist Chapel
BRO, ABN 1/1

Methodist
6 Aug. 1811

116/6
Archdeaconry
House of William Early, schoolmaster
Reg. by J. Kaves, James Negus, Henry Hekks, J. Mays, J. Hull
BRO, ABN 1/2; ABN 2/224; ABN 3/3, 73. PRO, RG 31/2, 245

10/18 Feb. 1826

116/7
Archdeaconry
House in occ. of Joseph Cave
Reg. by Joseph Cave, Edward Thomlinson, William Kadman, William Cave, (John Lambert *deleted*)
BRO, ABN 1/2; ABN 2/279. PRO, RG 31/2, 300
Certificate addressed to the Bishop of Lincoln

5 Aug./4 Sept. 1833

116/8
Archdeaconry
A Chapel newly built
Reg. by William Early, Richard Early, James Negus, William Keech, John Lovell, Henry Hekks, William Ashley (who with others built the chapel)
BRO, ABN 1/2; ABN 2/312. PRO, RG 31/2, 336

25/26 Mar. 1836

116/9
Archdeaconry
Mr Master's Granary
Reg. by W. Masters, John Plowman, Jesse Masters, Robert Warren, Samuel John Deeble
BRO, ABN 1/2; ABN 2/321. PRO, RG 31/2, 344
This entry assigned to Potton in ABN 1/1 & RG 31/2

Calvinists
6/6 Jan. 1838

116/10
Worship
Wesleyan Methodist Chapel
Reg. by William Henry Clarkson, Harpur St., Bedford, superintendent minister
Cancelled 3 Mar. 1876
OPCS, RG(W) 1865
Clarkson registered Wesleyan chapels at Bedford, Cardington, Clapham, Kempston. Milton Ernest, Pavenham & Wilshamstead on the same day

Wesleyan
9 Feb. 1854

116/11
Marriages
Baptist Chapel
OPCS, RG(M) 3828

Baptists
10 Aug. 1855

116/12
Worship
Wesleyan Chapel
Reg. by Hugh Jones, superintendent minister, Bedford Wesleyan Methodist Circuit
OPCS, RG(W) 20911

Wesleyan
12 Sept. 1872

116/13   **Wesleyan**
Marriages   **3 Aug. 1895**
Wesleyan Chapel
OPCS, RG(M) 14033

117. WRESTLINGWORTH

117/1
Archdeaconry   19/19 July 1814
Building in occ. of William Curtis
Reg. by Michael Saunderson, Thomas Winham, Richard Lunnis
BRO, ABN 1/1; ABN 2/162. PRO, RG 31/2, 161

117/2
Archdeaconry   20 Jan. 1821
House of Ann Lunnis
Reg. by Barnaby Boutell & others
BRO, ABN 1/2; ABN 3/3, 21. PRO, RG 31/2, 192

117/3   **Primitive Methodist**
Worship   **29 Nov. 1860**
Primitive Methodist Chapel
Reg. by James Young, Sun St., Biggleswade, Primitive Methodist minister
Cancelled on revision, 19 Apr. 1895
OPCS, RG(W) 9834
Young registered Primitive Methodist chapels at Arlesey, Bigleswade & Stotfold on the
same day

117/4   **Congregational**
Worship   **25 Apr. 1887**
Wrestlingworth Chapel, Congregational or Independent [Wrestlingworth
Evangelical Free Church]
Reg. by Charles Heath of Biggleswade, Congregational minister
OPCS, RG(W) 30098

118. WYMINGTON

118/1
Archdeaconry   15 June 1807
Dwelling house of George Mackeness
BRO, ABN 1/1

119. YELDEN

119/1
Quarter Sessions   10/15 June 1761
House & premises in occ. of Mary Williamson, widow
Reg. by Mary Williamson, William Grant, R. Tweltree, John Berrill, John Worlidge
BRO, QSP 43/2
Original certificate & draft licence

119/2
Archdeaconry   **22/25 Aug. 1789**
House of Joseph Wadsworth for occasional use
Reg. by Thomas Williamson, John Williamson
BRO, ABN 1/1; ABN 2/61. PRO, RG 31/2, 61

119/3
Archdeaconry   **29 Dec. 1797**
House of Thomas Mee
BRO, ABN 1/1

119/4
Archdeaconry   **10/17 Mar. 1834**
House of Thomas Sikes "to be used (occasionaly) as a place of Religious Worship"
Reg. by Henry White, William Knight, William Hodkings
BRO, ABN 1/2; ABN 2/283. PRO, RG 31/2, 306

119/5   **Wesleyan**
Worship   **29 May 1854**
Wesleyan Methodist Chapel
Reg. by Thomas Jeffery of Higham Ferrers (Northants.), Wesleyan Minister
Cancelled 8 May 1895
OPCS, RG(W) 5143
Jeffery registered a Wesleyan chapel at Riseley on the same day

119/6   **Wesleyan**
Worship   **8 Oct. 1884**
Wesleyan Chapel
Reg. by Jabez Wildes of Yelden (trustee)
OPCS, RG(W) 28142

APPENDIX 1

DISSENTING CONGREGATIONS IN THE EARLY EIGHTEENTH CENTURY

In 1715 the General Body of Ministers of the Three Denominations collected information about the number of dissenting congregations in England and Wales and the number of nonconformist voters, from local correspondents. The list, which received additions and amendments up to 1729, is known as the Evans List from the name of the secretary of the General Body. The intention was to demonstrate to the government of the day the strength of the dissenting interest. Because most of the information was received from Presbyterian and Independent ministers the Baptists tend to be under-represented in most counties, but not in Bedfordshire for which there are two lists. The second was compiled by Rev. John Jennings of Kibworth in Leicestershire. For further information about the list see *Congregational Historical Society Transactions*, vol. 19 (1961), pp. 72-79.

The Evans List is now in Dr Williams's Library (MS. 38.4). The following abbreviations were used by John Evans. BT - Borough Town, M - Market Town, I - Independent, P - Presbyterian, and A - (Ana)baptist.

BEDFORDSHIRE

			Hearers	Voters
Bedford BT	Ebenezer Chandler	I	1200	100
Biggleswade M		I		
Dunstable M	William Britten	A	100	12
	John Cook			
Stevington, near Bedford	Simon Harecock	A	400	18
Eversholt, near Woburn	Mathew Dutton	A	120	10
Charlton in Willy Hundred	Robert Church	A	300	20
Cranfield, between				
Ampthil & Newport Pagnel	William Jarvies	A	100	4
Ridgment	Samuel Butler	A	100	20
Luton M	Nathaniel Marsham	A	400	65
	Thomas Marsham			
	Samuel Chess			
	Francis Stone			
	Robert Hankins			
Goldington, near Bedford	Benjamin Scribner	A	35	7
	Skinner			
Charly-Wood	(supply'd from	A		
	Watford in Hertfordshire)			
Biggleswade M	Samuel Cole	A	300	6
Sharnbrook	Sam. Gurry	A	70	4
	Harper			
	Robert Page			

BEDFORDSHIRE *(continued)*

			Hearers	Voters
Southill, near Shifford	Thomas Killingworth	A	500	20
Cotton-end	Thomas Cooper	A	80	5
	Thomas Thompson			
Market street	(the same preachers			
	as Luton)	A	130	
Thorn, Winfield,	Ibid.	A	130	
Chalton alternately Keysoe	Lewis Norman	A	300	15
Blunham, near Bedford	(the same as Cotton			
	End)	A	200	7
Malden	Thomas Cooper	A	100	10
	Richard Jarvis			
	Samuel Butler Copperwheat			

The foregoing Account from Mr Eben. Chandler
of Bedford. The following, somewhat different,
from Mr John Jennings of Kibworth

Bedford	Ebenezer Chandler	I	1200	240
Biggleswade	Samuel Cole	A.P.	300	6
Luton, Market	Thomas Massum sen.	A	500	
street, Chalton,	Thomas Massum jun.		130	65
Thorn & Winfield			130	
Dunstable	William Brittain	A	100	12
Blunham	- Perry	A	200	7
Steventon	Simon Haircourt	A	400	18
Cranfield	Samuel Butler	A	100	4
Ridgmont	William Davies	A	100	20
Evershalt	Matthew Dutton	A	120	10
Keysoe	Lewis Norman	A	300	15
Carrington, Cotton End	Thomas Cooper	A	80	5
Charlton	Robert Church	A	300	20
Sharnbrooke	Samuel Gunney	A	70	4
Maldon	Richard Jarvies	A	100	10
Goldington	Benjamin Skinner	A	40	7
Southill	Thomas Killingworth	I	500	20
Leighton Buzzard			90	

APPENDIX 2

DISSENTING CONGREGATIONS
IN 1772

In 1772 Josiah Thompson also collected information about the number of dissenting congregations in England and Wales, as part of the political campaign to exempt nonconformists from the subscription required by the Toleration Act. He had access to a copy of the Evans List (App. 1), but made his own enquiries. Unfortunately he did not obtain information about the numbers of hearers and voters in each congregation.

This information is taken from the copy of the List in Dr Williams's Library (MS. 38.5). There are other copies extant. The following abbreviations are used by Thompson: B - Baptist, C - number of congregations, M - number of ministers.

1772 BEDFORDSHIRE 1773

		C	M	B C	B M
1)	Bedford	1	1		
2)	Blonham	1	1	1	1
3)	Biggleswade	1	1	1	1
4)	Cotten End	1	1	1	1
5)	Carlton	1	1	1	1
6)	Eversol & Ridgmont	1	1	1	1
7)	Keysoe	1	1	1	1
8)	Leighton & Dunstable	1	1	1	1
9)	Malden	1	1	1	1
10)	[Cranfelt *struck through*]				
11)	Stevington	1	1	1	1
12)	Sharnbrook	1	1	1	1
13)	Southall [Storton *added*]	1	1		
14)	Thorn	1	1	1	1
15)	Sutton & Gamlingay	1	1	1	1
16)	Cranfield	1	1	1	1
17)	Luton	1	1	1	1
18)	Chorley Wood &				
19)	Chippenfield	1		1	
20)	Market Street	1	1	1	1

Allmost all the Baptist Churches in this County admit of free Communion. The Number of Dissenters in Bedfordshire are computed to be about 3000. Dunstable, the interest exceeding low. Evershall and Ridgmont about 200. Luton about 500.

APPENDIX 3

DISSENTING CHAPELS IN 1842

Samuel Lewis published topographical dictionaries (or gazetteers) for England, Ireland, Scotland and Wales in the 1840s which are of considerable value for local historians. Most compilers of similar works, usually for an individual county, omitted any mention of dissenting chapels and meeting houses. Lewis, however, tried to include all such buildings, but was not always successful. The information given here is taken from the fifth edition of his *Topographical Dictionary of England* (London, 1842). 'Place of worship' must be assumed for each denomination mentioned, unless some other term is given. Cottages and rooms used for religious worship are not mentioned.

Ampthill	Independents, Society of Friends & Wesleyans
Arlsey	Wesleyans
Aspley-Guise	Wesleyans
Great Barford	Wesleyans
Barton in the Clay	Particular Baptists
Bedford	Baptists, Independents, Wesleyans & Moravians. Lately erected – a chapel for the Primitive Episcopal or Reformed Church of England, "the minister of which styles himself a Bishop."
Biggleswade	Baptists & Wesleyans
Blunham	Particular Baptists
Campton	Wesleyans. Catholic chapel
Cardington	Independents & Wesleyans. Particular Baptists at Cotton End
Carlton	Particular Baptists
Chalgrave	Wesleyans at Tebworth
Clophill	Wesleyans
Cranfield	Baptists & Wesleyans
Nether Dean	Wesleyans
Dunstable	Three places of worship for Baptists & one for Wesleyans
Eaton Bray	Wesleyans
Goldington	Independents
Harrold	Independents

Heath with Reach	Wesleyans
Hockliffe	Independents
Houghton Conquest	Wesleyans
Kempston	Wesleyans
Keysoe	Two places of worship for Baptists
Leighton Buzzard	Meeting-houses for Baptists, Society of Friends & Wesleyans
Lidlington	Wesleyans
Luton	Baptists, Society of Friends & Wesleyans
Marston-Moretaine	Wesleyans
Maulden	Baptists & Independents
Potton	Baptists & Wesleyans
Ridgmont	Baptists
Risley	Wesleyans. Also a Moravian establishment
Roxton	Independents
Salford	Wesleyans
Sharnbrook	Baptists
Shefford	A Roman Catholic chapel
Southill	Baptists
Little Staughton	Baptists
Stotfold	Wesleyans
Tempsford	Wesleyans
Thurleigh	Baptists
Toddington	Wesleyans & Baptists
Turvey	Independents & Wesleyans
Westoning	Baptists
Wilshamstead	Wesleyans
Woburn	Independents & Wesleyans
Wootton	Wesleyans

APPENDIX 4

BEDFORDSHIRE PLACES OF RELIGIOUS WORSHIP IN 1908

The first official list was published in 1908, although lists had been printed from 1837 onwards. The original list of 1908 is arranged by superintendent registrar's districts, and then numerically by the worship licence number. For the purposes of this appendix the entries have been re-arranged by parishes to match the calendar. An asterisk in place of the worship licence number shows that the licence was issued before 1852. 'AP' after the marriage licence number indicates that the congregation had appointed an authorised person.

AMPTHILL

Friends' Meeting House, Dunstable Street	W 4587
Primitive Methodist Chapel, Saunders' Piece Primitive Methodist	W 21622
Union Chapel, Dunstable Street Baptist & Congregational	W 24178 M 9560
Wesleyan Methodist Chapel, Dunstable Street Wesleyan Methodist	W 28162 M 11306 AP
Salvation Army Barracks, Arthur Street Salvation Army	W 37051
Strict Baptist Chapel, Oliver Street Strict Baptist	W 40623

ARLESEY

Wesleyan Chapel Wesleyan Methodist	W 3784
Primitive Methodist Chapel Primitive Methodist	W 22905
Salvation Army Barracks, Straw Street Salvation Army	W 32054

ASPLEY GUISE

Primitive Methodist Chapel, Woburn Sands Primitive Methodist	W 10308
Wesleyan Chapel, Chapel Street Wesleyan Methodist	W 15515 M 5213
Courtney Memorial Hall, The Square Christians not otherwise designated	W 42930

GREAT BARFORD

Wesleyan Methodist Church	W 39994
Wesleyan Methodist	

BARTON

Wesleyan Methodist Chapel, Barton in the Clay	W 1753
Wesleyan Methodist	M 17093
Primitive Methodist Chapel, Barton in the Clay	W 23070
Primitive Methodist	

BEDFORD

Primitive Methodist Chapel, Hassett Street	W 271
Primitive Methodist	M 3733
Howard Chapel, Mill Street	W 1256
Independents	M 11
Wesleyan Chapel, Harpur Street	W 1834
Wesleyan Methodist	M 4520 AP
Bunyan Meeting House, Mill Street	W 9403
Independents	M 3159 AP
Wesleyan Methodist Chapel, Cauldwell Street	W 17292
Wesleyan Methodist	M 6322
Moravian Chapel, St Peter's Street	W 18104
United Brethren	M 6387
Baptist Chapel, Mill Street	W 19488
Particular Baptist	M 7054
Southend Wesleyan Chapel, Ampthill Road	W 21527
Wesleyan Methodist	M 9261
Catholic Church of the Holy Child & St Joseph,	W 21723
Midland Road. Roman Catholic	M 9434
Bromham Road Wesleyan Methodist Chapel, Bromham Road	W 23777
Wesleyan Methodist	M 9843 AP
Congress Hall, River Street	W 31399
Salvation Army	
Catholic Apostolic Church, Gwyn Street	W 32586
Catholic Apostolic Church	M 12912
Providence Baptist Chapel, Rothsay Road	W 34613
Baptist	M 13803
Bedford United Mission, Costin Street	W 34616
Unsectarian	
Primitive Methodist Chapel, Park Road	W 35052
Primitive Methodist	M 14085
Primitive Methodist Chapel, Cauldwell Street	W 36120
Primitive Methodist	M 14729

BIGGLESWADE

Providence Chapel, Back Street	W *
Strict Baptist	M 8367
Wesleyan Chapel	W 1877
Wesleyan Methodist	M 191
Baptist Meeting, Hitchin Street	W 13264
Baptist	M 173
Primitive Methodist Chapel, Shortmead Street	W 22156
Primitive Methodist	M 14583
Gospel Room, Back Street	W 33948
Brethren	
St Peter's Catholic Chapel, York Terrace	W 41459
Roman Catholic	
Town Hall Schoolroom, Market Place	W 42450
Salvation Army	

BILLINGTON

Wesleyan Methodist Chapel	W 14203
Wesleyan Methodist	
Bethesda Primitive Methodist Chapel	W 16169
Primitive Methodist	

BLUNHAM

Baptist Meeting House	W 13845
Baptist	M 609

BROMHAM

Building in occupation of Odell	W 31514
Wesleyan Methodist	

CADDINGTON

Baptist Chapel, Woodside	W 15389
Particular Baptist	
Union Chapel	W 36280
Baptist & Independent	M 14807

CARDINGTON

Cotton End Meeting, Cotton End	*
Baptist	M 586
Wesleyan Methodist Chapel	W 1868
Wesleyan Methodist	M 14868
Congregational Chapel, Fenlake, Eastcotts	W 9417
Congregational	
Congregational Chapel	W 9422
Congregational	

Wesleyan Chapel, Harrowden, Eastcotts   W 40549
Wesleyan Methodist

CARLTON

Baptist Meeting House   *
Baptist   M 1143

CHALGRAVE

Wesleyan Methodist Chapel, Tebworth   W 1855
Wesleyan Methodist

CLAPHAM

Wesleyan Chapel   W 23077
Wesleyan Methodist   M 10072

CLIFTON

Clifton Chapel   W 5455
Baptist   M 3684

CLOPHILL

Primitive Methodist Chapel, Luton Road   W 758
Primitive Methodist

COLMWORTH

Primitive Methodist Chapel   W 2510
Primitive Methodist

CRANFIELD

Baptist Chapel, East End   W 10242
Baptist   M 885

Wesleyan Methodist Chapel   W 12870
Wesleyan Methodist

Mount Zion Chapel   W 18467
Particular Baptist   M 6538

DEAN

Wesleyan Methodist Chapel, Nether Dean   W 4687
Wesleyan Methodist   M 15643

Dean Congregational Church, Upper Dean   W 23745
Congregational   M 9322

DUNSTABLE

West Street Baptist Chapel, West Street   W 21
Baptist   M 3080

Wesleyan Chapel, High Street   W 1896
Wesleyan Methodist   M 2510 AP

Tabernacle, Edward Street   W 6488
Congregational   M 4264

Primitive Methodist Chapel, Victoria Street   W 15620
Primitive Methodist   M 6074

Mission Hall, King Street   W 20886
Who object to be designated

Salvation Army Hall, High Street North   W 37899
Salvation Army

Gospel Hall, Manchester Place   W 39329
Methodists

DUNTON

Baptist Chapel   W 13907
Particular Baptist

EATON BRAY

Baptist Chapel, Moor End   W 380
Baptist

Wesleyan Chapel   W 13534
Wesleyan Methodist   M 7617

Salvation Army Hall, Chapel Yard   W 40786
Salvation Army

EATON SOCON

Wesleyan Chapel   W 2636
Wesleyan Methodist   M 13839

Primitive Methodist Chapel, Wyboston   W 19829
Primitive Methodist

Primitive Methodist Chapel, Eaton Ford   W 20167
Primitive Methodist   M 17846

Wesleyan Chapel, Honeydon   W 20836
Wesleyan Methodist

EGGINGTON

Wesleyan Methodist Chapel   W 14204
Wesleyan Methodist

ELSTOW

Congregational Chapel   W 9418
Congregational

EVERSHOLT

Wesleyan Methodist Chapel   W 1969
Wesleyan Methodist

FELMERSHAM

Wesleyan Methodist Chapel, Radwell	W 2463
Wesleyan Methodist	

FLITTON

Wesleyan Methodist Chapel, Greenfield	W 1905
Wesleyan Methodist	

FLITWICK

Wesleyan Methodist Chapel	W 21546
Wesleyan Methodist	

GOLDINGTON

Congregational Chapel	W 9416
Congregational	

GRAVENHURST

Wesleyan Methodist Chapel, Upper Gravenhurst	W 1904
Wesleyan Methodist	M 15028

HARLINGTON

Wesleyan Methodist Chapel	W 1856
Wesleyan Methodist	M 18329

HARROLD

Harrold Chapel	*
Independents	M 1667
Mission Hall, High Street	W 27845
Unsectarian	M 12216

HAYNES

Wesleyan Methodist Chapel	W 22183
Wesleyan Methodist	
Baptist Chapel	W 34508
Calvinistic Baptist	

HEATH & REACH

Wesleyan Methodist Chapel	W 33438
Wesleyan Methodist	M 13165
Baptist Chapel	W 42894
Baptist	M 18795

HOCKLIFFE

Independent Chapel	*
Independent	M 2169

Wesleyan Methodist Chapel	W 1857
Wesleyan Methodist	
Primitive Methodist Chapel	W 15281
Primitive Methodist	

HOUGHTON CONQUEST

Primitive Methodist Chapel	W 14318
Primitive Methodist	
Wesleyan Methodist Chapel, Rectory Lane	W 24257
Wesleyan Methodist	M 16454

HOUGHTON REGIS

Wesleyan Methodist Chapel	W 1899
Wesleyan Methodist	
Wesleyan Methodist Chapel, Chalk Hill	W 1900
Wesleyan Methodist	
Primitive Methodist Chapel	W 15621
Primitive Methodist	
Baptist Chapel, High Street	W 16289
Particular Baptist	M 5549
Salvation Army Barracks, High Street	W 36178
Salvation Army	
Wesleyan Chapel, Waterlow Road, Upper Houghton Regis	W 41744
Wesleyan Methodist	

HUSBORNE CRAWLEY

Primitive Methodist Chapel	W 19720
Primitive Methodist	

KEMPSTON

Bunyan Chapel	W 33432
Congregational	M 13156
Primitive Methodist Chapel, Bedford Road	W 36727
Primitive Methodist	
Mission Hall, Duncombe Street	W 37160
Salvation Army	
Wesleyan Methodist Chapel	W 40675
Wesleyan Methodist	M 17492
Old Wesleyan Methodist Chapel	W 40962
Wesleyan Methodist Chapel	M 17745

KENSWORTH

Wesleyan Methodist Chapel	W 1897
Wesleyan Methodist	

KEYSOE

Brook End Meeting, Brook End	*
Particular Baptist	M 1179

KNOTTING

Wesleyan Methodist Chapel, Knotting Green	W 31500
Wesleyan Methodist	

LANGFORD

Wesleyan Chapel	W 14615
Wesleyan Methodist	M 7228
Salvation Army Barracks	W 30518
Salvation Army	

LEAGRAVE

Wesleyan Methodist Chapel	W 1901
Wesleyan Methodist	
Primitive Methodist Chapel	W 32458
Primitive Methodist	

LEIGHTON BUZZARD

Friends' Meeting House, North End	W 4638
Quakers	
Lake Street Chapel, Lake Street	W 16547
Protestant Dissenters	M 5686
Wesleyan Methodist Chapel, Hockliffe Street	W 16619
Wesleyan Methodist	M 5710 AP
Primitive Methodist Chapel, North Street	W 32158
Primitive Methodist	M 12541 AP
Hockliffe Road Baptist Chapel, Hockliffe Road	W 33470
Baptist	M 13181
Roman Catholic Church, Beaudesert	W 39916
Roman Catholic	M 17733
Atterbury Wesleyan Mission Chapel, Vandyke Road	W 40806
Wesleyan Methodist	
Salvation Army Hall, Lammas Walk	W 41257
Salvation Army	

LIDLINGTON

Wesleyan Methodist Chapel	W 2131
Wesleyan Methodist	M 16424
Bethel Primitive Methodist Chapel	W 16180
Primitive Methodist	

LUTON

Union Chapel	*
Baptist & Independent	M 1523 AP
Wesleyan Methodist Chapel, Church Street	W 1751
Wesleyan Methodist	
Wesleyan Methodist Chapel, Limbury	W 1754
Wesleyan Methodist	
Wesleyan Chapel, Chapel Street	W 1758
Wesleyan Methodist	M 3457
Friends' Meeting House	W 4740
Quakers	
Ceylon Chapel, Wellington Street	W 11637
Baptist	M 3294 AP
Wesleyan Methodist Chapel, Waller Street	W 16186
Wesleyan Methodist	M 9164 AP
Congregational Church, King Street	W 17404
Congregational	M 6261
Primitive Methodist Chapel, Brache Street, Park Town	W 17568
Primitive Methodist	M 11119
Primitive Methodist Chapel, High Town Road	W 17617
Primitive Methodist	
Baptist Meeting House, Park Street	W 17960
Baptist	M 6308 AP
Ebenezer Baptist Chapel, Hastings Street	W 20197
Particular Baptist	M 7434
Wesleyan Chapel, Albert Road, New Town	W 20910
Wesleyan Methodist	
Primitive Methodist Chapel, Church Street	W 24913
Primitive Methodist	M 13542
Primitive Methodist Church, Cardigan Street	W 25612
Primitive Methodist	M 14734
Mission Chapel, Ashton Street	W 27316
Wesleyan Methodist	
Salvation Army Barracks, Manchester Street	W 30842
Salvation Army	
Salvation Army Temple, Park Street	W 32493
Salvation Army	M 15168
St Mary Help of Christians, Castle Street	W 34530
Roman Catholic	M 13760
Wesleyan Chapel, Stopsley	W 34536
Wesleyan Methodist	
Mount Tabor Church, Castle Street	W 36531
Primitive Methodist	M 15323

Primitive Methodist Church, High Town Road	W 36607
Primitive Methodist	M 15011
Wesleyan Methodist Church, Baker Street, Bailey Hill	W 36799
Wesleyan Methodist	M 16587
Railway Mission Hall, Bridge Street	W 39302
Railway Mission (Luton Branch)	
Salvation Army Sunday School, Bridge Street	W 39370
Salvation Army	
Wesleyan Mission Chapel, Midland Road	W 39529
Wesleyan Methodist	
Melson Street Hall, Melson Street	W 40149
Christian Union (Unsectarian)	
Bury Park Church, Waldeck Road	W 40797
Congregational	M 17557
Baptist Mission House, 17 Old Bedford Road	W 40915
Old Baptist Union	
Primitive Methodist Chapel, Corner of Dunstable & Oak Roads	W 41614
Primitive Methodist	
Good Templars' Hall, Chapel Street	W 42515
Good Templars & Gospel Missioners	
Bethel Chapel, Chapel Street	W 43054
Strict Baptist	M 18888

MARSTON MORETAINE

Wesleyan Methodist Chapel	W 12469
Wesleyan Methodist	M 17914
Salvation Army Barracks, Upper Shelton	W 32086
Salvation Army	
Primitive Methodist Chapel, Church End	W 38244
Primitive Methodist	

MAULDEN

Maulden Meeting, Duck End	*
Baptist	M 991 AP
Wesleyan Methodist Chapel	W 2133
Wesleyan Methodist	
Primitive Methodist Chapel	W 13133
Primitive Methodist	

MILLBROOK

Wesleyan Methodist Chapel	W 12470
Wesleyan Methodist	

MILTON ERNEST

Wesleyan Methodist Chapel W 1871
Wesleyan Methodist

NORTHILL

Wesleyan Methodist Chapel, Upper Caldecote W 7590
Wesleyan Methodist M 16212

Wesleyan Methodist Church W 40360
Wesleyan Methodist

OAKLEY

Primitive Methodist Chapel W 36438
Primitive Methodist M 14909

PAVENHAM

Wesleyan Methodist Chapel W 12244
Wesleyan Methodist

POTSGROVE

Wesleyan Chapel, Sheep Lane W 15788
Wesleyan Methodist

POTTON

Congregational Chapel *
Independent M 3176

Wesleyan Methodist Chapel W 3322
Wesleyan Methodist M 8702

Baptist Chapel, Horsloe Street W 18801
Particular Baptist M 6714

Salvation Army Barracks W 32160
Salvation Army

RAVENSDEN

Zion Chapel W 1812
Particular Baptists M 16789

RENHOLD

Renhold Chapel W 40291
Baptist & Congregational

RIDGMONT

Wesleyan Methodist Chapel W 1970
Wesleyan Methodist M 2487

Baptist Chapel W 10196
Baptist M 473

RISELEY

Wesleyan Methodist Chapel
Wesleyan Methodist
W 5144

Moravian Chapel
United Brethren
W 8451
M 4288

ROXTON

Roxton Chapel
Independent
*
M 375

SALFORD

Wesleyan Chapel
Wesleyan Methodist
W 5393
M 18137

SANDY

Baptist Chapel
Baptist
W 5799

Wesleyan Chapel, Beeston
Wesleyan Methodist
W 18620
M 7185

Primitive Methodist Chapel, Girtford
Primitive Methodist
W 19093

Baptist Chapel
Particular Baptist
W 30946
M 12038

SHARNBROOK

Bethlehem Chapel, top of Barleycroft Lane
Particular Baptist
W 14805

Old Baptist Meeting House, High Street
Baptist
W 15064
M 2154

SHEFFORD

Catholic Chapel
Roman Catholic
*
M 1095

Union Meeting House, Little Hardwick
Baptist
*
M 1121

Wesleyan Chapel, Ampthill Road
Wesleyan Methodist
W 1875
M 14517

Salvation Army Barracks, Bridge Street
Salvation Army
W 38352

Gospel Hall, New Street
Christian Brethren
W 41193

SHILLINGTON

Union Chapel
Independent
*
M 4691

Wesleyan Methodist Chapel, Pegsden Wesleyan Methodist	W 1902
Wesleyan Methodist Chapel Wesleyan Methodist	W 20920 M 14820
Primitive Methodist Chapel, Bury Road Primitive Methodist	W 42872

SOUTHILL

Southill Meeting Particular Baptist	* M 3391

STAGSDEN

Congregational Chapel Congregational	W 9420

STANBRIDGE

Primitive Methodist Chapel Primitive Methodist	W 11814
Wesleyan Methodist Chapel Wesleyan Methodist	W 19785

LITTLE STAUGHTON

Baptist Meeting Baptist	* M 2118

STEPPINGLEY

Wesleyan Methodist Church Wesleyan Methodist	W 40106 M 17644

STEVINGTON

Baptist Meeting House, West End Baptist	* M 1668 AP
Primitive Methodist Chapel Primitive Methodist	W 15920

STOTFOLD

Primitive Methodist Chapel Primitive Methodist	W 9836
Old Baptist Chapel, Rook Tree Lane General Baptists	W 16642 M 5856
Wesleyan Chapel Wesleyan Methodist	W 19339 M 7386
Hope Baptist Chapel, Mill Lane Strict Baptist	W 29167

Salvation Army Barracks   W 31983
Salvation Army

STREATLEY

Primitive Methodist Chapel, Sharpenhoe   W 11638
Primitive Methodist

STUDHAM

Wesleyan Methodist Chapel   W 14538
Wesleyan Methodist

SUNDON

Wesleyan Methodist Chapel   W 1898
Wesleyan Methodist

SWINESHEAD

Wesleyan Methodist Chapel   W 16892
Wesleyan Methodist

TEMPSFORD

Wesleyan Chapel   W 3323
Wesleyan Methodist   M 1135

THURLEIGH

Baptist Chapel   W 38335
Baptist   M 16104

TILBROOK

Moravian Chapel   W 1294
United Brethren

Wesleyan Methodist Chapel   W 8254
Wesleyan Methodist

TILSWORTH

Wesleyan Chapel   W 15326
Wesleyan Methodist

TODDINGTON

Wesleyan Methodist Chapel   W 1854
Wesleyan Methodist   M 5190
Wesleyan Methodist Chapel, Chalton   W 1858
Wesleyan Methodist

Baptist Chapel, Ampthill Street W 30644
Baptist M 11904

Wesleyan Methodist Chapel, Chalton W 42355
Wesleyan Methodist

TOTTERNHOE

Wesleyan Methodist Chapel W 14391
Wesleyan Methodist

Primitive Methodist Chapel W 16046
Primitive Methodist

TURVEY

Wesleyan Methodist Chapel W 1870
Wesleyan Methodist

Independent Chapel W 14614
Independent M 1361

WESTONING

Wesleyan Chapel W 15829
Wesleyan Methodist M 18734

Particular Baptist Chapel W 34375
Particular Calvinistic Baptist M 13669

WILDEN

Baptist Chapel W 19484
Baptist

WILLINGTON

Wesleyan Chapel W 18670
Wesleyan Methodist M 6952

WILSHAMSTEAD

Wesleyan Chapel W 1867
Wesleyan Methodist M 7042

Mission Hall W 34805
Free Methodists

WOBURN

Independent Chapel *
Independent M 2123

Wesleyan Chapel W 12752
Wesleyan Methodist

WOOTTON

Baptist Chapel	*
Baptist	M 3828
Wesleyan Chapel	W 20911
Wesleyan Methodist	M 14033

WRESTLINGWORTH

Congregational Chapel	W 30098
Congregational	M 16926

YELDEN

Wesleyan Chapel	W 28142
Wesleyans	

APPENDIX 5

NONCONFORMIST TRUST DEEDS
1736-1865

The Mortmain Act of 1736 (9 Geo. II, c.36) required devises of property in trust to be enrolled in Chancery. In 1871 the 32nd *Report of the Deputy Keeper of the Public Records* printed an index to all the deeds so enrolled on the dorse of the Close Rolls. The index was compiled from the original annual indexes to the Rolls and no attempt was made to check these against the original entries. Since the annual indexes were apparently made from the endorsements on the original deeds there was considerable opportunity for errors to creep in. The printed index therefore contains even more errors and entries can vary from two or three words to two or three lines of details. Although the arrangement of this index is alphabetical by the first letter of the parish or hamlet it is then chronologically arranged, making it necessary to read through all the entries. For more information about the enrolment of trust deeds in Chancery see R.W. Ambler, 'Enrolled Trust Deeds' (*Archives*, vol 20, 1993, pp. 177-186)

The references given here are to the year (regnal or calendar) followed by the number of the roll, and the number of the deed on the roll. If more than one number is given for the deed there is usually a lease and release. To consult the originals at the Public Record Office these references have to be converted to the new C54 reference numbers. For deeds after 1865 there is an index in the search room.

AMPTHILL

Wesleyan Methodists	1854, 15, 13
Methodists	1863, 81, 1

ARLESEY

Wesleyan Methodist chapel	1846, 8, 7

ASPLEY GUISE

Two cottages for Primitive Methodists at Hogstye End	1849, 31, 9

BARTON

Particular Baptists	11 Geo. IV, 37, 2
Methodists	6 Will. IV, 170, 6
Methodist chapel	1865, 77, 15

BEDFORD

Methodists	6 Geo. IV, 65, 2
Protestant Dissenters	5 Will. IV, 156, 1
Particular Baptists, St Pauls par.	5 Will. IV, 157, 15
New Episcopalian, St Pauls par.	5 Will. IV, 194, 9

Calvinistic Baptists	6 Will. IV, 184, 14,15
Chapel in St Pauls par.	1840, 216, 2
Messuage for Howard chapel	1846, 102, 6
Dissenting chapel, St Pauls par.	1862, 63, 7, 8
Dissenters' buildings, St Pauls par.	1862, 157, 16
Particular Baptist chapel, St Marys par.	1862, 178, 4
Primitive Methodist chapel	1862, 228, 4
House for Particular Baptist minister, St Pauls par.	1863, 2, 4
Methodist chapel, St Marys par.	1864, 77, 9

BIGGLESWADE

Wesleyan Methodist	5 Will. IV, 173, 3
Particular Baptist chapel	1846, 97, 8
Primitive Methodist	1854, 46, 1
Baptist burial ground	1862, 146, 1

BLUNHAM

| Calvinistic Baptists | 7 Will. IV, 186, 3 |

CADDINGTON

| Particular Baptists at Woodside | 1863, 12, 1 |

CARDINGTON

| Baptist minister at Cotton End | 29 Geo. II, 2, 11,9 |
| Methodists | 6 Geo. IV, 64, 1 |

CARLTON

| Baptists | *c 1828*   8 Geo. IV, 84, 8 |
| Primitive Methodists | 1846, 24, 8 |

CHALGRAVE

Methodists in Tebworth	53 Geo. III, 29, 18
Wesleyan Methodist chapel	1842, 76, 2
Methodist school	1860, 51, 2

CLAPHAM

| Methodists | 3 Will. IV, 53, 4 |

CLIFTON

| Calvinistic Baptists | 1856, 65, 8 |
| Particular Baptist chapel | 1858, 73, 9 |

CLOPHILL

| Primitive Methodists | 1852, 65, 8 |

COLMWORTH

| Primitive Methodists | 1853, 103, 8 |

CRANFIELD

Methodist chapel at Church End	1840, 168, 9, 10
Particular Baptist chapel	1862, 202, 5

DEAN

Methodists in Nether Dean	50 Geo. III, 41, 2
Methodists in Nether Dean	57 Geo. III, 57, 12

DUNSTABLE

Methodists	2 Will. IV, 75, 16,17
Particular Baptists	1838, 167, 4
Methodist chapel	1839, 202, 12, 13
Temperance Hall	1841, 171, 7
Primitive Methodists	1852, 106, 11
Independents	1854, 37, 1
Methodists	1859, 12, 6, 7
Primitive Methodist chapel & school	1861, 148, 10
Methodists	1862, 155, 12
Primitive Methodist chapel & school	1863, 4, 3

DUNTON

Particular Baptist chapel	1857, 45, 7

EATON BRAY

Enlarged meeting house	46 Geo. III, 17, 10
Particular Baptists	6 Will. IV, 163, 10,11
Methodist school	1860, 119, 2
Primitive Methodist chapel & school	1865, 28, 5

EATON SOCON

Wesleyan Methodists	1851, 11, 10

EVERSHOLT

Wesleyan Methodists	1849, 65, 9

FELMERSHAM

Methodists	48 Geo. III, 29, 2

HARLINGTON

Methodists	7 Will. IV, 194, 13

HARROLD

Independents	*c1832*	2 Will. IV, 67, 3
Paedobaptists		2 Will. IV, 67, 5
Independents		1864, 48, 5

HAYNES

Congregational chapel	7 Geo. IV, 88, 5
Methodists	8 Geo. IV, 80, 6
Methodist chapel	1840, 208, 19

HEATH & REACH

See also Leighton Buzzard	
Methodists	3 Geo. IV, 62, 2
Primitive Methodist chapel in Leighton Buzzard	1863, 53, 20
Methodist chapel in Leighton Buzzard	1865, 13, 10

HOCKLIFFE

Paedobaptists	6 Geo. IV, 64, 1
Methodists	4 Will. IV, 57, 13
Primitive Methodist chapel	1862, 153, 8

HOUGHTON CONQUEST

Methodists	58 Geo. III, 71, 1
Primitive Methodist chapel	1855, 24, 6

HOUGHTON REGIS

Wesleyan Methodists	1851, 28, 12
Primitive Methodist chapel & school	1861, 148, 11

KEMPSTON

Methodists at Bell End	3 Geo. IV, 69, 2
Methodist chapel	1839, 207, 12
Wesleyan Methodist chapel at Up End	1859, 100, 10
Wesleyan Methodist chapel	1860, 95, 1

KENSWORTH

Methodists	10 Geo. IV, 85, 12
Wesleyan Methodists	1847, 50, 12

KEYSOE

Particular Baptists	10 Geo. IV, 80, 9, 10
Particular Baptist chapel & burial ground	1853, 92, 1

LANGFORD

Methodists	5 Will. IV, 195, 12
Wesleyan Methodist chapel	1861, 129, 3

LEAGRAVE

Methodists	5 Geo. IV, 67, 7
Methodists	1862, 94, 9

LEIGHTON BUZZARD

See also Heath & Reach	
Baptists	49 Geo. III, 25, 11
Methodists	50 Geo. IV, 41, 8
Wesleyan Methodists in Billington	1838, 168, 12
Methodist cottage	1839, 199, 17
Methodist chapel	1841, 165, 12
Friends' meeting house & burial ground	1844, 47, 2
Dissenting chapel at Heath	1846, 1, 17
Particular Baptist chapel	1846, 127, 13
Primitive Methodists	1852, 88, 20
Wesleyan Methodists	1853, 30, 2
Primitive Methodists	1860, 88, 8
Methodists	1864, 139, 16
Wesleyan Methodists	1864, 139, 17
Particular Baptist chapel	1865, 37, 11

LIDLINGTON

Methodists	55 Geo. III, 78, 2, 3
Primitive Methodist chapel	1863, 71, 9

LUTON

Assistant Wesleyan minister	20 Geo. III, 23, 1
Methodists	48 Geo. III, 31, 12,13
Methodists	6 Geo. IV, 69, 19
Particular Baptists	4 Will. IV, 56, 24
Trinitarian Baptist chapel & school	1837, 179, 3
Primitive Methodist chapel & school	1839, 213, 12, 13
Wesleyan Methodist chapel at Stopsley	1845, 3, 8
Wesleyan Methodist chapel	1847, 6, 11
Wesleyan Methodists	1847, 69, 6
Particular Baptists	1848, 136, 12
Primitive Methodists	1852, 65, 11
Particular Baptists	1853, 121, 14
Baptists	1860, 60, 17
Methodist chapel at Limbury	1862, 234, 8
Particular Baptists	1862, 96, 11
Quakers	1862, 118, 13
Wesleyan Methodist chapel	1863, 128, 3
Wesleyan Methodist chapel	1863, 128, 4
Calvinistic Baptists	1863, 141, 6
Primitive Methodists at West Hyde	1864, 44, 15
Quaker burial ground	1865, 13, 7
Independent chapel	1865, 50, 7
Independent chapel	1865, 50, 8

MARSTON MORTEYNE

Methodists	53 Geo. III, 33, 5

MAULDEN

Methodists	54 Geo. III, 55, 3
Methodists	6 Geo. IV, 65, 3
Methodists	6 Will. IV, 183, 8
Primitive Methodist chapel	1860, 2, 17

MILTON ERNEST

Methodists	1 Geo. IV, 53, 11

NORTHILL

Calvinistic Baptists	1856, 67, 3
Wesleyan Methodists in Upper Caldecote	1857, 48, 3

OAKLEY

Primitive Methodists	1849, 71, 10

PAVENHAM

Primitive Methodists	1862, 135, 10
Wesleyan Methodist chapel	1864, 29, 12

POTSGROVE

Paedobaptist chapel	1863, 92, 15
Wesleyan Methodists, Sheep Lane	1865, 118, 7

POTTON

Wesleyan Methodists	1842, 48, 17
Particular Baptists	1850, 11, 11
Wesleyan Methodist land in Bull St.	1852, 20, 8
Wesleyan Methodists	1853, 59, 1
Independents	1854, 5, 5
Wesleyan Methodists	1861, 158, 10

RAVENSDEN

Free Communion Baptists	1853, 112, 12

RIDGMONT

Baptists	5 Will. IV, 194, 3, 4

RISELEY

Methodists	27 Geo. III, 20, 18
Particular Baptists	1843, 74, 8

SALFORD

Methodists	1840, 160, 13, 14

SANDY

Methodist chapel	1862, 47, 5
Particular Baptist chapel	1862, 109, 12

SHARNBROOK

Particular Baptists	1843, 4, 4
House for Baptist minister	1843, 136, 4
Particular Baptist chapel	1862, 157, 4

SHEFFORD

Enlarged chapel	4 Geo. IV, 67, 8
Methodists	7 Will. IV, 172, 7

SHILLINGTON

Meeting house for Evangelical Protestant Dissenters	1842, 43, 1
Wesleyan Methodist chapel	1842, 76, 1

SOUTHILL

Baptists	45 Geo. III, 22, 10

STANBRIDGE

Primitive Methodist chapel & school	1862, 43, 2

LITTLE STAUGHTON

Protestant Dissenters	43 Geo. III, 30, 7
Protestant Dissenters	43 Geo. III, 35, 13
Protestant Dissenters	8 Geo. IV, 80, 10
Baptist chapel & minister	5 Will. IV, 104, 7
Dissenters	1862, 146, 20

STEVINGTON

Particular Baptists	c 1824	3 Geo. IV, 54, 10
Primitive Methodist chapel & school		1864, 65, 2

STOTFOLD

Primitive Methodist chapel	1847, 154, 14

STREATLEY

Primitive Methodist chapel & school at Sharpenhoe	1858, 89, 14

STUDHAM

Wesleyan Methodist chapel	1858, 72, 21
Wesleyan Methodists	1860, 81, 3

SUNDON

Wesleyan Methodists at Upper Sundon	1848, 72, 1

SWINESHEAD

Methodists   1865, 52, 2

TEMPSFORD

Methodists   53 Geo. III, 25, 12
House for Methodist preacher   1842, 58, 9
House for Methodist preacher   1861, 158, 11, 12

THURLEIGH

Particular Baptist chapel   1844, 46, 3

TILBROOK

Wesleyan Methodist chapel   1858, 17, 15

TILSWORTH

Wesleyan Methodists   1860, 22, 12

TODDINGTON

Protestant Dissenters   53 Geo. III, 21, 10
Methodists   4 Geo. IV, 69, 8
Methodists in Chalton   7 Will. IV, 201, 4
Wesleyan Methodist chapel   1846, 108, 11
Wesleyan Methodist chapel   1861, 94, 6
Wesleyan Methodist chapel in Chalton   1862, 24, 14

TOTTERNHOE

Methodist chapel   1840, 208, 17
Primitive Methodist chapel & school   1863, 130, 6

TURVEY

Methodists   10 Geo. IV, 91, 1
Paedobaptists   c 1830 10 Geo. IV, 75, 1, 2
House for Paedobaptists   1846, 77, 16

WESTONING

Particular Baptists   58 Geo. III, 67, 4
Calvinistic Baptists   6 Will. IV, 185, 4
Baptists, Middle or Cranfield field   1851, 69, 19
Wesleyan Methodist chapel   1863, 110, 24

WILDEN

Protestant Dissenting chapel   1846, 32, 14

WILSHAMSTEAD

Methodists   54 Geo. III, 55, 4
Methodists   6 Geo. IV, 65, 4

WOBURN

Paedobaptists	4 Geo. IV, 68, 12,13
Wesleyan Methodists	1861, 6, 18

WOOTTON

Methodists	52 Geo. III, 33, 1
Particular Baptists	7 Will. IV, 200, 16
Wesleyan Methodist chapel	1862, 218, 2

WRESTLINGWORTH

Independent chapel	1845, 122, 3
Primitive Methodists	1852, 74, 10
Independent chapel	1862, 196, 14

INDEX

In this index the numbers 1-14 refer to the pages of the introduction, and numbers 'App 1' or 'App 2' to those two appendices. All other entries are to the individual licences in the calendar. All parishes named are (or were) in Bedfordshire unless otherwise indicated.